FRAGMENTED ASIA

Fragmented Asia: Regional Integration and National Disintegration in Pacific Asia

Edited by

IAN G. COOK
MARCUS A. DOEL
REX LI

Avebury *1996*

Aldershot · Brookfield USA · Hong Kong · Singapore · Sydney

Published by
Avebury
Ashgate Publishing Ltd
Gower House
Croft Road
Aldershot
Hants GU11 3HR
England

Ashgate Publishing Company
Old Post Road
Brookfield
Vermont 05036
USA

British Library Cataloguing in Publication Data

Fragmented Asia: Regional Integration and
National Disintegration in Pacific Asia
I. Cook, Ian G.
337.11823

Library of Congress Catalog Card Number: 95-83728

ISBN 1 85972 194 X

Printed in Great Britain by the Ipswich Book Company, Suffolk

Contents

Figures and tables

Contributors

Anne Booth is Professor of Economics at the School of Oriental and African Studies, University of London. A graduate of Victoria University, Wellington, and the Australian National University in Canberra, she has specialized in the economic development of Southeast Asia, and has published extensively on Indonesia, and the ASEAN region. Her recent publications include *Agricultural Development in Indonesia* (Sydney, 1988) and, as editor, *The Oil Boom and After: Indonesian Economic Policy and Performance in the Soeharto Era* (Singapore, 1992). She is currently completing a study of Indonesian economic development in the nineteenth and twentieth centuries.

John Bray is Head of Research at Control Risks Information Services, a London-based political risk consultancy. After graduating from Cambridge University, he taught in Northern India for two years, and joined Control Risks in 1983. His professional interests include South and Southeast Asian affairs, the principles of political risk analysis, and energy politics. His most recent publications include *Burma: The Politics of Constructive Engagement* (Royal Institute of International Affairs, 1995).

Terry Cannon is Reader in Third World Development Studies at the University of Greenwich in London. He has published many papers and chapters on various aspects of the Chinese economic reforms. His recent publications include, as co-editor, *The Geography of Contemporary China: The Impact of Deng Xiaoping's Decade* (Routledge, 1990). With Le-Yin Zhang, he is involved in a research project on regional tensions in China.

Ian G. Cook is Reader in Urban and Regional Issues, Head of Human Geography, and Head of the Centre for Pacific Rim Studies at Liverpool John Moores University. From 1983 to 1990 he co-edited the journal *Contemporary Issues in*

Geography and Education. His research interests include community based economic development, as well as urban and regional issues in Pacific Asia, and he has written many papers on these topics. Dr Cook has given presentations at the Department of Geography, Peking University and the Chinese Academy of Social Science, Beijing, and, more recently, was invited by the Chinese Ministry of Civil Affairs to present a paper on China's metropoles as the sole British representative at the First International Symposium on Urbanization in China, Shunde City, September 1995.

Marcus A. Doel is Lecturer in Human Geography at Loughborough University. He was previously Lecturer and Research Fellow at Liverpool John Moores University, where he published widely on new theoretical directions in cultural, economic, and political geography in such journals as *Environment and Planning A & D, Political Geography,* and *Transactions of the Institute of British Geographers.* He is currently completing a book entitled *The Harsh Law of Space: Deconstruction, Geography, Postmodernism.*

Glenn D. Hook is Professor of Japanese Studies at the University of Sheffield, and an Honorary Research Associate at Hiroshima University, Japan. He has been a Visiting Professor at Peking University, Tampere University, and the University of Tokyo, a Research Associate at the University of California, and Fellow at the Australian National University. His research interests are in Japanese international relations, security, and language and politics. He has published extensively in both Japanese and English. His recent English publications include *Militarization and Demilitarization in Contemporary Japan* (Routledge, 1996) and, as co-editor, *The Internationalization of Japan* (Routledge, 1992).

Tim Huxley is Director of the Centre for South-East Asian Studies, University of Hull. He was educated at Oxford, Aberystwyth and the Australian National University. Before joining the Centre at Hull in 1989, he had worked in the Australian Parliamentary Research Service, taught at Aberystwyth and Lancaster, and spent two years as a Fellow at the Institute of Southeast Asian Studies in Singapore. Dr Huxley has written widely on security issues in Southeast Asia. His most recent publications include *Insecurity in the ASEAN Region* (Royal United Services Institute for Defence Studies, 1993). He is currently working on a project on arms proliferation in East Asia.

Cho-Oon Khong is Senior Economist with Group Planning, Shell International Limited, London. He is responsible for the Asia-Pacific region in Shell's scenario planning, and was a member of the team which developed *Global Scenarios 1995-2020* for the Shell Group. Dr Khong is a Singaporean citizen, and received his doctorate from the London School of Economics. He was previously Lecturer in Development Studies/International Relations at the University of Bath (where he is now on long-term leave of absence), Lecturer in Political Science at the

National University of Singapore, Senior Economist at the Commonwealth Secretariat in London, and Laski Senior Scholar at St John's College, Cambridge.

Rex Li is Senior Lecturer in International Relations and Deputy Head of the Centre for Pacific Rim Studies at Liverpool John Moores University. Educated in Hong Kong and London, he worked as a journalist for a number of newspapers and magazines before joining the academic community. He was UK editor of *East and West*, and has written widely on international relations and East Asian affairs. His most recent publications include an article on China and Asia-Pacific Security in *Security Dialogue* (International Peace Research Institute). He has research interests in Pacific economic and security cooperation, and is currently completing a study of China's role in the changing global order.

Fu-Kuo Liu is an Associate Research Fellow at the Institute of International Relations, National Chengchi University, Taipei, where he works on regional economic integration, East Asian regionalism and industrial development, with particular reference to the influence of industrial groups on the emergence of Greater China. He studied political science, diplomacy, and international relations at National Chengchi University and the University of Southampton, and received his doctorate from the Department of Politics, University of Hull, in 1995.

Ngai-Ling Sum is Alex Horsley Research Fellow at the Political Economy Research Centre, the University of Sheffield. She has research interests in the political economy of Pacific Asia, newly industrializing countries, and the relationship between political economy and cultural politics. Dr Sum's most recent publications include an article on identity politics and 'political reform' in Hong Kong in *Economy and Society*, and a chapter on East Asian regionalism in *Regionalism and World Order*, edited by Andrew Gamble and Anthony Payne (Macmillan, 1996). She is currently working on a book entitled *Capitalism in East Asian Newly Industrializing Countries: A Regional Perspective*.

Le-Yin Zhang studied for her first and Master's degrees at Beijing Normal University, and received her doctorate on foreign investment in Guangdong Province from University College London, in 1990. She has worked as a consultant and researcher for various projects on China. She is currently working with Terry Cannon on regional conflicts in China.

Preface

The 'economic miracle' of Japan and the Newly Industrializing Countries of East Asia, and more recently, of China and some Southeast Asian countries has attracted a huge amount of attention from Western scholars, businesses, and governments. Pacific Asia is now widely regarded as a region of economic growth and dynamism. However, it is also a region of instabilities and uncertainties, especially in the post-Cold War era. Indeed, the pace and complexity of the changes in the area are increasingly beyond the scope of any one individual, institution, or even one discipline, to comprehend. Stimulated by our awareness of the need to develop and integrate research findings on constituent countries and regions of the Pacific Rim, we established the Centre for Pacific Rim Studies at Liverpool John Moores University, and initiated the British Pacific Rim Research Group in 1993, obtaining funding from the Economic and Social Research Council (ESRC) to organize a series of national and international research seminars on the region. The seminars brought together established and younger scholars from a host of disciplines and academic institutions in Britain and Pacific Rim countries, as well as government officials and representatives of the business community. A wide range of topics have been covered by these seminars, including economic development, business challenges and opportunities, sustainable development, security issues, regional integration, transnational organizations, and, Europe and Pacific Asia.

This volume is the first of the Pacific Rim Research Series emanating from the seminar series, which took place from 1993 to 1995. Most of the chapters in the volume are revised and updated versions of the papers presented to one of the seminars held at the School of Oriental and African Studies (SOAS), University of London, in May 1994. Other chapters have been specially commissioned for the book. The aim of this volume is to analyse the internal and external challenges to the states in Pacific Asia in the light of the rapid pace of change both within these countries and in the international system. More specifically, the authors examine the parallel trends in Pacific Asia of economic integration and security cooperation on the one hand, and growing pressures for decentralization, and even disintegration, in certain states, on the other. They also consider the response of Pacific Asian countries to these challenges, and the regional and global implications. We hope that the book will make a useful contribution to the continuing debate on the future of Pacific Asia and its likely impact on the world.

The diverse and vibrant programme of the Pacific Rim seminar series has been made possible by the participation and involvement of a large number of colleagues throughout the country and from Pacific Asia. We are extremely grateful to all the paper presenters, discussants and participants, especially the local organizers at SOAS, University of London, the School of East Asian Studies, University of Sheffield, and the Centre for South-East Asian Studies, University of Hull. Special thanks are due to Professor Anne Booth, Professor Ian Gow, and Dr Mike Parnwell. We are also grateful to the contributors for sending us the final drafts of their chapters within a fairly short period of time. In addition, we wish to thank a number of people at Liverpool John Moores University: Professor David McEvoy, Director of the School of Social Science, for his support and encouragement; Yongjiang Wang, Senior Lecturer in Japanese Language and Business, who was fully involved in the initiation and organization of the seminar series but is not in a position to work on this particular volume; Phil Cubbin, for his excellent cartographic, computer, and production skills, and to Steve Lawler, for his technical assistance, which were indispensable at the final stage of producing this book; Cathy Renton, Linda Pringle, Lesley Jenkins, Lynnette Heppard, for their assistance in organizing those seminars taking place in Liverpool.

Acknowledgements are also due to the University of Queensland Press, Cornell University Press and the Centre for International Studies, University of Ohio for extracts from *The Development of Indonesian* Society, *Decline of Constitutional Democracy in Indonesia*, and *Financing Local Government in Indonesia*, respectively. Finally, we would like to acknowledge the financial support from the ESRC for the seminar series.

Ian Cook, Marcus Doel, and Rex Li
Liverpool, November 1995

Abbreviations

ABSDF	All Burmese Students' Democratic Front
ADB	Asian Development Bank
AMM	ASEAN Ministerial Meeting
ANIC	Asian Newly Industrializing Country
AFTA	ASEAN Free Trade Area
APEC	Asia-Pacific Economic Cooperation
ARATS	Association for Relations Across the Taiwan Straits
ARF	ASEAN Regional Forum
ASEAN	Association of South-East Asian Nations
BSPP	Burma Socialist Programme Party
CCP	Chinese Communist Party
CEA	Chinese Economic Area
CNP	Chinese New Party (Taiwan)
CPB	Communist Party of Burma
CSBM	Confidence and Security Building Measure
CSCA	Conference on Security Cooperation in Asia
CSCE	Conference on Security and Cooperation in Europe
DAB	Democratic Alliance of Burma
DDSI	Directorate of Defence Services Intelligence (Burma)
DEA	Drug Enforcement Agency
DKBO	Democratic Kayin Buddhist Organization
DPP	Democratic Progressive Party (Taiwan)
EAEC	East Asian Economic Caucus
EC	European Community
EU	European Union
FAPA	Formosan Association for Public Affairs (Taiwan)
FDI	Foreign Direct Investment
FELG	Finance and Economic Leadership Group (of the

	Central Committee of the CCP)
FPS	First Party Secretary
FYP	Five-Year Plan
G-5	Group of Five Industrialised Democracies (France, Germany, Japan, UK, US)
G-7	Group of Seven Industrialised Democracies (Canada, France, Germany, Italy, Japan, UK, US)
GATT	General Agreement on Tariffs and Trade
GDP	Gross Domestic Product
GLF	Great Leap Forward (China)
GNP	Gross National Product
GSP	Generalized System of Preference
HPAE	High-Performing Asian Economy
IAEA	International Atomic Energy Agency
IBM	International Business Machines
IMF	International Monetary Fund
INPRES	Indonesian Central Government Infrastructure Funding Programmes
KIO	Kachin Independence Organization (Burma)
KNPP	Karenni National Progressive Party (Burma)
KNU	Karen National Union (Burma)
KMT	Kuomintang (Taiwan)
KNIL	Royal Dutch Indies Army
MNDAA	Myanmar National Democratic Alliance Army
MTA	Mong Tai Army (Burma)
NAFTA	North American Free Trade Area
NDF	National Democratic Front (Burma)
NIC	Newly Industrializing Country
NIE	Newly Industrializing Economy
NLD	National League for Democracy (Burma)
NU	Islamic Scholars Party (Indonesia)
NUP	National Unity Party (Burma)
ODA	Official Development Assistance (Japan)
OECD	Organization for Economic Cooperation and Development
OMA	Orderly Marketing Agreement
OPEC	Organization of Petroleum Exporting Countries
PAD	Provincial and District Own-Revenues (Indonesia)
PAFTA	Pacific Free Trade Area
PBB	Land and Property Tax (Indonesia)
PBEC	Pacific Basin Economic Council
PDF	People's Democratic Front (Burma)
PECC	Pacific Economic Cooperation Conference
PLA	People's Liberation Army (China)
PMC	Post-Ministerial Conference (ASEAN)

PNI	Indonesian Nationalist Party
PRC	People's Republic of China
PTT	Petroleum Authority of Thailand
SAR	Special Administrative Region (China)
SEA-10	South-East Asia Grouping of Ten Countries
SEE	State Economic Enterprise
SEF	Straits Exchange Foundation
SEZ	Special Economic Zone (China)
SLORC	State Law and Order Council (Burma)
SOE	State-owned Enterprise (China)
SOM	Senior Officials' Meeting
SUA	Shan United Army (Burma)
TNB	Transnational Bank
TNC	Transnational Corporation
TVE	Township and village enterprise (China)
UK	United Kingdom
UN	United Nations
UNDCP	United Nations Drugs Control Programme
UNDP	United Nations Development Programme
US	United States
UWSP	United Wa State Party (Burma)
VER	Voluntary Export Restraint
WTO	World Trade Organization
ZOPFAN	Zone of Peace, Freedom and Neutrality (Southeast Asia)

Introduction

Ian Cook, Marcus Doel and Rex Li

It is now well known that Pacific Asia is the most dynamic part of the global economy, and that the next century may well be the 'Pacific Century' as the focus of global affairs shifts from the North Atlantic to the (North) Pacific. The implications of this dynamic transformation for the economies, political regimes, societies and geographies of the countries of Pacific Asia are manifold, as they help shape the world of the twenty-first century in ways that are complex, multifaceted and uncertain. The essentially bipolar world of the second half of the twentieth century has already given way to the multipolar world of the next, with consequent implications for global security as policymakers and decision takers from government and business alike strive to understand the vagaries of a New World Order. They are now required to deal with diverse and diffuse demands from the socio-economic structures and political economies which are emerging so rapidly within this new and more volatile context of change .

A range of new questions are increasingly coming to the fore in Britain, Europe, North America and Pacific Asia itself. These include: can the nation-state be sustained; which country/countries will lead the global economy; what are the implications for our country/company of the high rates of growth in Pacific Asia; should we foster new supra-national regional entities such as the EU in other parts of the globe; and what are the constraints and opportunities which block or stimulate the emergence of new forms of governance? We would suggest that these and other questions can no longer be tackled by experts from a single discipline only; rather, they require multidisciplinary and interdisciplinary analysis in order to fully outline and interpret the range of factors and perspectives which bear upon each question. The contributors to this volume, therefore, are drawn from such disciplines as human geography, political science and international relations, political economy and development economics, and also represent a wide spread of expertise. Further, many of the authors are from Pacific

Asia itself, in the spirit of multicultural cooperation of the type which will become more and more necessary as we move into the next century.

The book takes as its focus the integration and disintegration of Pacific Asia. Integration is occurring at various levels, from what we might term the macro-regional to the micro-regional, as cross-border cooperation proceeds apace. New linkages are developing, between economies, political systems and social structures, and these may threaten the viability of the states across whose borders these connections develop. Flows of natural resources, manufactured goods, investment, concepts and ideas provide new opportunities for interactions in a number of spheres, but for the state, the multiplicity of these interactions, and their diffuse and inchoate nature, makes them difficult to control. The new situation can result in regional concepts and regional identities supplanting national concepts and national identities, and regionalism may supplant nationalism for the people in the areas most affected by these changes. The interweaving of this 'new regionalism' with economic development, globalization and political change presents new challenges for the peoples and governments of Pacific Asia.

Our first chapter is contributed by Professor Glenn Hook of the School of East Asian Studies, University of Sheffield. He draws upon his extensive experience of one of the key actors in the region, Japan, to highlight some practical and theoretical aspects of regionalism from a Japanese perspective, in particular its socio-economic and spatial heterogeneity. He 'point[s] to the need to understand regionalism by taking into account the complex nature of regional identities', viewing 'regions as the outcome of political as well as economic processes, where social forces vie in order to establish their own versions of a region' (p. 13), a perspective with which we concur. This leads neatly to the focus on the contested nature of regionalism in which alternative regional identities and concepts are constructed and presented by governments, business and other institutions for their own ends. In the Japanese case, these ends have varied considerably over time, with the main focus of controversy being whether Japan should be part of some greater East Asian region (such as the pre-World War II 'Greater East Asia Coprosperity Sphere') or part of a trans-Pacific entity, including North America (such as the recent suggestion of a 'Pacific Free Trade Area'). Hook explores Japan's links with Asia and with the Pacific over time, illustrating the importance of such factors as Japan's post-war economic and political restructuring, export focus, overseas investment patterns, government policy, and resource requirements, on shaping the direction in which Japan should move as a major regional player. For Japan, the debate in all its ramifications continues, with links to the global economy tending to lead the country towards the US and APEC, whereas more localized factors are encouraging sub-regional linkages, at prefectural level, with partners in East Asia. This has a knock-on effect on the Japanese state itself, as alternatives to the state are developed. Hook concludes that: 'How this process evolves will affect the balance of Japan's relations with

2

Asia and the West. In this can be seen the global importance of sub-regionalism in East Asia' (p. 26).

Japan is a strong state, both internally and externally. In the next chapter, Tim Huxley of the Centre for South East Asian Studies, University of Hull, examines that regional organization, the Association of South East Asian Nations (ASEAN), which is largely composed of weak states. Huxley notes that ASEAN 'is by far the most successful Third World regional organization' (p. 29) and has become a model for other such regions, particularly due to its successful interventions over the Cambodian situation and its recent incorporation of Vietnam into the organization. Notwithstanding such undoubted success, Huxley argues that the future of ASEAN is uncertain due to the internal contradictions resulting from its composition as a group of weak states. Thus, for example, although the organization has ensured that, to-date, conflict between member states has been minimized, and has introduced the Zone of Peace, Freedom and Neutrality (ZOPFAN) concept to the Southeast Asian region, its unwillingness to institute a range of policies both within and between its constituent states aimed at strengthening the 'national resilience' of these states on the one hand, and of ensuring that intra-mural disputes are resolved (rather than merely being contained) on the other: 'prevents ASEAN from evolving into a strong security regime, in which institutional mechanisms for conflict resolution are activated, and ultimately into a security community in which internecine violence would be inconceivable' (p. 34). Huxley, therefore, argues strongly that ASEAN states need to reduce their internal inequalities, and hence internal tensions, and to considerably speed up and deepen recent moves towards confidence- and security-building measures (CSBMs), and the ASEAN Regional Forum (ARF). If this is not done, ASEAN may ultimately prove to be incapable of responding to the complexities of the new security situation in the region, including the potential threat of an increasingly powerful and assertive China.

Tim Huxley's chapter is a timely reminder of the contrasting myths and realities that underpin regionalism. There would seem to be considerable schismatic tendencies underlying the veneer of unity ASEAN presents. 'Unity in diversity' is of course the famous phrase that has traditionally been applied to Southeast Asia in general and to Indonesia in particular. Our next chapter considers the third apex in the 'great triangle' of Pacific Asia: China. Due to China's great importance to the future of Pacific Asia it is considered in different facets in several chapters. The first of these, by Ngai-Ling Sum of the Political Economy Research Centre of the University of Sheffield, is concerned with the politics of identity around the contested construction of the 'Greater China' bloc, comprising of Hong Kong-Macau, Taiwan and Southern China. Dr Sum argues that this newly emerging bloc can be understood neither in terms of the geo-political discourses of the Cold War, nor of the developing geo-economic discourses of the post-Cold War. Rather, it must be analysed via a structure-strategy-agency schema, which can adequately deal with the 'multi-faceted, multi-layered coupling of geo-economics, and geo-politics' (p. 53). Her analysis, therefore, considers such features as the US' new 'insurance' strategy of risk reduction via bilateralism, the encouragement of the democratization agenda of Governor Patten in Hong Kong, and the continued independence and democratization processes in Taiwan. Sum points out that the coupling of these principally Western driven (i.e. US and UK) geo-political strategies are made more complex by the parallel geo-economic strategies of China and Japan. China, for example, has presented the concept of Greater China as a means both of strengthening China's economic development, via the incorporation of Hong Kong and Taiwanese investment and management expertise into the spatial economy of South China, and fostering this 'imagined community' as what we can term a nationalized and essentialized political and terrritorial claim on Hong Kong and Taiwan. Japan's agenda, meanwhile, is to penetrate the Chinese market by 'piggy-backing' on these economic linkages. The Chinese government has strongly played the patriotic card to encourage the huge investments of recent years by overseas Chinese, but the dilemma which faces the people of Hong Kong and Taiwan includes democratization vis-à-vis the 'pragmatic nationalism' of a Greater China. The identity struggle of both Hong Kong and Taiwan is then reviewed, with competing discursive formations interpreted. Sum suggests that the dialectical interface between global, regional and local forces gives rise to identity struggles in which new articulations of social bases of support arise. The political, opportunity *structure* may thus be significantly changed by the *strategies* adopted by *agents* in reconstructing meanings and identities.

China is so vast that it is necessary to consider not only the expansionist features of this Greater China concept, but also the internal dynamics of regionalization within the country. To this end, Terry Cannon and Le-Yin Zhang of the University of Greenwich focus on regional tensions within China, examining and evaluating their underlying causes, the response of central and local governments to the resultant intra-regional conflicts up to 1993, and summarising the detailed reforms introduced to the economy by central government in 1994. The focus is on the political economy of regionalism in China, and they show the contribution of the economic reforms of the 1980s to intra-provincial tension, wherein some provinces utilise their new-found autonomy to obstruct flows of goods and materials or to compete wastefully for state investment funds, for example. Government policy that encouraged rapid growth in the coastal provinces via a range of favourable measures, fiscal opportunities for and pressures on local authorities that stimulated their increased linkages with local enterprises, and the intertwining of such factors with the wider political controversies and debates concerning the shape, scope and direction of market reforms, combined to lead to a difficult situation by the early 1990s in which, as Cannon and Zhang put it, "the centre pretends to rule and the provinces pretend to be ruled" (p. 85). This situation led to intensive debate within China, as regional imbalances threatened to destabilize the country and fears grew of a possible break-up of China on the same lines as had happened in the USSR. The debate crystallized over the tax and fiscal reforms introduced in 1994, coupled with the further expansion of the market economy. As the authors note, central government is seeking to first, 'redistribute power and financial resources from local authorities to central government and enterprises; second, detach enterprises from government' (p. 93). It is too soon to say whether these measures will be successful, but Terry Cannon and Le-Yin Zhang conclude that the pro-market, neo-liberal approach is unable to fully deal with the regional issue. Rather they suggest that China is a commercializing rather than a market economy, with no guarantee that central government can recoup revenues from the provinces, nor deal adequately with regional poverty. Regional tensions, therefore, are likely to continue in one form or another despite the reform package.

Indonesia is another vast country (although Westerners often forget just how large it is). Professor Anne Booth of the School of African and Asian Studies, University of London, employs her twenty years of expertise in the study of development questions within Indonesia to analyse its regional issues and policies since Independence in 1949. As she tellingly begins: 'Indonesia is, by any standard, an improbable country' (p. 102). The Dutch colonial power sought to extend its power and suzerainty far beyond Java, as much to prevent more distant islands falling into the hands of other European powers as for any intrinsic desire for conquest. Similarly, the newly formed Indonesian state chose a unitary system as much because of the tainted Dutch experiment in federalism in 1945-46 as any real desire for a centralized system. Growing frustration with the domination of Java grew, however, as the island consumed the bulk of imports despite its low level of export activity, unlike many of the outlying islands, and armed regional-based conflicts occurred. The advent of Soeharto's New Order regime in 1965 led on the one hand to even more centralization of power in Java, and on the other hand to the resources to grapple with regional disparities via the new oil revenues. The INPRES programmes were utilized to provide local infrastructure, ranging from schools and health facilities to road and irrigation provision. Strong central control was exerted to minimize waste and corruption and these programmes made a generally positive contribution to developing rural areas in the 1970s and 1980s, even after the cutbacks due to falling oil prices in the late 1980s. Booth provides an analytical update of a previous study to show, however, that allocations in 1993-94 were skewed towards provinces with a higher proportion of the population below the poverty line. Similarly, her analysis of the own-revenues of provinces and districts illustrates considerable spatial variation, with Jakarta (motor vehicle tax) and Bali (hotel tax) being the main beneficiaries, contrasting markedly with Eastern Indonesia for example, notwithstanding that a few very poor provinces have also done well in raising local revenues.

These two points of spatial contrast relate to Anne Booth's findings on the development gap in Indonesia, in which Eastern Indonesia is markedly lagging behind Java, the mineral-rich provinces and other parts of the country, such as Bali. She states that 'Eastern Indonesia has benefited little from any of the three main forms of industrialization that have occurred in Indonesia over the past twenty-five years' (pp. 116-7), nor do its inherent socio-economic and environmental disadvantages suggest that this dismal situation can be easily remedied. Further, even in the mining provinces, which rank highly in terms of per capita Gross Domestic Product (GDP), per capita consumption expenditures show that poverty is widespread, for example in Irian Jaya, where the gap between the two indicators is great, due in turn to the gap between exports from, and imports into, the province. In this and other provinces, unrest is found as 'indigenous people have so little say in the disposition of their resource wealth, and, consequently, a desire for greater control over their own futures' (p. 119). The causes may be slightly different, but here, as in China, regional tensions require the state to tread carefully lest it instigate or continue policies which exacerbate spatial inequalities and thus fuel fissiparous tendencies. Booth concludes by summarising three basic options for the Indonesian government: to make minimal change to the status quo; to deal with regional problems on an ad hoc basis; or to develop a federalist direction involving fundamental reforms in the centre-regions relationship. She herself would seem to be in favour of both poorer and wealthier provinces securing a greater degree of control over their resources, but she concludes by noting that fiscal measures alone would be insufficient without accompanying political changes, principally towards democratization and the consequent regulation of a more regionalized government via the ballot box. To this we would add that, at present, such alternatives would seem to be some way off.

Notwithstanding the importance of political factors in the previous two chapters, economic development issues are central to their analyses. This latter perspective is also found, and to a greater degree, in the following chapter by Fu-Kuo Liu of the Institute of International Relations, Taipei, Taiwan. Western observers, and others, have rightly been struck by the tremendous success of the Asian Newly Industrialized Countries (ANICs) of Hong Kong, Singapore, Taiwan and South Korea, but Dr Liu's thesis is twofold, namely: that the drive to regionalism in East Asia, especially at the sub-regional level, is driven by economic rather than political motives; and that the involvement of the ANICs in this process of regionalization is a reflection of the pressure of industrial restructuring on their economies. The ANICs are caught in what we might term a 'double bind', in which on the one hand they are squeezed by increased protectionism in their key export markets of the US and the EU, allied to their lack of access to the highest level of advanced technology, and on the other hand faced with the pressure emanating from, inter alia, the much lower labour costs, land prices, and less concern for environmental issues, of developing countries such as Indonesia or, especially, China. The loss of comparative advantage and the need to maintain competitiveness has required the ANICs to invest heavily in the latter group of countries and to set up 'growth triangles' that combine the capital and know-how of the ANICs with the local cost, resource and regulatory advantages of the host country. Liu quotes the then Trade and Industry Minister of Singapore, speaking at an investors meeting in 1990 with regards to the proposed Singapore-Johor-Riau growth triangle, to the effect that Singapore lacks land and labour, but has a developed infrastructure and higher concentration of manufacturing and service industries, while both Indonesia and Malaysia have abundant labour and natural resources *'and potential for tremendous growth once these are organized and developed'* (p. 152) [our emphasis]. The implication of this is of course that it is Singapore that will do the organizing and developing, operating in a similar manner to a transnational corporation for example. In a similar vein, Taiwan exports capital, and low and middle-level technology and management experience, combining them with the labour and raw material resources of their partner(s).

The value of Liu's perspective is that he shows that the ANICs are operating from a position of weakness rather strength, in the sense that they are simultaneously encountering a 'ceiling' to their export performance (comprised of protectionism in the developed economies as well as a technological threshold that prevents them from engaging in what we might term the 'frontier zone' of hi-tech), while the 'floor' is being pushed rapidly upwards via the entry of the 'new' economies into the global economy in general, and Pacific Asia in particular. The challenges which the ANICs face Fu-Kuo Liu generalises as "exogenous industrial structural problems"; these provide the 'momentum of regionalization' and create new sub-regional divisions of labour which provide complementarity. Unlike the 'talking shop' of APEC and other Pan-Pacific groupings the sub-regional groupings which Liu describes are driven by private sector interests, and provide 'an extensive economic space' (p. 158) in which, he argues, the ANICs overcome their labour shortages, retain their comparative advantage, and balance differences in regional economic development.

Fu-Kuo Liu's chapter is followed by one from the first of our representatives from the world of business (albeit an economist on long-term leave of absence from the world of academe at the University of Bath), Cho-Oon Khong of Shell International. Dr. Khong presents a business view of Pacific Asian as a region, delving deeply into the myths and stereotypes of the contemporary situation in order to unravel the dynamics of change in Asia. He notes, for example, that there is no single 'East Asian Growth Model', and in any case that any such model would be on the verge of major change in order to cope effectively with current and unfolding scenarios. Just as there is no single growth model so too is there no single set of much-vaunted Confucian values to underpin any model. Rather, he makes the pertinent point that the presentation of Confucianism by East Asian governments to define a common regional identity is selective, based on a narrow conception of Confucianism, and used to 'justify certain forms of government rule, which are believed to be necessary to maintain order and stability against

7

both internal and external pressures for change' (p. 172). Further, Confucian values comprise only one possible set of 'anchor points' among the many which are possible in the creation of new regional 'imagined communities'.

In addition to interest in the models of economic growth found in East Asia, and the role of Confucianism, for example, within these, Western business is deeply concerned with the sustainability of East Asian development. Dr. Khong therefore utilizes the concept of 'total factor productivity' to show that, notwithstanding the potential synergy of Asia-Pacific regionalism (or the sub-regionalism to which Fu-Kuo Liu refers), or the high savings ratios of East Asia, limitations of, for example, the low value-added approach, of state intervention in economic development, and of capital input will preclude the indefinite linear extrapolation of current growth rates.

Another major focus is on the operation of Overseas Chinese Networks, which Cho-Oon Khong suggests provides the 'glue' of regional identity, rather than the institutions of APEC or ASEAN. He supports Liu's analysis that it is the spontaneous integration by the market rather than the political system which is the key factor. He debunks the myth that these are networks of open liberalization, as they can appear from the outside, but instead are networks which operate from behind a 'barricades' mentality in which personal contact and trust of an intensely private nature, excluding foreigners, has been the essential feature. The thrust of globalization, however, allied to the need for high technology, is pressuring these networks to open up, providing potential linkages with Western firms who can provide expertise and access to Western markets. Another point that Khong makes, and one which is also made in a different way by Hook and Liu in previous chapters, is that Asia-Pacific regionalism is open and outward-oriented. In part this reflects the spatial expansion of these Overseas Chinese Networks which stretch especially to the United States and Canada but also elsewhere. It also reflects, echoing previous authors, the crucial importance of North American markets, and even the expansion of intra-regional trade is often in intermediate products where the final destination is North America.

These economic and cultural issues have strategic implications. Uncertainties concern the continuing role of the United States in Asia - a 'spectre' which the diners would prefer to remain at the East Asian banquet but also 'the spectre of a hegemon in decline, impelled by growing isolationism at home and a feeling of being rebuffed abroad' (p. 177) as Khong eloquently expresses it. Other uncertainties concern the current or imminent regime transitions in North Korea, China and, at some point, Indonesia, and contribute to the climate of uncertainty which renders policy-making difficult. The economic stakes are high, 'but the political commitment to Asian regionalism is as yet fragile: either absent, wavering or suspicious. It is this political lacuna which makes the long-term future of Asian regionalism so unclear' (p. 177). according to Khong. On strategic issues, therefore, it is necessary to temper optimism with caution, and Dr. Khong concludes that, instead of a dichotomy between opening up to change or resisting

8

it we have mutual dependence, like Yin and Yang, and he concludes that 'Both expanding horizons and an exclusive identity, feeding off each other, may be the critical drivers of Asia-Pacific regionalism' (p. 179).

If such a feeding process achieves mutual balance then future scenarios can be, essentially, optimistic. Our last two chapters focus on two countries for which the balance may not, however, hold. Firstly, our other representative of the world of business, John Bray of Control Risks International, focuses on Burma (Myanmar) to exemplify two themes which run through this volume, namely the fear of fragmentation at the national level, combined with increasing pressure for greater economic and political integration at the regional level.

Firstly, at the national level, the 'Burmese Path to Socialism' under General Ne Win was followed, in 1988, by the State Law and Order Restoration Council (SLORC) comprised entirely of army officers. Both of these regimes utilized autocratic policies, largely in response to the threatened break up of Burma via conflict with the many ethnic minorities who fell within the boundaries of this particular colonial map-makers fiction. SLORC has, as Bray notes 'of necessity', introduced economic liberalization policies and has insisted that in due course it will hand over power to civilians. In 1990, however, it ignored the resounding electoral success of Aung San Suu Kyi's National League for Democracy and continued her house arrest, begun in 1989, ending it only in summer 1995. In 1993 SLORC set up a National Convention to draw up the guiding principles of a new constitution but loaded the membership heavily in favour of its own appointees, and the mass of the Burmese people would seem to regard the Convention, in consequence, as a sham. Where SLORC has had some political success is in arranging ceasefires with many of its ethnic minority opponents, but as Bray notes these ceasefires are fragile, and in any case some other conflicts continue. The economic changes may prove to be more fruitful. Outside investors are attracted by Burma's rich natural resource base and tourism potential, and SLORC has declared 1996 as 'Visit Myanmar Year'.

At the regional level, Burma's pivotal position relative to both India and China, coupled with its undoubted economic potential, has led to pragmatism from most of its Asian neighbours, in marked contrast to United States and other Western nations which have heaped opprobrium on Burma due to its human rights record. Thus China, for example, which shares this experience of criticism from the West, has become a major ally and is encouraging cross border economic links with Yunnan province, and economic expansion into north Burma to the alarm of many Burmese. Also, ASEAN has been engaged in a policy of 'constructive engagement', which Bray attributes largely to 'commercial self-interest'. This is leading to an invite from Thailand to attend the December 1995 regional security summit. Also the proposed 'golden quadrilateral' developments along the Mekong River, brokered by the Asian Development Bank, may further draw Burma into a regional futures. Against such trends, however, Bray notes that Burma needs China more than China needs Burma, and that China would probably drop its backing for the Burmese regime should it obtain greater benefits elsewhere by doing so, while Thailand-Burma relations are fraught with tensions, and the US can exert considerable leverage to block IMF or World Bank funding unless political change occurs. Bray concludes that the apparent strength of the regime masks deep divisions in Burmese society, and the increased links with the region may put in train processes which further tears apart the fabric of the state. Unless a more democratic situation is established, therefore, Bray suggests: 'regional integration and national fragmentation may prove to be two sides of the same coin' (p. 197).

Our final chapter, by Dr Ian Cook and Rex Li of the Centre for Pacific Rim Studies, School of Social Science, Liverpool John Moores University, also considers these 'two sides of the coin' with regards to the future of China, the importance of which has such serious implications not only for Pacific Asia but also for the world in general. They identify the factors which underpin centralist and decentralist tendencies within China, and present alternative scenarios for the Chinese state. Centralist tendencies include: the legacy of the imperial system with its hierarchical structure; the reaction of the Chinese Communist Party (CCP) to the humiliations, by outside powers, of the 19th and early 20th centuries; and the dominance of the Han culture, both numerically and spatially. After the communist revolution, for example, a rigid Centrally Planned Economy was introduced, run on Soviet lines, prior to the Sino-Soviet split, and the CCP has continued to exert a strong control over the political system, notwithstanding the economic liberalization of recent years. As against that, decentralist tendencies include: the legacy of economic development which before the People's Republic was primarily located along the coast, along the Chiang Jiang (Yangzi) and Manchuria; schismatic tendencies in provinces such as Guangdong or Sichuan; the Maoist legacy of 'one unit-ism'; and regional disparities which include the association of ethnic minorities with poorer and spatially extensive peripheral regions. Such internal factors combine with other centrifugal tendencies arising from external linkages to ensure that fragmentation of China is, indeed, possible..

Nevertheless, Cook and Li present three alternative scenarios for the future. Scenario one is based on the assumptions that the post-Deng political transition is smooth, that economic growth continues unabated, that China continues to improve its diplomatic relations with other countries while building up its military strength, and the People's Liberation Army (PLA), whose role will be crucial in whatever outcome, continues to support the status quo. In such a scenario the Chinese state would face various internal and external pressures but would be able to tackle these via the combination of economic carrot and neo-authoritarian political stick. Scenario two is the break-up scenario, occurring under either a leftist or new-rightist turn in the post-Deng era. Regional and popular pressures would build up to such an extent that fragmentation took place, with at least regional units of the PLA supporting breakaway regions. China would return to its 1920s and 1930s situation, and this, to Cook and Li would be a 'nightmare scenario', for the 1990s involves weapons of mass destruction. The resultant loss of life and population displacement would not only be serious in itself but would also have a tremendous impact in Pacific Asia in particular, but also, via the interdependence of the global economy, on many other countries of the globe including those of Europe and North America.

In scenario three, China does not shrink, as in scenario two, but expands to a 'Greater China' similar to that discussed by Ngai Ling Sum above, but not just limited to South China with Hong Kong/ Macau and Taiwan. The consequences of such an expansion are difficult to predict: one possibility is that China becomes such a strong state economically and politically that it becomes 'a major force of economic progress and a responsible member of the international community' (p. 214). The fears of other countries are found to be groundless in such a scenario. The second outcome, conversely, is that a strong China has the economic and political power to assert militarily its historic claims to the Nansha/Spratly and Diaoyutai/Senkaku islands. This may then lead to military confrontations with neighbouring countries, further militarization in Japan and Russia and potential conflict with the US. Such scenarios, then, have profound regional and global implications. Ian Cook and Rex Li conclude that the potential cost (in human life, economic wealth and political instability) of a break-up scenario means that the West must be cautious lest it actively encourages such an outcome. And on the other side, 'the Chinese government would be well advised to be sensitive to perceptions of other countries in its pursuit of great power status'. Their final plea, therefore, is for 'deeper mutual understanding and cooperation in an increasingly interdependent world' (p. 215).

Hopefully, this volume makes a small contribution towards this objective. The contributors take different perspectives on the importance of the economic as opposed to the political, and have contrasting viewpoints on current and future outcomes. However, we are not seeking to introduce some new orthodoxy; rather to raise issues for discussion, reflection and further analysis. The themes of regionalism, sub-regionalism, economic development, and political change which recur through this text ensure that a multiplicity of perspectives are required in order to fully understand them. These can be found in the chapters that follow.

1   Japan and contested regionalism

Glenn Hook

Against the background of decline in United States hegemony and the end of the Cold War division of the world, the question of Japan's global and regional roles in politics and economics continues to be raised. Some predict the twenty-first century will be dominated by a 'bigemony' between the US and Japan; others see the world coming under Japanese hegemony; still others fear that Japan is already on the path to forging a regional bloc (On future scenarios, see Inoguchi, 1990). In all of this, Japan's relations with the US, on the one hand, and East Asia, on the other, are central. Indeed, ever since the US ended the empire's attempt to use force as a means of creating the Greater East Asian Coprosperity Sphere, bilateralism and regionalism have been at the heart of Japan's relations with the outside world. In the post-Cold War world of the 1990s, the Pacific at the centre of bilateralism and East Asia at the centre of regionalism are taking on new identities in the process of the competitive attempts to reconstitute regions as 'Asia Pacific' or 'East Asia.'

In the wake of the economic success of first Japan, then of the 'four tigers' (Hong Kong, Singapore, South Korea, and Taiwan), and now of the Association of South East Asian Nations (ASEAN) members Indonesia, Malaysia, and Thailand, East Asia is being trumpeted as the economic growth region of the global economy. The economic success of the four tigers, and in the last two decades of what the World Bank now calls the Newly Industrializing Economies (NIEs) of Indonesia, Malaysia and Thailand, has led the Bank to coin a new acronym, HPAEs, the 'high-performing Asian economies', to refer to these East Asian 'miracle' economies (The World Bank, 1993). Although East Asia is seen to be made up of 'all the low- and middle-income economies of East and Southeast Asia and the Pacific, east of and including China and Thailand', the Bank's focus is placed squarely on the HPAEs (The World Bank, 1993, p. xvi). It is in respect of Japan's relations with the tigers and the ASEAN 'miracle' economies that, in our own discussion of East Asia, regions and regionalism will be problematized.

Despite the economic success of East Asia, however, the legacy of Japanese imperialism, together with the unfolding competition to establish regions with different memberships and boundaries, point to the need to understand regionalism by taking into account the complex nature of regional identities. We thus view regions as the outcome of political as well as economic processes, where social forces vie in order to establish their own versions of a region. While changing patterns of trade and investment are important indices for demonstrating the emergence of an East Asia or Asia Pacific region, with growth in intra-regional trade and investment — particularly as witnessed after the 1985 Plaza Accord and the 1987 Louvre Accord currency realignments — being used to bolster the regional idea, the powerful challenge to an East Asian regional identity, as seen in the increasingly prominent role played by the US in the Asia Pacific Economic Conference (APEC) (See Miura, 1995), highlights the political nature of regionalism. By examining Japanese involvement in regionalism on different levels, we intend to show how, in the Cold War as well as in the emerging post-Cold War era, regions are contested in East Asia and the Pacific.

Contested regionalism

Without doubt, the ending of the Cold War has stimulated a growing interest in the political economy of regionalism. Whether in Europe, with the deepening and widening of the European Union (EU); in North America, with the signing of the North America Free Trade Agreement (NAFTA); or in Asia Pacific, with the strengthening of the organizational base of APEC, observers and practitioners alike see the possibility of the global political economy splintering into three competing meta-regional groupings centring on the most powerful economies in these three regions — Germany in Europe, the US in the Americas, and Japan in East Asia. Some even go so far as to warn of the possibility of the world fragmenting into a confrontational triad of economic blocs.

Such 'inward-looking regionalism', which is seen to characterize the regional initiatives in Europe and North America (Okita, 1989, p. 10), differs from the 'open regionalism' of Asia Pacific (Elek, 1994; Garnaut and Drysdale, 1994). Insofar as economic approaches to regionalism view a region as resulting from increasing levels of economic cooperation, through in particular an expansion in regional trade and investment, then inward-looking regionalism can be distinguished by discrimination against those outside the region, and open regionalism by non-discrimination (Garnaut and Drysdale, 1994). In this respect, the emergence of an economic bloc appears less likely in Asia Pacific than in the other core regions of the globe, as the region comprises the industrially developed, the newly industrializing, and the developing, making the abolition of custom duties between national economies, and other such steps along the way to

13

establishing a bloc, fraught with difficulty. What is more, the dependence of East Asian economies on global, not just regional, exports suggests open regionalism is in their interests. Certainly, the Japanese government supports open regionalism, as demonstrated by Foreign Minister Hata's speech at the 1993 meeting of APEC in Seattle (Cited in Furukawa, 1994a, p. 64).

The emergence of powerful economies in East Asia has fuelled the debate on regionalism, with the Malaysian Prime Minister Mahathir's 1990 proposal for an East Asian Economic Caucus (EAEC) acting as a lightning-rod (On EAEC, see Shima, 1993). This would seek to build a regional identity centring on East Asia, with Japan as a crucial linchpin in a new grouping including ASEAN and the three Chinas. In the face of US opposition to any attempt to create an exclusive, closed form of regionalism centring on an East Asian identity, the Japanese government has refused to support the Malaysian initiative, preferring instead to support APEC (e.g. *Nihon Keizai Shimbun*, 17 January 1993). While concern has often been expressed by Japan's neighbours over the possibility of it dominating regional institutions, the proposal by Malaysia to include it in EAEC highlights the crucial role Japan plays as the economic hub of the region. The success of East Asian export-led growth strategies means that the follower economies now share many of the same needs as Japan in maintaining open markets for exports on a global scale. In this sense, the initiative by a member of the newly industrializing ASEAN countries points to a perception of East Asia as a viable region for the development of cooperation on issues in the global political economy.

These references to both Asia Pacific and East Asia symbolize the contested nature of regional boundaries and identities. For regions are not pre-existent spatial entities, or merely geographic nomenclatures, but identities constructed through socio-cultural, political and economic processes and activities. Social forces work to construct or destroy specific regional identities, as well as to highlight, shade or obfuscate different elements of identity. Hence the boundaries of regions remain flexible. Depending on the motivation and elements used in defining a region, certain areas will be excluded or included, with regions often 'fraying' at the edges. Membership in regional organizations can be used as a way to create or reconstitute a regional identity, as is occurring now in the competition between APEC and EAEC. Certainly, the increasingly prominent role being played by the US in nurturing APEC as the regional organization is indicative of the attempts being made to construct a regional identity linking the US economy to the HPAEs. By in this way taking on a lead role in tying together Asia and the Pacific, the US no doubt aims to benefit from strengthening links with the growth economies of East Asia.

Japanese perspectives on East Asia and the Pacific

The contested nature of regions is evident from how Japan has constructed and reconstructed East Asia and the surrounding area as a region. The present perception of the region is not clear-cut, but generally is seen to include the Korean peninsula, the three Chinas, and sometimes Mongolia, with Southeast Asia including ASEAN, Indochina and Mynmar. How have these areas been perceived in the past? To start with, 'island Southeast Asia' (*nanyo*) has been recognized historically in Japan. But whereas Southeast Asia started to be perceived as a region in the West at the time of the Pacific War, it already had been recognized as such in Japan after the First World War, as evidenced by the appearance of 'Southeast Asia' in school textbooks in 1919. This followed a division of the region into *nai nanyo* (Micronesia and other islands) and *gai nanyo* (present-day Southeast Asia). Essentially, the appearance of Southeast Asia as a region at this time 'resulted from the expansion of Japanese economic interests through the First World War' (Yamaguchi, 1991, pp. 19-20).

Similarly, when Japan attempted to reconstitute 'East Asia' around the concept of the Greater East Asian Coprosperity Sphere, other parts of the region were brought within a contested view of a 'Greater East Asia'. In the case of Manchuria, for instance, the economic and political reconstitution of East Asia meant the 'outsider' (Japan) was competing with the 'insider' (China) in defining the spatial identity of a part of the region. Needless to say, for the Chinese the construction of 'Manchuria' (*Manshu*) was resisted as the imposition of an identity from the outside, but Manchuria gained international currency in the political restructuring of the region carried out by the Japanese empire. In this sense, new identities can be legitimized as well as delegitimized by acceptance or rejection in the international community.

Finally, East Asia has been regarded as an historical or cultural space, thereby bringing within its embrace Japan, China (including Taiwan and Hong Kong), the Korean peninsula, Vietnam, and Singapore; namely, those cultures seen to be influenced by traditional Confucian values and social practices. Thus, a cultural definition of the region need not coincide with a regional identity giving priority to economics or politics. During the Cold War the political division of the Korean peninsula and Vietnam meant that a cultural understanding of the East Asian region was overlaid with a regional division based on Cold War political considerations. With the end of the Cold War, culture has started to reappear as a key element in linking Japan and the fast growing economies of East Asia, with Confucian social practices and values viewed as being at the core of an economic culture where hard work, education, respect for elders, and so on, help explain, wholly or in part, the success of these nations (Berger and Hsiao, 1988). In this, culture and economic success tend to overlap, with interest focusing more on Confucian success stories, like Singapore, than on 'Confucian' Vietnam

Historically speaking, the Japanese empire's conquest of other parts of Asia and the attempt to create the Greater East Asian Coprosperity Sphere has left an indelible sense of distrust amongst Japan's neighbours. It is true that the Cold War division of the region put Japan on the same political side as the non-communist regimes of East and Southeast Asia, but any regional role emerging from the nation's economic success, as recognized by its entry into the

Organization for Economic Cooperation and Development (OECD) in 1964, was undermined by the initiative taken by other Asian nations, particularly the creation of ASEAN in 1967. The difficulty for Japan was in exercising power, which confirmed its Asian identity, for Japan's historical legacy precluded its neighbours from sharing a sense of solidarity with the old imperial power. This made other Asian nations reluctant to strengthen links with Japan, especially in the areas of politics and security. At the same time, in the area of economics, the disparity between Japan and the developing nations of East Asia at the outset linked Japan and the region in a classic centre-periphery relationship, with the natural resources of the region being of central concern to the former empire. In this sense, one of the major endogenous forces for institution-building in the region, ASEAN, excluded Japan amidst general distrust of the imperialist past and fears of neo-colonialism.

Thus, the political as well as economic links with the US strengthened Japan's Pacific identity. The concept of an Asia Pacific region initially arose outside of East Asia as a way of linking Asia to the Pacific through bilateral security arrangements. During the Cold War the US set about building a 'hub and spokes' security system, linking East Asia and the Pacific through bilateral security treaties with Japan, the Philippines, the Republic of Korea, and so on. Such exogenous sources for the links between East Asia and the Pacific were complemented by Japan's own struggle to join the West. Within the region, Japanese policy makers and business leaders paid particular attention to reconstituting Japan — the newly emerging economic superpower — as a Pacific power in the wake of its entry into the OECD. Thereafter, a boom occurred in Pacific initiatives, as with the proposal for a Pacific Free Trade Area (PAFTA) made by Kojima Kiyoshi (Korhonen, 1994). In a sense, Japan's entry into the OECD signified a further step along the road to 'leaving Asia and entering the West' (*datsua nyuo*), but at heart this confirmed the nation's ambivalent position as part of both Asia and the Pacific. For instance, in hosting the Southeast Asia Development Ministerial Meeting in 1966, the Japanese government confirmed its membership of the economically advanced OECD countries as a member of the Pacific. For the first time Japan played a role in promoting cooperation and economic development, positioning itself as the most advanced economy of Asia. At the same time, its development as a Pacific power meant the Japanese and American economies grew closer. Whilst this gave economic substance to the later development of APEC, the successful export of made-in-Japans to the US intensified trade conflict and rivalry between the two nations. Still, the security links at the heart of the relationship ensured that, in the end, the Japanese government usually submitted to pressure from the US to restrict exports, as we will see below.

The defeat of Japan in the second world war and the subsequent emergence of the Cold War was instrumental in restructuring the nation's political and economic links with East Asia and the Pacific. The integration of Japan into the capitalist camp in the Cold War confrontation in the region meant bilateral relations with the US became the pillar of Japan's reconstituted relations with the outside world. In this, the Pacific took precedence over Asia. On the one hand, the security treaty system centring on bilateral relations between the US and East Asia restricted links between Japan and its Asian neighbours. On the other hand, the legacy of imperialism distorted the relations that the nation gradually rebuilt with the region, from the 1950s onwards.

To start with, during the Occupation and in the early years after its end the US played a crucial role in rebuilding the Japanese economy. Joseph Dodge's pegging of the yen at 360 yen to the dollar in 1949 ensured that exports became an essential ingredient in the recovery of Japan's economic strength (Tsuru, 1993, pp.78ff.). Still, it was not clear at the time that, as a result of the Japanese success in rebuilding the economy, expanding exports, and then becoming an economic superpower, the US' own economy would be challenged in sector after sector by the might of the new Japan. Although the role of the American market as an absorber of made-in-Japans was important to the successful challenges mounted by the Japanese economy as an eventual rival of the US, this was essentially one of the hidden costs of America's restructuring of East Asia along Cold War lines. The 'special procurements' made by the US during the Korean War meant that, from the very start, the Japanese economy was able to take advantage of the hot wars arising out of the Cold War division of East Asia. Similar benefits accrued to Japan as a result of the Vietnam War (Havens, 1987). The boost to the economy brought about by America's two wars symbolized how Japanese development benefited from conflicts in the region. In essence, and given the Cold War ideological framework of US policy making, which placed security at the very heart of relations with East Asia, Japan's stability as a capitalist bastion against communism was needed for the development of capitalist East Asia. Furthermore, since economic growth was seen as essential to Japanese stability, the US supported Japan's entry into the International Monetary Fund (IMF) in 1952, and the General Agreement on Tariffs and Trade (GATT) in 1955. Such actions facilitated the recovery, growth and expansion of the Japanese economy, as did the 'divine winds' of the two wars in the region.

The high growth era of roughly the mid-1950s to the early 1970s was a period of major expansion in Japanese exports, with the dollar volume of exports between 1955 and 1975 increasing 27.7 times (Tsuru, 1993, p. 82). During this period, Japan's main exports moved from low technology textiles to steel, radios and televisions. After the twin oil shocks of 1973 and 1978, exports of automobiles and electrical machinery came to occupy an increasingly important share of Japanese exports, becoming major export items in the 1980s. The increasing

17

sophistication of Japanese industry is evident from the export of industrial items, which moved from sewing machines and cameras, to televisions and automobiles, and then to communication equipment and other high technology products. From the mid-1950s onwards, about a quarter to a third of total exports were destined for the US. The increasing trade conflict between the US and Japan as a result of the latter's surge in exports highlighted the changed nature of the economic relationship, with cooperation in an anti-communist security policy going hand in hand with competition in economics. Indeed, the economic success of Japan over the years has posed a challenge to the US economy, with Japanese exports being subject to Orderly Marketing Agreements (OMAs) as well as Voluntary Export Restraints (VERs), as in the cases of colour televisions, steel, machine tools and automobiles (Ito, 1993).

The other major destination for Japanese goods was Southeast Asia, with about a quarter of exports destined for these economies from the mid-1950s onwards. Japan's emergence as an economic superpower was integrally tied to the role of the region's developing economies in absorbing exports and supplying natural resources and minerals for Japanese industrialization. Up until the mid-1960s, the developing East Asian economies were particularly important as absorbers of the heavy industrial products at the base of Japan's economic reconstruction, as these lacked a competitive edge in the markets of the advanced economies. With the rise of the tigers and then the other East Asian economies, however, Japanese exports of machines and tools came to take on an increasingly important role. In 1993, for instance, 66.3 per cent of Japanese exports to ASEAN were machines and tools, especially general machines and electric machines (Tsusho Sangyosho, 1994, p. 265). At the same time, the surge in exports of components for communication equipment and integrated circuits highlighted the close links between Japan-based companies and their subsidiaries in other parts of East Asia, with intra-company trade on the upswing.

In all of this, Japanese Official Development Assistance (ODA) has played a crucial role in providing an opportunity for Japanese exporters, on the one hand, and in funding the infrastructure projects making investments in East Asia more attractive for Japanese enterprises, on the other. The path was opened for a new post-empire relationship with Asia, through the payment of war reparations from the mid-1950s onwards, starting with reparation and economic cooperation agreements with Burma (1954), the Philippines (1956), Indonesia (1958), and South Vietnam (1959). Economic cooperation agreements were also signed with Laos and Cambodia (1958-59), South Korea (1965), and others. These agreements served to open the door for Japanese exports to the region, and provided opportunities for Japanese construction companies involved in infrastructure projects to spread their wings overseas and reap commercial benefits in the future (see Ensign, 1992). The regional focus on Asia was particularly strong in the 1960s and 1970s, with over ninety per cent of Japanese ODA going to Asian countries in 1970, with Indonesia (33.8 per cent) and South Korea (23.3 per cent) receiving the giant's share in that year. These figures illustrate the dual role

Japanese ODA has played in the exploitation of natural resources in Indonesia and in the penetration of the economy in South Korea. The percentage of ODA destined for Asia continued at over two-thirds in the early 1980s, and was still a majority in the 1990s. By 1980, Indonesia's share of Japanese ODA had dropped to 17.9 per cent and South Korea's to 3.8 per cent, with China becoming an increasingly important destination for ODA from the late 1980s onwards, in line with the burgeoning interest of Japanese business in the Chinese economy (Yamada, 1992, p. 222).

Although Japanese Foreign Direct Investments (FDI) started in 1951, the rush to meet expanding domestic demand, along with government restrictions on the availability of foreign currency more generally, limited the appeal to companies of investing in East Asia. What investment did occur largely focused on the development of natural resources. It was not until the early 1970s that Japanese companies began to invest heavily overseas. Domestically, the success achieved in pursuing a policy of high economic growth had led to a rise in the cost of production, especially labour, making investment in East Asia attractive to business. At the same time, the 'Nixon shocks' of 1971 brought an end to the gold standard and the fixed rate of exchange Japan had enjoyed following Dodge's pegging of the yen at 360. The yen immediately appreciated by nearly seventeen per cent. With the move to floating rates in 1973, the currency was destined to move ever upwards. The high yen led to a decline in Japan's international competitiveness making overseas investments even more appealing, especially in labour-intensive manufacturing industries such as textiles. The growing trade conflict with the US in textiles and other products gave added incentive to move overseas. From this time on, the region started to act as a major launch platform for the export of products to third countries, in line with the export promotion strategies of tigers such as Taiwan and South Korea (Kobayashi, 1992).

Another major wave of Japanese investment in East Asia followed the restructuring of Japanese companies after the second oil shock. At this time, investment not only continued into other parts of East Asia, but also increased in the US and Europe. In the area of auto production, for instance, Honda and Toyota went into production in the US. In Europe, Hitachi set up a plant in West Germany in order to produce video tape recorders. Investments in the automobile and electronic industries in these developed regions reflected the increasingly global strategy of Japanese corporations, which were strengthening their investments in the three core regions of the global economy — Europe, North America, and Asia itself (Inoue, 1993). At the same time, this strategy helped to avoid trade friction and, in the case of investments in Europe, most of which were located in West Germany and the United Kingdom, provided access to the markets of the members of the European Community.

The increase in the value of the yen after the Plaza Accord of 1985, from around 250 yen to the dollar in April 1985 to 150 yen to the dollar in July 1987, again led to a boost in overseas investments. In the US, for instance, Toyota expanded production and other companies such as Mitsubishi and Mazda made investments in automobile plants (Shimokawa, 1992). In East Asia, as a result of the economic success of the four tigers, pushing up the price of producing in these areas, ASEAN became increasingly popular with Japanese business. The main Asian recipients of FDI from the late 1980s were Thailand and Malaysia, and later Indonesia. This strengthened the web of relationships between Japan, Japanese transplants in the tigers, and the NIEs of ASEAN, with small- and medium-sized Japanese companies also starting to move overseas in large numbers, with a peak of 1,625 cases in 1988 (JETRO, 1993, p. 73). In essence, component producers for Japanese electronics and automobiles were increasingly relocating to offshore East Asia in order to follow the giant Japanese companies which, under domestic and global pressures, had moved offshore. As a result, there was an almost doubling in the export of manufacturing goods from the HPAEs of ASEAN between 1985 and 1989.

After the downturn in the Japanese economy following the bursting of the Japanese bubble, overseas investments picked up again, especially in the wake of the rise in the value of the yen in the mid-1990s. What is striking about the investment now being made is the growth of investment in China. In 1990, China gained only 0.6 per cent of Asian investments (accounting for 12.4 per cent of total investment), well behind the top three destinations of Hong Kong (3.1 per cent), Thailand (2 per cent), and Indonesia (1.9 per cent) (JETRO, 1992). In 1993, however, of the 18.4 per cent of Japanese FDI in Asia, the highest percentage of 4.7 per cent was in China, marking a 58 per cent increase over the previous year (JETRO, 1995, p. 511). The cheap labour available in China, along with the high performance of the Chinese economy, made investments in China attractive for small- and medium-sized enterprises, as well as large Japanese corporations. In 1993, the investments by these companies in manufacturing picked up after a decline from 1990, with the majority of them being made in China. Increasingly, both large and small Japanese companies are establishing production facilities in China, especially in the coastal regions.

Finally, Japan was linked to East Asia as a result of the need to import natural resources, especially energy and mineral resources. The lack of resources at home ensured that, even though Japan was at the outset locked into a transPacific relationship for about a third of the end products of its production system, East Asia was crucial to heavy industrialization and the growth of trade. From an economic point of view, therefore, the Japanese government had to rebuild relations with the victims of Japanese imperialism as an integral part of rebuilding the economy. The shared belief of the Japanese and American leadership in anti-communism and pro-capitalism meant that, in seeking access to resources, the anti-communist, authoritarian regimes of Southeast Asia appeared as the ideal partners. Cooperation between Japan and the authoritarian developmentalist regimes of Indonesia and the Philippines, for instance, was essential in order to gain access to the region's oil, bauxite, copper, and so on. Later, with the economic development of the region, manufactured goods made up an increasingly large part of imports. For instance, whereas in 1985 manufactured

20

goods made up only 8.4 per cent of imports from ASEAN, the rate had shot up to twenty-three per cent by 1989 (Sekiguchi and Ono, 1991, p. 38). The changing nature of the exports from the ASEAN HPAEs can be seen from the growing percentage of industrial exports, with increases in Thailand, Malaysia and Indonesia between 1970 and 1990 of 22.3 per cent to 74.9 per cent, 27.2 per cent to 58.9 per cent, and 6.9 per cent to 38.4 per cent, respectively (Yokota, 1992, p. 70). In this way, reverse imports of electronic goods and automotive parts strengthened the links between Japan and the ASEAN HPAEs.

The post-Cold War and sub-regionalism

The ending of the global Cold War and the erosion, if not complete breakdown, of the Cold War structures in East Asia have destroyed the bipolar framework of international relations in the region. These changes mean that the certainty at the base of the security treaty system, the 'Soviet threat', no longer pertains. In its place is fertile ground for competitive attempts to define an Asia Pacific as well as an East Asian identity on different regional levels. The shared commitment of policy makers on both sides of the Pacific to a bilateralism rooted in anti-communism and pro-capitalism has lost one of the two pillars of the post-1945 relationship. Although the Japanese government still sees military cooperation and the continuation of the US presence in the region as essential for maintaining regional stability, as do most of the other East Asian nations (Soeya, 1993, pp. 26-8), the emerging regional organizations offer the Japanese a way to balance bilateralism with multilateralism. In this sense, multiple identities are starting to emerge to challenge the bilateralism of the Cold War, with Japan linked to a variety of regional groupings.

Indeed, the Cold War's end has further highlighted the contested and overlapping nature of regionalism. There are attempts to create different kinds of regions, ranging from sub-regionalism linking national regions across the boundaries of states up to meta-regions embracing national entities within spatial groupings. This is giving rise to 'patchwork regionalism', with a multitude of overlapping links and interests. In other words, sub-regions often form part of a larger regional or meta-regional grouping. At the meta-regional level, for instance, social forces promoting an economic and political understanding of Japan's identity with Asia and the Pacific are seeking to promote Japan as part of the Asia Pacific. The institutional framework offered by APEC gives substance to this regional identity at the level of the state, with the political leaders of member states and economic areas (Hong Kong and Taiwan) seeking, with varying degrees of commitment, to create a regional identity for Asia Pacific. The challenge to APEC by Mahathir's EAEC is an attempt to push forward with a narrower, regional identity focused on East Asia. Given the present lack of Japanese support for EAEC, APEC remains a possible forum for negotiating on economic issues, gradually breaking out of bilateral economic negotiations with the US, with the ASEAN Regional Forum increasingly becoming the forum for multilateral discussions of security issues (Furukawa, 1994b).

With the ending of the global Cold War and the erosion of the Cold War framework in East Asia, links at the sub-regional level between Japan and Russia, China, and the Korean peninsula are emerging as the basis for creating a new, sub-regional identity. A distinctive feature of the post-Cold War regional restructuring is the role national regions are playing in pushing forward with links across national boundaries, so that parts of the former Soviet Union, China and North Korea, which were once locked behind the bipolar Cold War division of the world, are now being included in newly defined regions with Japan. Within Japan, a number of prefectures, cities and enterprises have taken the lead in pushing forward with the development of sub-regional economic groupings. The most important of these is the 'Pan Japan Sea Economic Zone'. Although this was first proposed in 1968 (*Nihonkaiken Keizai Kenkyukaihen*, 1992, p. 207), it was the ending of the Cold War that created a political environment capable of strengthening the economic and other links at the sub-regional level. Activities especially involve the Japanese prefectures on the Japan Sea coast, such as Niigata; the Korean Peninsula, the Russian Far East, and Northeast China. The development of market economies in Russia and China, the normalization of relations between South Korea and Russia, the joint entry of the two Koreas into the United Nations, the overall relaxation of regional tensions, and similar factors, have all served to stimulate Japanese interest in building such a zone in the early 1990s.

Nevertheless, symbolic of the way the legacy of Japanese imperialism can continue to cast a shadow over regional relationships, identifying the region using the expression 'Japan Sea' has been resisted in China and especially on the Korean peninsula. Instead, 'Northeast Asia Economic Zone' is preferred, as the use of 'Japan Sea' is intertwined with Japanese imperialist expansion to other parts of Asia. In the eighteenth and nineteenth centuries, for instance, European maps of Northeast Asia marked part of this sea as the Japan Sea and part as the Korea Sea. Traditionally, the sea had been given different names in Korea, Japan and Siberia; respectively, East Sea, West Sea, and South Sea. At the beginning of the Meiji period, moreover, the sea was referred to as the Korea Sea (*Chosenkai*) on official maps in Japan. Thereafter, the sea close to Japan was referred to as the Japan Sea (*Nihonkai*), and that close to Korea as the Korea Sea (*Chosenkai*). It was only after the colonization of Korea in 1910 that the whole sea became known as the Japan Sea (*Nihonkaiken Keizai Kenkyukaihen*, 1992, p. 133). It is for this reason that, in academic and other discussions promoting regional links, alternatives such as the 'Green Sea' (*seikai*) have been proposed (*Asahi Shimbun*, 11 April 1995).

Despite these difficulties over naming, a variety of activities have been taking place between Japan and other parts of the region. Exchanges of people, the opening of charter air routes, trade promotion, sister city agreements, and so on, are examples of the type of links being forged. As the focus on an 'economic zone' suggests, the possibility of pushing forward with new regional links — for instance, using Japanese capital and technology, Chinese labour, and Russian natural resources — has captured the imagination of local communities along the Japan Sea. Moreover, the development of the Tumen River Delta Project (See Park, 1993) is seen to provide Japan with new opportunities, both through participation in infrastructure projects as well as through the further development of the Japan Sea Economic Zone. The joint development of the Tumen River basin recently took a major step forward when China, Russia, South Korea, North Korea, and Mongolia agreed to establish a joint committee in order to resolve policy differences in regard to the introduction of foreign capital, trade promotion, and so on (*Nihon Keizai Shimbun*, 18 July 1995).

What is particularly noteworthy about these activities is the leading role played by prefectural and other local governments in Japan, rather than the central government, as key actors in promoting links at the sub-regional level. Illustrative of these efforts is the 1992 signing of friendship agreements between Toyama Prefecture, as well as Osaka, and the coastal region of the Russian Far East. Similarly, the Kansai Japan Committee for Economic Development has taken the initiative in proposing the provision of relevant information, training programmes, and other initiatives, to promote the Japan Sea Economic Zone (*Hokkaido Shimbun*, 15 January 1992). To facilitate sub-regional trade links, moreover, Yamagata Prefecture has been granted approval to expand the size of Sakata port in order to take vessels of up to 50,000 tons (*Kohoku Nippo*, 7 May 1993). On the other hand, Niigata City, along with businesses with offices in Niigata, have agreed to cooperate in the upgrading of the facilities at the airport serving Vladivostok (*Nihonkaiken Keizai Kekyukaihen*, 1992, p. 19). This is one example of how local governments in Japan are becoming involved in infrastructure projects in the Russian Far East, with local governments thus playing a role in carrying out 'aid projects' (Hagai and Otsu, 1994). For prefectural and city governments along the Japan Sea coast, the possibility of building links across national boundaries, enmeshing the local economy in international or transnational networks, serves not only as a way to revitalize the local economy, but also as a way to balance the overwhelming power of the central government in Tokyo. In other words, sub-regionalism provides local governments with an opportunity to promote decentralization through the internationalization of the local economy, challenging the centralized role of the Japanese state.

Along with local governments, private sector enterprises have been active in building links on the sub-regional level, taking the initiative in crossing state boundaries in the region in order to take comparative advantage of resources and labour, as well as to exploit market opportunities. In 1992, for instance, the trading company Marubeni opened an office in Vladivostok. Other large Japanese companies have set up joint venture businesses. At the same time small- and medium-sized enterprises are taking a lead role in pushing ahead with new projects in the region. Examples include operating hotels in Vladivostok, exporting used cars and tyres, and establishing information and communication companies. This is not to suggest that in pushing forward with business between Japan and the other economies in the region, problems do not occur. For instance, due to difficulties with payment, an Hokkaido exporter of used cars to the Russian Far East suspended operations in 1992 (*Hokkaido Shimbun*, 14 August 1992). However, during the few years since the end of the Cold War, an increasing number and variety of Japanese companies in the Japan Sea region are taking the initiative in exploiting business opportunities in the region. The trend seems set to grow.

Conclusion

The growth of sub-regionalism in the post-Cold War world demonstrates how changes in the international political environment can exert a powerful influence on the perception of regions as well as on the possibility of constructing new regional links and identities. What our discussion of meta-regions, regions, and sub-regions suggests is the patchwork, overlapping nature of Japanese regionalism in the 1990s. The same trend can be identified in other parts of East Asia. Thailand, for instance, is a member of the meta-regional APEC, the regional ASEAN, and the sub-regional Baht Economic Zone. In this way, these emerging regions are creating overlapping interests and identities within and between the regional members.

With the certainties of anti-communism and pro-capitalism as the basis for Japanese identity eroded, regionalism is emerging as a source for new identities, with the boundaries of the various regions remaining contested. As we have seen, on the meta-regional level, Japan is identifying with APEC, indicating the still powerful legacy of Cold War bilateralism. This gives the US leverage over Japan. As no Japanese government has proposed ending the US-Japan security treaty, the US' leverage can be expected to continue, with Japan seeking to limit its influence through APEC-type multi-lateral forums. In this sense, the bilateral security links act as a constraint on Japan's development of an independent role in East Asia, with the political economy of regionalism being permeated with security concerns, despite the end of the Cold War. Needless to say, the regional role of China, now as a political power, and increasingly as a military power, remains a key reason for Japan and other East Asian nations to support a continued US presence in East Asia.

The EAEC proposal is important for our discussion of regionalism as it indicates a change in attitude in the region, where at least some of Japan's neighbours no longer view the legacy of the war as an insurmountable obstacle for Japan in carving out a regional role. Certainly, other Asian leaders, especially in China and on the Korean peninsula, still harbour suspicions about Japan's role. The failure of the Murayama government to pass a clear-cut apology for aggression in commemoration of the fiftieth anniversary of the war's end highlights the difficulty in Japan in coming to grips with the legacy of imperialism. At the same time, however, the fact that the Malaysian prime minister called on Prime Minister Murayama to stop apologizing for the war indicates that a change in attitude is underway in parts of East Asia. Similarly, at the time of the Gulf War, when some of Japan's neighbours were willing to accept port calls by Maritime Self-Defence Forces on the way to the Gulf, and in support of the deployment of Japanese troops in Cambodia, we increasingly find Asian nations no longer ready to immediately charge Japan with reviving militarism or recreating the Greater East Asian Coprosperity Sphere. In this sense, the possibility of Japan acting as the 'voice of Asia' has increased, at least in areas of common concern, where Japan is the only Asian voice, as at meetings of the G-5 or G-7.

We thus can expect areas of closer cooperation between Japan and the other HPAEs to emerge, but this does not mean the emergence of a regional bloc. It is true that, especially in the 1990s, the amount of intra-regional trade has increased dramatically. For instance, East and Southeast Asia account for over ninety-six per cent of Japanese exports in the Asian region, with the total amount exported to East and Southeast Asia as a percentage of its global exports having risen from 26.7 per cent in 1989, to 32.5 per cent in 1993, on a US dollar basis. However, Japan remains a global trader, with the advanced economies of North America and Western Europe still acting as core absorbers of Japanese consumer and other products. Despite a decline from 20.5 per cent in 1989, Japan continued to export 17.7 per cent of total exports to Western Europe in 1993, with automobiles, motorcycles, and electrical machinery being key export items. Similarly, in the case of North America, despite a decline from 36.3 per cent in 1989, Japan continued to export 30.9 per cent of total exports to Canada and the US in 1993, with a similar focus on transport machinery and electrical machinery (Tsusho Sangyosho, 1994). The export focus of the other HPAEs suggests that, as with Japan, access to the other two core regions of the global economy will continue to be crucial to the healthy development of their economies.

At the same time, however, the trade friction witnessed between Japan and the US is increasingly emerging between Japan and the other East Asian economies. In the same way that the US imposed VERs on the importation of Japanese automobiles, for instance, Taiwan has called on Japan to implement VERs in exchange for lifting trade barriers against Japan. In the case of Chinese textiles, moreover, the government is investigating imposing import restrictions through the Multi-Fiber Arrangement (Sasaki and Shimane, 1994). Along with cooperation, therefore, the follower economies of East Asia also are in competition with Japan. In this sense, the new institutions of the region have a long way to go before they are able to play a role like that of European institutions in seeking to resolve issues between member states.

In the end, Japanese responses to competing forms of regionalism can be said to have crystallized around the question faced by respective governments since the Meiji era: how relations with Asia, on the one hand, and the West, on the other, should be balanced. The balance at the time of writing seems still to be tilted to the West, with Japan's international political economy being mostly shaped through links with the US and APEC. At the same time, however, we have seen how a tentative start has been made to build links on the sub-regional level. This is a challenge to the primacy of the Japanese state as the major, if not the sole, actor both domestically and internationally. It indicates how, in the post-Cold War era, an increasing number of actors are complementing, if not directly challenging, the role of the state. By linking the prefectural regions of Japan with what, to some at the heart of the state, are still the nation's 'enemies', these actors are forming common interests in a way that may serve to facilitate the formation of identities that do not target nations in the region as 'enemies'. In this respect, the overlapping, patchwork regionalism emerging in East Asia is reshaping the image and nature of the Japanese state, both internally and externally. How this process evolves will affect the balance of Japan's relations with Asia and the West. In this can be seen the global importance of sub-regionalism in East Asia.

Acknowledgement

This is a revised version of a paper presented at the Centre for Japanese Studies, the University of Sheffield's thirtieth anniversary international symposium, 'Japan, Asia-Pacific and Regionalism: Global and Regional Dynamics into the 21st Century', held 13-15 September 1995. I would like to thank the participants for their comments and the Toshiba International Foundation for support of this research and the symposium.

References

Berger, P. and Hsiao, M. H. H. (eds) (1988), *In Search of an East Asian Development Model*, Transaction Books, New Brunswick, NJ.

Elek, A. (1994), 'Trade policy options for the Asia Pacific region in the 1990's: the potential of open regionalism', in Garnaut R. and Drysdale, P. (eds), *Asia Pacific Regionalism. Readings in International Economic Relations*, Harper Educational, Pymble, pp. 212-7.

Ensign, M. (1992), *Doing Good or Doing Well? Japan's Foreign Aid: Japan's Foreign Aid Programme*, Columbia University Press, New York.

Furukawa, E. (1994a), 'APEC Shiatoru Kaigi no Dorama: Ajia Taiheiyo Chiiki Kyoryoku wa Doko e Iku ka' ('The drama at the Seattle meeting of APEC: where is regional cooperation heading?'), *Boeki to Kanzei*, Vol. 42, No. 1, pp. 60-7.

Furukawa, E. (1994b), 'Higashi Ajia no Chiiki Anpo de Omowaku ga Zureru Nishigawa to ASEAN. Hossoku shita ARF no Unei wa Tairitsu no Shippo o Hiku' ('Regional security in East Asia falls short of the West's and ASEAN's expectations. Conflict remains over the operation of the recently launched ASEAN Regional Forum'), *Sekai Shuho*, 30 August, pp. 16-19.

Garnaut, R. and Drysdale, P. (1994), 'Asia Pacific Regionalism: the Issues', in Garnaut R. and Drysdale, P. (eds), *Asia Pacific Regionalism. Readings in International Economic Relations*, Harper Educational, Pymble, pp. 1-7.

Hagai, M. and Otsu, H. (eds) (1994), *Jichitai Gaiko no Chosen* (The Challenges of Local Government Diplomacy), Yushindo Kobunsha, Tokyo.

Havens, T. R. H. (1987), *Fire Across the Sea. The Vietnam War and Japan*, Princeton University Press, Princeton.

Inoguchi, T. (1990), 'Four Scenarios for the Future', in Newland, K. (ed.), *The International Relations of Japan*, Macmillan, London, pp. 206-25.

Inoue, H. (1993), *Takokuseki Kigyo to Gurobaru Senryaku* (Multinational Corporations and Global Strategy), Chuo Keizaisha, Tokyo.

Ito, T. (1993), 'U.S. Political Pressure and Economic Liberalization in East Asia', in Frankel, J. A. and Kahler, M. (eds), *Regionalism and Rivalry: Japan and the United States in Pacific Asia*, University of Chicago Press, Chicago, pp. 391-422.

JETRO (1992), *Sekai to Nihon no Kaigai Chokusetsu Toshi, 1992* (Overseas Direct Investments of the World and Japan, 1992), *JETRO Hakusho*, Japan External Trade Organization, Tokyo.

JETRO (1993), *Sekai to Nihon no Kaigai Chokusetsu Toshi, 1993* (Overseas Direct Investments of the World and Japan, 1993), *JETRO Hakusho*, Japan External Trade Organization, Tokyo.

JETRO (1995), *Sekai to Nihon no Kaigai Chokusetsu Toshi, 1995* (Overseas Direct Investments of the World and Japan, 1995), *JETRO Hakusho*, Japan External Trade Organization, Tokyo.

Kobayashi, H. (1992), *Tonan Ajia no Nikkei Kigyo* (Japanese Enterprises in Southeast Asia), Nippon Hyoronsha, Tokyo.

Korhonen, P. (1994), *Japan and the Pacific Free Trade Area*, Routledge, London.

Miura, K. (1995), 'Bei Shido no Blokkuka Tsuyomeru APEC' ('APEC strengthens the creation of blocs under American leadership'), *Zenei*, No. 655, pp. 129-138.

Nihonkaiken Keizai Kenkyukaihen (1992), *Kan Nihonkai Keizaiken* (The Pan Japan Sea Economic Zone), Sochisha, Tokyo.

Okita, S. (1989), *Emerging Forms of Global Markets and the Nature of Interdependence in an Increasingly Multipolar World*, OECD Development Centre, Paris.

Park, J. (1993), 'Korea and North-East Asia Economic Cooperation: The Tumen River Project', in De Bettignies, H. C. (ed.), *Changing Relationships in the Asia-Pacific Region: Implications for European Corporations*, INSEAD, Fontainbleau, pp. 103-21.

Sasaki, T. amd Shimane Y. (1994), 'The New Dynamics of the Asian Economy', *Japan Research Quarterly*, Vol. 3, No. 3, pp. 50-88.

Sekiguchi, S. and Ono, A. (eds) (1991), *Ajia Keizai Kenkyu. Boeki, Toshi, Gijutsu Seisaku no Tenkai* (Research on Asian Economics. The Development of Trade, Investment, and Technology Policies), Chuo Keizaisha, Tokyo.

Shima, S. (1993), 'Nihon-ASEAN Kankei no Shintenkai: Higashi Ajia Keizai Kyogitai (EAEC) Koso o Megutte' ('New development in Japan-ASEAN relations: the concept of EAEC'), *Waseda Seiji Koho Kenkyu*, No. 41, pp. 29-56.

Shimokawa, K. (1992), 'The Internationalization of the Japanese Automobile Industry', in Hook, G. D. and Weiner, M. A. (eds), *The Internationalization of Japan*, Routledge, London, pp. 149-70.

Soeya, Y. (1993), ''Reisengo' no Ajia Taiheiyo to Nihon Gaiko' ('Asia Pacific in the post-Cold War era and Japanese diplomacy'), *Gaiko Jiho*, No. 1294, pp. 18-32.

Tsuru, S. (1993), *Japanese Capitalism: Creative Defeat and Beyond*, Cambridge University Press, Cambridge.

Tsusho Sangyosho (1994), *Tsusho Hakusho Heisei 6 Nen Ban (Kakuron)* (Ministry of International Trade and Industry White Paper, 1994), Okurasho Insatsu Kyoku, Tokyo

World Bank (1993), *The East Asian Miracle. Economic Growth and Public Policy*, Oxford University Press, Oxford.

Yamada, S. (1992), 'ASEAN Shokoku e no Nihon no Keizai Kyoryoku' ('Japanese economic cooperation with the members of ASEAN'), in Ohata, Y. and Urata, S. (eds), *ASEAN no Keizai. Nihon no Yakuwari* (ASEAN Economics. Japan's Role), Yuikaku, Tokyo, pp. 217-48.

Yamaguchi, H. (1991), *Chiiki Kenkyuron* (Area Studies), Ajia Keizai Kenkyujo, Tokyo.

Yokota, K. (1992), 'ASEAN Shokoku no Boeki Kozo' ('Trade structure of ASEAN members'), in Ohata, Y. and Urata, S. (eds), *ASEAN no Keizai. Nihon no Yakuwari* (ASEAN Economics. Japan's Role), Yuikaku, Tokyo, pp. 63-90.

2 ASEAN's role in the emerging East Asian regional security architecture

Tim Huxley

This chapter sets out to investigate the security role of the Association of South East Asian Nations (ASEAN) and its place in the regional security architecture which is emerging in East Asia in the 1990s. ASEAN rather than Southeast Asia as a whole has been chosen as the focus for several reasons. Firstly, ASEAN has an intrinsic significance in that it is by far the most successful Third World regional organization. Its diplomatic cohesion and apparent intra-mural harmony, together with the increasing economic prosperity of most of its members relative to the rest of the Third World, have led to it becoming something of a model for other regions aspiring to similar success. The Association's status has been boosted not only by the high profile role it assumed in relation to the Cambodian issue during the 1980s, but also by the collapse of Vietnam's previous aggressive ideological and military posture following the withdrawal of Soviet support at the end of the decade. Vietnam became a full member of ASEAN in July 1995, and it is conceivable that before the end of the decade ASEAN will expand its membership to include Laos, Cambodia and Myanmar as well. Secondly, although ASEAN has never claimed to be a security organization as such, it has clearly functioned as one, by setting out to realize a range of ambitions in relation to the enhancement of security at national, regional and international levels. Thirdly, in the 1990s, ASEAN is attempting to play a pivotal role in the creation of a new, post-Cold War security system in East Asia.

ASEAN's security role: ambitions and limitations

In 1967, when ASEAN was inaugurated, its members (then Indonesia, Malaysia, the Philippines, Singapore and Thailand; Brunei joined in 1984) faced a wide range of security threats. These included domestic insurgencies, latent bilateral disputes between the new Association's own members, the potential impact of communist victories in Indochina, and the danger of interference by extra-regional powers. ASEAN's members were economically and militarily weak developing states in an unstable and conflict-ridden region. While ASEAN was never supposed to be the basis for a *defence* community, from the beginning it was the repository for a variety of ambitions in relation to the resolution (or at least management) of its members' security problems. To a significant degree, these security objectives have been conceptually and practically inter-related. But while ASEAN was always intended to perform a variety of security roles, and has been called an 'emerging security regime with a tendency towards community' (Wiseman, 1992, p. 46; Leifer, 1992a, p. 167), its record in achieving its security-related ambitions has been mixed. Strictly speaking, even in the 1990s ASEAN constitutes only a limited security regime and is — at best — many years away from becoming a security community.[1]

National and regional resilience

Since ASEAN was established, there has been widespread acknowledgement by its member governments of the validity of the Indonesian concept of 'national resilience', involving the use of economic and social development to undermine any impetus for radical political change. Thus, the Association's primary declaratory objective of furthering its members' economic growth and social progress was aimed particularly at eliminating the socio-economic deprivation which had so enhanced the appeal of communist revolution, and to a lesser extent ethnically-based separatism. There has also been consensus amongst ASEAN leaders that the attainment of 'resilience' at the national level will contribute to a wider 'regional resilience' which will eventually form the basis for Southeast Asia's security against external as well as domestic threats.

The collapse of the non-communist Indochinese regimes in 1975 reinforced ASEAN members' view that economic and social development were essential weapons in the continuing struggle against the communist threat. ASEAN's 1976 Treaty of Amity and Cooperation in Southeast Asia expressed a determination to strengthen 'national resilience' in 'political, economic, socio-cultural as well as security fields' and to 'co-operate in all fields for the promotion of regional resilience' (see Appendix B to Broinowski, 1982, pp. 273-7).

ASEAN's most widely-perceived significance in security terms has been related to its role in controlling intra-regional conflict (both between its own members, and more widely within Southeast Asia) and to its potential role in the broader management of regional security through the ZOPFAN (Zone of Peace, Freedom and Neutrality) concept. However, the failure to implement more wholeheartedly policies in support of its most fundamental, but often overlooked, security objective — the creation of national and regional resilience — may have undermined progress towards achieving ASEAN's wider security aims.

Rapid growth characterized the ASEAN economies for most of the 1970s and 1980s, although there was a decade-long depression in the Philippines from the early 1980s and a short-lived region-wide recession in the mid-1980s. Economic dynamism has continued to be one of the most striking features of most ASEAN members in the early 1990s. Gross Domestic Product (GDP) growth figures for Indonesia, Malaysia, Singapore and Thailand in 1994 were all in the seven to ten per cent range, and authoritative forecasts suggest that they will remain there for at least the rest of the decade. Singapore is now essentially a developed country. Malaysia and Thailand are both approaching Newly Industrialized Country (NIC) status. Even the Philippines' economy achieved 4½ per cent growth in 1994 (EIU, 1995, p. 4), and Brunei is wealthy on the scale of the smaller Gulf states.

The prosperity of most ASEAN members can only marginally be ascribed to the success of ASEAN policies aimed at enhancing regional economic cooperation. 'Cooperative enterprise directed against protectionist practice by industrialized states' (Leifer, 1992b, p. 379) has become more important with the rise of nascent trading blocs since the 1980s, and has certainly had a positive impact on ASEAN members' economic development. But, in general, attempts at economic cooperation within ASEAN have not been either far-reaching or successful.[2] The ASEAN region's prosperity is largely the result of economic policies pursued at the national level by individual governments.

Despite most ASEAN members striking economic success in terms of rapid GDP growth, these impressive aggregate figures tend to camouflage dangerously high levels of socio-economic inequity between both classes and regions in economically booming Malaysia and Thailand, and relatively prosperous Indonesia, as well as in the depressed Philippines (Booth, 1993). The attainment of 'national resilience' will require a much greater degree of social justice — especially in the sense of a fundamental amelioration of the basic rural problems of landlessness, indebtedness and underemployment, and of urban poverty — in the four largest ASEAN countries.

The spatial dimension to poverty has particularly serious implications for 'national resilience'. Socio-economic inequality between regions has always been a problem for the governments of the larger ASEAN states, and undoubtedly contributed in the past to insurgencies in areas such as Thailand's Northeast and Mindanao in the southern Philippines. Since the 1980s, there have been indications that unfair development policies — manifested in the form of a 'resource drain', whereby higher than average regional GDP based on exploitation of local primary resources is paralleled by a higher than average incidence of poverty (Booth, 1993, pp. 23-4) — have accentuated pre-existing centre-periphery tensions based on ethnic and political differences. In Indonesia, economic grievances rooted in the perception that the local community was deriving little benefit from the massive exploitation of natural gas resources almost certainly triggered the large-scale armed revolt by an Islamic separatist movement in Aceh (the Northernmost part of Sumatra) in 1989 (Kell, 1995). The problem of Aceh may foreshadow long-term problems for the Indonesian regime's efforts to maintain national unity. The memory of previous severe difficulties in centre-periphery relations has inclined the Suharto regime to over-centralize power, seriously impeding development outside Java. A continuation of the present policy of centralizing political power and economic decision-making could, over a fifteen to twenty year period, lead to Indonesia becoming 'a reluctant union held together by military force' (Booth, 1992, p. 45). Rather similarly, tensions in Malaysia between the federal government and the resource-rich but relatively impoverished Borneo states of Sabah and Sarawak have become increasingly serious since the late 1980s (Kahin, 1992, pp. 30-49). The recently-mooted idea of creating economic 'growth triangles' between, for example, Phuket province in Southern Thailand, Northern Sumatra in Indonesia and the Malaysian state of Penang, focusses on the development of peripheral regions. However, these projects could have the unintended effect of reinforcing centrifugal impulses, particularly if new economic bonds parallel existing transnational ethnic or religious links.

However, the most fundamental obstacle to the enhancement of 'national resilience' in the four largest ASEAN countries is that the very nature of their regimes has often tended to impede implementation of the policies necessary to ameliorate tensions between classes and between regions. These regimes' rather narrow power bases have been located principally in the military, business, landowning, bureaucratic and technocratic elites, which have often seen their interests as coincidental with the maintenance of a social, economic and political status quo tolerant of exploitation and corruption. Given that the regimes have depended for their survival on the support of these elites rather than the population as a whole, there has often been little incentive to undertake fundamental reforms. In Thailand, for example, 'public policy tends to be shaped by the interests of small, usually urban-based higher-income groups, rather than the declared social and economic priorities of the nation' (Ho Kwon Ping, 1982, p. 218).

Political development, in the sense of building more democratic and responsive political structures, is clearly necessary if the eradication of poverty and the resolution of centre-periphery tensions in the larger ASEAN states are to remain feasible objectives. But the sort of fundamental political change which is probably necessary to ensure social justice and fair treatment of peripheral regions has never been on the agenda of either individual ASEAN regimes or ASEAN as an organization. Indeed, the very concept of 'national resilience' revolves around the use of performance legitimacy — based on tangible improvements in aggregate living standards — to maintain the existing ASEAN regimes' hold on power. There is much truth in the argument that the ASEAN states' economic successes have owed much to the firm direction which could probably only have been provided by authoritarian regimes. But there is also a strong argument that the necessity of responding to the sectional and regional pressures which would result from a broadening of effective political participation might help to overcome some of the ASEAN states' serious socio-economic problems. It is also true, though, that such a degree of political change would necessitate radical curtailment of the privileges of the elites which presently dominate the larger ASEAN states' political systems.

Pressures for political change to match economic progress have been growing in most ASEAN countries since the 1970s and 1980s. But so far these pressures generally have not resulted in either the broadening of political participation or increased regional input into economic decision-making on a scale sufficient to affect the direction of government socio-economic policies fundamentally. Singapore is the only ASEAN member to have achieved a level of economic *and* social development which might justifiably be considered to constitute 'national resilience'. Though problems of social justice remain, Singapore's prosperity is fairly well-distributed, and in such a geographically compact state there are, of course, no centre-periphery problems. The People's Action Party government, while by no means universally popular, has considerably greater legitimacy than any of its ASEAN counterparts, polling almost sixty per cent of the vote in the 1991 general election. It seems likely that future political change in Singapore will be conducted democratically and peacefully.

In contrast to the enviable state of national resilience achieved by Singapore, it may not be overly far-fetched to question whether the attainment of such a condition could prove chimerical for some ASEAN members, except in the very long term. Thailand, with its long pre-colonial history of nationhood, relatively high levels of ethnic and religious homogeneity, and economic prosperity, seems likely to succeed in consolidating its national resilience. But despite the very strong argument that the survival record of post-colonial states in Southeast Asia suggests that the region has 'a good chance of continuing to sustain its paradoxical condition of ethnic separatism and continuity of political forms' (Leifer, 1993, p. 19), perhaps there should be some concern over the long-term viability of the other larger ASEAN states, and especially Indonesia and Malaysia, in view of their multiple problems of geographical extensiveness, ethnic and religious complexity, and emerging economically-based centre-periphery strains. The possibility that these artificial and unwieldy post-colonial states, together with Brunei, may not survive the next twenty years should not be ruled out. In an admittedly very different region, the Yugoslavian catastrophe has demonstrated that rapid aggregate economic growth does not necessarily preclude the eventual disintegration of an ethnically and religiously fragmented society.[3]

Intra-ASEAN tensions

The second aspect of ASEAN's implicit security role was, from the beginning, to act as a framework for overcoming the legacy of its members' disputes with one another. The Treaty of Amity and Cooperation was 'intended to provide a code of conduct for relations among regional states and also an institutional mechanism for the peaceful settlement of disputes' (Leifer, 1992a, p. 167). ASEAN has indirectly contributed to the prosperity of its members by helping them to subdue disputes amongst themselves: greater tension or open conflict between ASEAN member states would have diverted resources away from development and made the region unattractive to foreign investors. ASEAN's formation was made possible by the cessation in 1966 of Indonesia's 'Confrontation' against Malaysia, but numerous intra-ASEAN disputes have continued to exist beneath a veneer of neighbourliness.

The most important intra-ASEAN problems have involved the Philippines' claim to the Malaysian state of Sabah, and the failure to resolve long-term suspicions between Malaysia and Singapore following the 'separation' of the latter in 1965. But Malaysia also has territorial disputes with Indonesia, Thailand and Brunei (David, 1995). A widespread interpretation is that ASEAN's single most important success has been as a confidence-building regime, under which these intra-mural disputes have become muted to the point of insignificance. One regional specialist has gone so far as to claim that 'ASEAN has become a security community in Karl Deutsch's sense, in which there no longer is an expectation of the use of force by one member against another' (Simon, 1988, p. 68). Such a degree of optimism is almost certainly misplaced, as at least one ASEAN member (Singapore) bases its defence strategy primarily on the deterrence of one or more ASEAN neighbours (Malaysia and Indonesia) (Huxley, 1991).

A more accurate assessment might be that ASEAN has very successfully *contained*, but has made little effort to *resolve*, intra-mural disputes. ASEAN members' wish to continue using informal measures to manage disputes amongst themselves is clear from their failure to establish and use the formal machinery for dispute settlement provided for in the Treaty of Amity and Cooperation in the form of a 'High Council'. While some would argue that ASEAN's long-term cohesion has been based to a large degree on its members' conscious eschewing of any potentially divisive attempt to use the Association to resolve underlying problems between themselves, it is also true that the effective absence of mechanisms for the settlement of disputes means that ASEAN remains weak as a 'security regime'.

The nub of the problem that prevents ASEAN from evolving into a strong security regime, in which institutional mechanisms for conflict resolution are activated, and ultimately into a security community in which internecine violence would be inconceivable, is that most of its members remain in some senses what Barry Buzan (1989, pp. 16-23; 1991a, pp. 96-107; 1991b, pp. 45-6) and others have called 'weak states', possessing relatively low levels of socio-political cohesion.[4] The failure to create 'national resilience' in terms of social justice and the resolution of centre-periphery tensions reflects what Buzan highlights as the weakness of both the 'idea' and the institution of the state, so typical of post-colonial Third World countries.

Buzan has pointed out that 'because they lack cohesion themselves, weak states are poorly placed to make any contribution to the order of the [international] system as a whole', and that 'their domestic insecurity frequently spills over to disrupt the security of neighbours' (Buzan, 1989, pp. 22-3; Buzan 1991b, p. 46). It is clear that even the 'weakest' of ASEAN's members (the Philippines) is much stronger in terms of socio-political cohesion than very weak Southeast Asian states such as Cambodia and Burma. It is also clear that ASEAN's members have collectively made a considerable contribution to regional order (and hence indirectly to wider international security) by preventing intra-ASEAN conflicts of interest from becoming more overt. However, unless most of its members become considerably 'stronger' states, it is hard to see how ASEAN can develop into a more effective and significant security organization. The ASEAN states' 'weakness' means that the conduct of intra-mural relations within ASEAN remains closely linked to domestic social, economic and political problems.

Its members' weakness as states detrimentally affects the conduct of intra-ASEAN relations in two connected senses. Firstly, some members' domestic vulnerabilities provide opportunities for interference from ASEAN neighbours by way of support for discontented ethnic or religious factions. For example, Malaysian state or federal governments have been implicated since the 1970s in providing political and material support to Muslim-based separatist movements in nearby parts of the Philippines (Mindanao), Thailand (Pattani) and Indonesia (Aceh). Secondly, some ASEAN governments derive political benefit from the continued existence of territorial and other disputes with their neighbours. The assertion of territorial claims provides an easy means of gaining domestic political legitimacy without making concessions to sectional or regional forces. For example, until the Philippines is considerably more developed, in terms of political stability as well as economic prosperity, there can be no assurance that a government in Manila will not feel pressured to revive and assert the country's claim to the Malaysian state of Sabah. Similarly, there will always be the danger that Singapore might be used as a domestic political 'football' in Malaysia, until the latter becomes a much more cohesive, mature, and self-confident state.

ASEAN evolved out of the recognition by its five original members, all 'weak states' at the time, that it was in their common interest to mute their disputes with one another in the face of a threatening environment in the wider region. This sense of common interest has been sufficient to allow ASEAN's members to forge a limited security regime. The further development of ASEAN as a security regime would require a willingness to resolve, rather than merely de-emphasize, intra-mural disputes; a security *community* would necessitate that Singapore and Malaysia, for example, cease planning for war against one another. Even the former development would require most of the ASEAN states to become considerably more cohesive domestically. But, as Buzan (1991b, p. 46) says, 'existing strong states are gifts of history, and as yet we have little knowledge about how to create others like them'. Social and political development in most ASEAN countries lag behind economic growth, and there may be considerable domestic turmoil before 'strong states' become the regional norm. In the meantime, any such turmoil could accentuate intra-ASEAN problems.

Relations with Indochina

ASEAN's third security objective entailed the extension of its framework of regional order to include the rest of Southeast Asia. The Bangkok Declaration, which established ASEAN, talked of the Association being 'open for participation to all states in the South East Asian region': it was evident that ASEAN's founders thought that it might be a useful instrument for coping with whatever post-war situation emerged in Indochina. However, attempts to engage with Indochina were rebuffed by the victorious communist regimes there in the mid-1970s. But by 1978 the intensifying conflict between Vietnam (supported by the Soviet Union) and Cambodia (backed by China) had inclined each side in the dispute to attempt to win ASEAN's support. ASEAN's members all refused initially to be drawn into the emerging Third Indochina War, but there were nuances in their individual attitudes, though, reflecting different strategic perspectives. In brief, there were — and in some senses still are — divergent 'regionalist' and 'globalist' security conceptualizations within ASEAN. These have been based essentially on divergent threat perceptions. The enduring concern of Indonesia, and to a lesser extent Malaysia, with China as a serious long-term security threat — best resisted by regional countries of whatever ideology acting in unison — inclined them to empathize with Hanoi's concept of regional order (involving in particular a substantial Vietnamese political and military role in Cambodia and Laos). Indonesia and Malaysia, the 'regionalist' ASEAN members, were also concerned — at least in principle — to exclude the military influence of all extra-regional major powers from Southeast Asia. The viewpoint held in Singapore and Thailand tended towards China's view of Vietnam as a dangerous, expansionist power closely allied with the Soviet Union. From this globalist viewpoint, regional security was best maintained by linking the ASEAN states to the anti-Soviet entente led by the US and China. These differences foreshadowed deeper divisions which emerged within ASEAN — at times straining its unity — after the Vietnamese invasion of Cambodia at the end of 1978.

The Vietnamese invasion and subsequent occupation of Cambodia provided ASEAN with its diplomatic finest hour, as the Association successfully strove during the 1980s to maintain international opposition to Hanoi's role in Cambodia and to resist challenges to the diplomatic status of the ousted Democratic Kampuchea regime. But while the Cambodian issue gave ASEAN's members an extremely important focus for political cooperation — to the extent that the Association seemed at times to have become virtually a single issue organization — there were some fundamental drawbacks to ASEAN's Cambodian policy (Huxley, 1985). The tension which divergent strategic perspectives generated within ASEAN was especially clear in the evident desire of the Indonesian armed forces' leadership that Vietnamese as well as Thai security interests in Cambodia should be recognized. But this tension was moderated by Indonesian president Suharto's willingness effectively to subordinate Indonesia's vision of an ideal regional order to Thailand's security interests so as to maintain ASEAN's unity. ASEAN, in the Suharto regime's view, was potentially an extremely valuable framework within which to exert Indonesia's regional primacy in the longer term (Leifer, 1983, pp. 142-71). But while the Indonesian government acquiesced in ASEAN's steadfast support for Thailand, the Indonesian armed forces kept open channels of communication with Hanoi.

Ultimately, the impasse over Cambodia was broken not as the result of ASEAN's efforts but rather as the consequence of factors beyond ASEAN's control, and particularly the unwillingness of the Soviet Union under Gorbachev to continue underwriting — financially and diplomatically — Vietnam's dominant role in relation to its smaller neighbour. The withdrawal of Soviet support, the dictates of Hanoi's economic renovation process, and the wish to avoid a tributary relationship with China lent Vietnam's foreign policy what Michael Leifer (1992a, p. 169) has called a 'supplicant quality'. But the resolution of the Cambodian problem as an international issue with the October 1991 Paris agreement did open the way for the eventual integration of Vietnam and Laos — and potentially Cambodia as well, when and if its apparently intractable problems of domestic power-sharing are resolved — into an ASEAN-led system of regional order. The eagerness of some ASEAN members, most notably Thailand and Singapore, to reap the benefits of close economic links with their former regional adversaries reinforced the trend towards closer relations with the Indochinese states. In July 1992, the fact that Vietnam and Laos now had little choice but to play the game of regional international relations according to ASEAN's rules (in terms of attempting to mute and contain intra-regional tensions) was reflected in their accession to the Treaty of Amity and Cooperation in Southeast Asia.

The inadequacy of ZOPFAN

The fourth sense in which ASEAN has attempted to perform a security function is related to the role of extra-regional powers in Southeast Asia. ASEAN's collective suggested solution to the problem of external interference in the region was the Zone of Peace, Freedom and Neutrality (ZOPFAN) proposal, enunciated in 1971. The ZOPFAN declaration called for ASEAN's members to use their commitment to national and regional resilience as the basis for the 'neutralization' of Southeast Asia aimed at preventing 'any form or manner of interference by outside Powers'. Because of the reliance of all ASEAN members except Indonesia on continuing security links with the United States and other Western powers, there was never any consensus within ASEAN that ZOPFAN was desirable except as a vague long-term aspiration. ZOPFAN pretended to an ability on the ASEAN states' part to manage their own region's security, but it was not underpinned by any semblance of adequate corporate capability, particularly in military terms (Leifer, 1989, p. 7). Nevertheless, many government politicians, and opinion-makers, in Indonesia and Malaysia have over the years continued to portray ZOPFAN as a realistic and worthy objective.

ASEAN's stance in opposition to Vietnam's role in Cambodia during the 1980s necessitated that the Association and its members go against the grain of the ZOPFAN proposal by aligning themselves with China and the West against Vietnam and the Soviet Union. This alignment was not merely diplomatic. The

ASEAN states' inability — or unwillingness — to deploy countervailing military power meant that they were unwilling and unable to provide any credible deterrent to possible further Soviet-backed Vietnamese aggression, with the result that Thailand came to depend on Chinese and American security guarantees. The establishment of Soviet naval and air facilities in Vietnam in the early 1980s provided an additional justification, from the ASEAN governments' viewpoint, for the reassuring continued presence of US naval and air bases in the Philippines. Thailand allowed itself to be used as a conduit through which Chinese arms and other material support could be passed to the Cambodian resistance, including the Khmer Rouge. ASEAN was a participant in the ultimately successful campaign against Vietnam's role in Cambodia, but could not have pursued this campaign without cooperating closely with China and the US.

By the early 1990s, though, the end of the Cold War in Southeast Asia — characterized by the Vietnamese military withdrawal from Cambodia, the virtual cessation of Soviet military aid to Hanoi, the scaling down of Soviet naval and air deployments in Vietnam, and the closure of the American bases in the Philippines — meant that conditions for the implementation of ZOPFAN were in some senses more promising than ever. But other factors — notably the emergence of China as an increasingly assertive and powerful player in the region — have underlined ZOPFAN's continuing inadequacy as a framework for potentially managing regional security in the absence among the ASEAN states of regional resilience in the sense of 'a more homogeneous outlook, buttressed by corporate military capability' (IISS, 1993, p. 160). Nevertheless, the extreme unlikelihood that ZOPFAN would ever be realized in practical terms paradoxically inclined ASEAN and its members to retain it as a long-term declaratory objective.

The tyranny of weak statehood

As Michael Leifer (1992a, p. 169) has pointed out, while ASEAN's policy-makers have paid 'more than lip-service to the values of common security', 'the realist persuasion' has persisted amongst them. The *declaratory* emphasis of the individual ASEAN states' security priorities, as well as of the Association as a collectivity, has been on building 'resilience', the renunciation of national priorities in bilateral relations for the greater good of ASEAN solidarity, the extension of this pattern of neighbourliness to Indochina, and the ultimate removal of the extra-regional powers' military presence from the region in the interests of the regional self-management of security issues. But this approach's limitations were revealed by the crisis created for ASEAN by the Vietnamese invasion of Cambodia, which constituted a clear rebuttal of all that the Association stood for in security terms. ASEAN's response involved an implicit renunciation of its own principles: regional security became dependent on the construction of a balance of power, using countervailing force supplied by the US and China. The availability of a multilateral ASEAN force for deployment on Thailand's border with Cambodia might have reduced Thailand's need for such heavy reliance on US and Chinese security guarantees. This was, however, utterly unfeasible not only because the ASEAN states were weak powers, but also because their weakness *as states* and their divergent threat perceptions meant that they were unable to cooperate effectively, other than at the grand diplomatic level, on security and defence matters.

The new regional security architecture

Global and regional developments since the late 1980s have transformed the ASEAN states' strategic environment, raising the question of whether and how ASEAN can play a useful security role in the 1990s and beyond.

Southeast Asia's strategic transformation has removed old threats (from Vietnam and the Soviet Union), but has simultaneously cast doubt on the reliability of the regional states' principal strategic partner (the US). It has also produced serious new potential challenges to regional security from nascent great powers — China, Japan, and perhaps also India — which are likely, because of their relative proximity to Southeast Asia, to be more or less permanent factors in the ASEAN states' future security calculations. There is great uncertainty regarding the form that external security threats might take in this new environment: how the various peri-regional actors will 'play their cards' and how they will relate to each other remain unclear. But the most serious new concern is with China's growing power and assertiveness, particularly in relation to its extensive territorial claims in the South China Sea.

While *immediate* external security threats have virtually disappeared, this radically changed, more multi-polar strategic environment is hardly less threatening in the medium to long term. In response, ASEAN's members have adopted a range of policies. Most of the ASEAN states have attempted to maintain or enhance their defence links with the US. They have also continued the efforts which they have been making since the late 1970s to enhance their own military capabilities (Huxley, 1994, pp. 136-55). But although Vietnam's behaviour in relation to Cambodia exposed the limitations of ASEAN's ability to pursue what might be called 'common security' aspirations for the region, the member governments have sought to place the organization at the centre of efforts to construct a new security 'architecture', not just for Southeast Asia, but also for the wider East Asian region. ASEAN's new, more institutionalized putative security role is an extrapolation of the organization's long-held ambitions in relation to both the intensification of the intra-ASEAN security regime and its expansion to include the rest of Southeast Asia. At the same time, it attempts (as ZOPFAN, at least in theory, has in the past) to create a framework for the restraint of those extra-regional powers which have strategic interests in the region.

ASEAN's avoidance of the multilateral defence cooperation role suggested occasionally by politicians and officials in the region is hardly surprising in view of continuing bilateral tensions and the absence of strongly-held common threat perceptions. Rather more surprising, however, has been ASEAN's failure until recently to provide even an informal confidence-building framework for the more explicit multilateral discussion by its members of threat perceptions, defence plans, and security links with extra-regional powers. As recently as 1990, representatives of the ASEAN states seemed 'puzzled by calls for confidence-building measures in their region' and argued that 'ASEAN itself is an overarching confidence-building measure which has so improved relations between them as to preclude the need for military confidence-building' (Findlay, 1990, p. 9).

The relatively recent glimmers of official recognition in the region of the need for rather more explicit confidence- and security-building measures (CSBMs) within ASEAN may indicate concern inside ASEAN governments that the dangerous combination of bilateral disputes and fairly intensive military modernization programmes has the potential to spiral out of control. The loss of Cambodia as a focus for intra-ASEAN security collaboration may have increased the danger of this happening. In June 1993, Malaysian defence minister Najib argued that 'there is a real need to establish confidence ... confidence must not be assumed, but instead, instituted'.[5]

Thus, the Association's new security role has at its most parochial level involved an effort to institutionalize the multilateral discussion of security matters among ASEAN members, and to involve defence officials as well as foreign ministers and foreign ministry officials in these discussions. Following the ASEAN Ministerial Meeting (AMM) in Singapore in July 1993, Najib announced that 'there is an ASEAN move to get defence officials to meet to discuss ... only discuss, regional security', stressing that the proposed discussions were a 'confidence-building measure' and not a 'defence pact or alliance' (*Straits Times*, 28 July 1993). At about the same time, Singapore's foreign minister spoke of 'preparing for the day' when ASEAN's defence ministers could meet (*Straits Times*, 27 July 1993). There has been no indication of when ASEAN defence officials and ministers will meet or precisely what they will talk about. But it is clear that the sensitivities and suspicions which have prevented multilateral functional military cooperation within ASEAN are also likely to circumscribe defence discussions.

Concrete intra-ASEAN CSBMs will be even more problematic to set up than generalized discussions. In 1993, Malaysia's defence minister suggested one such CSBM which might usefully be instituted under the auspices of an intra-ASEAN defence forum: a regional arms register.[6] In early 1994, the Philippine government endorsed a proposal by ASEAN's strategic studies 'think-tanks' for the exchange of information on defence spending and arms procurement (*Asian*

Defence Journal, April 1994, p. 126). The ASEAN states, together with other members of the ASEAN Regional Forum (ARF), agreed in principle at ARF's first meeting in July 1994 to 'promote the eventual participation of all ARF countries in the UN conventional arms register' (*Thailand Foreign Affairs Newsletter*, July-September 1994, p. 13). But to be of any use as a confidence-building measure, a regional arms register would need to contain more detailed information than the UN register and at least one other ASEAN member, Singapore, is probably unsympathetic to this idea.

In view of the persistent bilateral suspicions between ASEAN members and their divergent threat perceptions in relation to extra-regional powers, multilateral functional military cooperation is not on ASEAN's agenda (Huxley, 1993, pp. 66-7). Even a Malaysian suggestion for a joint ASEAN peacekeeping force was rejected by Indonesia's defence minister in early 1995 (*Straits Times*, 16 February 1995). It is clear that major obstacles stand in the way of any significant intensification of the existing limited intra-ASEAN security regime.

The expansion of ASEAN?

In the early 1990s, and particularly in the wake of the July 1994 ASEAN ministerial conference and the related first ARF meeting, the ASEAN governments have shown rather more concrete interest in expanding their existing limited regional security regime, involving a tradition of avoiding and managing conflict, than they have in intensifying security collaboration amongst themselves. This process of attempting to expand the regime has been conducted on two levels: within Southeast Asia, and within the wider East Asian region.

Within Southeast Asia, the ultimate aim is to expand ASEAN to include the other four regional states. In 1992, Vietnam and Laos acceded to the Treaty of Amity and Cooperation and were invited to be observers at future AMMs. These developments were widely interpreted as steps in the direction of eventual ASEAN membership, which both countries appeared to be enthusiastic about. But although Malaysian prime minister Mahathir Mohamed spoke in April 1992 of the need for a 'bigger ASEAN', including all ten Southeast Asian states, no timetable for the future progress of Vietnam, Laos, Cambodia and Myanmar (Burma) towards ASEAN membership was laid down.

Support for Vietnamese membership was strongest in the Philippine, Malaysian and Indonesian governments, all of which may harbour implicit geopolitical motivations for wishing to see a larger ASEAN as China grows more powerful and confident, particularly in relation to the South China Sea. But Thailand and Singapore were less enthusiastic, and there was fairly widespread concern within ASEAN over Vietnam's relatively backward economy, the potential for political instability in Vietnam, bilateral problems between ASEAN members and Hanoi, and Sino-Vietnamese tensions (Gainsborough, 1993, p. 386). Nevertheless, at their meeting in July 1994, ASEAN's foreign ministers agreed in principle to admit Vietnam.[7] In October 1994, Hanoi formally applied for membership and the July 1995 AMM approved this application.[8]

The integration of the other Southeast Asian states into ASEAN will not be so rapid. Financial and personnel constraints have prevented the Laotian government from applying for ASEAN membership precipitately. The question of Cambodia's potential membership is even more problematic. Apart from possible long-term difficulties in establishing a stable power-sharing system within Cambodia, the country's economic dereliction and possibly even domestic political opposition to ASEAN membership may present serious obstacles.[9] Nevertheless, Cambodia attended the 1993 and 1994 AMMs as a 'guest'. Having already indicated in December 1994 that it hoped to become a full member within two years, Phnom Penh was granted ASEAN observer status at the July 1995 AMM (Ching, 1994, p. 23; *Straits Times Weekly Edition*, 5 August 1995).

Despite the Thai foreign minister's rhetoric concerning the desirability of the 'speedy integration of Myanmar into ASEAN' (*Straits Times Weekly Edition*, 25 September 1993), which probably represented an incentive for the Yangon regime to behave less aggressively in its bilateral relationship with Thailand, obstacles remain which are at least as significant as those in the way of Laotian and Cambodian membership. ASEAN has pursued a policy of 'constructive engagement' towards the SLORC (Burma's State Law and Order Restoration Council) regime since the late 1980s, and Myanmar was allowed to attend the 1994 AMM as a guest of Thailand, the host state. But Yangon's atrocious behaviour towards the country's Rohingya Muslims, which caused over 270,000 of them to flee to Bangladesh in 1991-92, enraged the Malaysian government and caused unease in other ASEAN capitals (Siemers, 1993, p. 263). In broader terms, the Myanmar regime's illegitimacy in the eyes of most of the country's ethnic minorities, and a high proportion of Burmans as well, and its virtual ostracization by the West, imply that it is almost inconceivable that it will be admitted to ASEAN membership before there is a fundamental, internationally-recognized resolution of the country's profound domestic political problems. The release of Aung San Suu Kyi from long-term house arrest in July 1995 was only a first step in this direction.

At the 1994 AMM, the Thai government proposed establishing a pan-Southeast Asian grouping, referred to as SEA-10 or Southeast Asia Community, as a 'half-way house' to full ASEAN membership for the Indochinese states and Myanmar. Though the Philippines supported this idea, Malaysia — seeing it as a potential threat to ASEAN's role as the leading Southeast Asian regional organization — strongly opposed it (*Straits Times*, 21 July 1994; Schwarz, 1994, p. 24). Although Vietnam's unexpectedly fast movement towards full ASEAN membership has further undermined the SEA-10 concept, the Thai government seems intent on pursuing the idea, which it apparently sees as a means of providing an overarching political confidence-building framework for its important economic relationships with its smaller neighbours in mainland Southeast Asia.[10]

However, there are limits on how far the intensification of relations between the ASEAN states and their regional neighbours can contribute to the development of a Southeast Asia-wide security regime. Despite their intense economic involvement in Indochina, those states which adopted the toughest rhetorical line regarding Vietnam's role in Cambodia during the 1980s and are less concerned than their ASEAN partners regarding China's role in the South China Sea — Thailand and Singapore — may still harbour reservations over Vietnam's membership of ASEAN. In particular, the Thai armed forces' leadership has not significantly revised its view of Vietnam 'as a potential adversary and 'trouble-maker' (Paribatra, 1994, p. 255). The Thai military's concern relates principally to the possibility of Vietnamese re-intervention in Cambodia in the event of large-scale conflict erupting between the rival Khmer factions.[11] Thailand also disputes the demarcation of land boundaries with Cambodia, Laos and Myanmar (*Straits Times*, 19 June 1993). Moreover, Vietnam disputes sovereignty over maritime territory with Indonesia, Thailand, Malaysia, the Philippines and Brunei, and the issue of border demarcation between Thailand and Laos remains unresolved. The focus of the ASEAN countries and Vietnam has so far usually been on their maritime disputes with China. But intra-Southeast Asian maritime conflicts of interest, and the aura of mutual suspicion and distrust which accompanies them, are unlikely to disappear in the foreseeable future despite efforts by Hanoi and the ASEAN governments to de-emphasize the importance of their disputes, and in some cases to resolve them. The inclusion within ASEAN of Vietnam — the principal challenger to Beijing's territorial claims in the South China Sea — may also seriously complicate the group's relations with China, in some circumstances seriously straining its unity.

The Indochinese states and Myanmar are considerably weaker as states than their somewhat weak ASEAN counterparts. The glaring contradiction between increasing economic freedom in Vietnam and Laos and these countries' ideologically-bankrupt communist parties' attempts to maintain an exclusive hold on power is a sure indication of extremely low levels of socio-political cohesion. In Cambodia, socio-political cohesion is clearly almost completely absent. The Cambodian state is so weak that there is a danger that it will again become one of what Buzan (1991b, p. 46) has called the 'holes in the fabric of international order', disrupting the security of its neighbours, Thailand and Vietnam, and tempting them to re-intervene.

ASEAN's expansion will complicate and possibly slow down its decision-making process. It is by no means a foregone conclusion that ASEAN's new members will integrate easily into the grouping's club-like atmosphere. Indeed, some existing members apparently fear that Vietnam may bring a more adversarial diplomatic style to the Association's proceedings (Paribatra, 1994, p. 253). In sum, the inclusion of the Indochinese states and Myanmar in ASEAN, which has often been talked about as if it were a panacea for regional security problems, can hardly strengthen the existing weak security regime within the Association, and may actually undermine it.

The second way in which the ASEAN governments have attempted to expand their limited security regime in a geographical sense has been by sponsoring a forum for the discussion of security in the wider East Asian region. The origins of this role can be traced back to President Gorbachev's call in his 1986 Vladivostok speech for an Asia-Pacific equivalent to the successful Conference on Security and Cooperation in Europe (CSCE) process, which had helped to ensure a more stable security system in Europe since the mid-1970s. In 1990, Gareth Evans, the Australian foreign minister, proposed more specifically a 'Conference on Security Cooperation in Asia' (CSCA). Initially, the ASEAN governments were not enthusiastic about these proposals: not only was there a widespread view that the East Asian region was too complex for confidence and security-building measures along CSCE lines, but there was also concern (as there was initially also in relation to the Asia-Pacific Economic Cooperation concept) that new Asia-Pacific institutions might detract from ASEAN's role as the pre-eminent regional body. Another worry was that a CSCA might create a forum where Western participants could exert pressure on the ASEAN countries with regard to human rights issues, which were a central issue in the CSCE process (Acharya, 1993, pp. 59-60).

Though reluctant to support the CSCA idea, the ASEAN governments did recognize that the evolving strategic environment contained potential opportunities for the enhancement of regional security as well as new, emerging threats. There was particular concern that emerging regional powers — essentially China and Japan — should somehow be integrated into a system of regional order and thereby 'domesticated'. So the general idea of the need for multilateral discussions regarding security issues in the Asia-Pacific region was not dismissed out of hand. Within weeks of Evans' proposal for a CSCA, Indonesia's defence and security minister, Benny Murdani, called for a 'forum on regional security' (*Straits Times*, 11 September 1990).

During 1991, the various semi-official strategic studies 'think-tanks' in the ASEAN region promoted the idea of using ASEAN's Post-Ministerial Conference (PMC), which follows the annual AMM and involves discussions between ASEAN members and their 'dialogue partners' (by 1991 the US, Canada, Australia, New Zealand, the European Community, Japan and South Korea)[12] as the institutional framework for discussions on regional security. The principal advantages of this idea from ASEAN members' viewpoints was that it would allow them substantial control over the scope and direction of the regional security dialogue and would maintain ASEAN's focal role. At the July 1991 PMC, Japan's foreign minister proposed using future PMCs for 'a process of political discussion to improve the sense of security among us', and ASEAN ministers tentatively supported this suggestion, while underlining the continuing relevance of ZOPFAN and the Treaty of Amity and Cooperation as 'appropriate bases for addressing ... regional peace and security issues' (Vatikiotis, 1991, pp. 10-11).[13] Indeed, by this time, all the major interested powers supported the idea of the

PMC becoming a security forum. The US administration had been unenthusiastic when the idea of a CSCA was first suggested, fearing the possible impact of such a multilateral initiative on its bilateral security arrangements in the region, but found the PMC's role expansion much more palatable.

The Singapore Declaration, issued by ASEAN's fourth summit meeting of heads of government in January 1992, confirmed that the agenda of future PMCs would be expanded to include security issues (Vatikiotis, 1992, p. 11). The first concrete discussions of security matters under PMC auspices occurred after the July 1992 AMM in Manila, when the participants exchanged views on matters such as Myanmar, Cambodia, North Korea, Indochinese refugees, the South China Sea, piracy and drug-trafficking (*Straits Times*, 25 July 1992).

A year later, the 1993 AMM in Singapore agreed to establish an even wider, ministerial-level forum: this ARF would involve countries with observer status at the AMM and PMC (Vietnam, Laos, and Papua New Guinea) and the two 'guests' (China and Russia) in security-related discussions with the existing PMC participants (the six ASEAN members and their seven dialogue partners) (*Straits Times*, 22 July 1993).

The ARF was lauded in grand terms in the region even before its inaugural meeting. With uncharacteristic naivety, Singapore's *Straits Times* claimed on 27 July 1993 that ASEAN had 'accomplished the feat of fashioning a regional order for the Pacific Rim'. Realistically, though, there was from the beginning a danger that the ARF would lack bite because of the diversity of its membership and the great variety of security problems in East Asia which it might reasonably be expected to manage. As Patrick Cronin (1992, p. 214) suggested, 'busy policymakers ... gravitate toward a problem-solving approach' and have little time for such 'all-encompassing fora'. The ARF's potentially huge ambit soon led US assistant secretary of state Winston Lord, amongst others, to argue that separate sub-regional fora, most obviously in Northeast Asia, would be needed to deal with specific problems such as the inter-Korean issue (*Straits Times*, 20 August 1993). The ARF might thus ultimately find its purview limited to Southeast Asia and the South China Sea, with APEC possibly widening its role to become an umbrella security — as well as economic — forum for the entire Asia-Pacific region.[14]

The ARF's first, three-hour meeting in July 1994 reinforced doubts over its potential usefulness as an element in the emerging regional security architecture. The discussions touched on important issues such as the conflicting claims in the Spratlys and tension in the Korean peninsula. It was agreed that the ARF would be convened annually (with the 1995 meeting planned for Brunei), and that ideas such as 'confidence and security building, nuclear nonproliferation, peacekeeping cooperation including a regional peacekeeping training centre, exchanges of nonclassified military information, maritime security issues [sic] and preventive diplomacy' might be worthy of 'further study' by the ARF senior officials' meeting (SOM) and ultimately the ARF itself. There was also concurrence that all ARF countries should eventually participate in the United Nations' Conventional

Arms Register (*New Straits Times*, 26 July 1994).[15] Overall though, the meeting's proceedings were bland and its concrete achievements decidedly limited.

The 1994 ARF meeting prompted a renewed call, by South Korea, for a 'North East Asia Security Dialogue' (*New Straits Times*, 27 July 1994). But a new problem also emerged as it became clear that participants' attitudes towards 'the purpose and pace of the ARF' (Couchman, 1995, p. 4) diverged widely. While China acknowledged the usefulness of the Forum for consultative purposes, it staunchly opposed any notion that it could be used for multilateral discussion, let alone resolution, of issues such as conflicting territorial claims in the South China Sea. Partly out of recognition of the need for the ARF to develop gradually in order to ensure continuing Chinese participation, but also to some extent because of their own weak statehood (implying an unwillingness to subordinate sovereignty and national self-assertion to notions of international interdependence), the ASEAN governments broadly agreed with Beijing, although some may have hoped that the ARF could play a role in conflict resolution in the medium to long term. But other participants, including the US, Japan, Russia, Australia and South Korea clearly viewed the ARF's problem-solving potential in more ambitious terms than China and the ASEAN states (Couchman, 1995, p. 5). Significantly, these more ambitious ARF participants were all, to a greater or lesser extent, democracies and (with the arguable exception of Russia) strong states.

The ARF SOM in May 1995, held in preparation for the second ARF (to be held the following August) underlined the reluctance of China, and to a lesser extent the ASEAN states, for the ARF to take on the more concrete regional security role desired by the US and Australia in particular (Karniol, 1995, p. 31). While the SOM proposed that the forthcoming ARF should proceed with discussions on security perceptions, the publication of defence White Papers and participation in the UN Conventional Arms Register, more demanding ideas concerning the creation of a regional arms register, and a maritime information database were effectively sidelined for further consideration by non-official 'Track Two' meetings. Unsurprisingly, the achievements of the Second ARF meeting itself, held in August 1995, were hardly spectacular: the focus remained on 'diplomacy driven by process rather than results' (Couchman, 1995, pp. 6-8).

The greatest challenge to the ARF's viability as a pan-East Asian regional security regime comes from China's growing regional role. While Beijing may hope that participating in the Forum will reinforce its 'status as a benevolent great power' (Couchman, 1995, p. 9), there is no evidence that ARF membership has in any way constrained its international behaviour. China's role in the South China Sea has become a particularly important concern for ASEAN members, especially since its forces occupied a reef claimed by the Philippines in the Spratlys in early 1995. The forward-based naval and air presence which the US had maintained in the Philippines until 1992 might well have deterred such Chinese adventurism, but ASEAN's attempts to 'domesticate' China through multilateral security discussions were ineffectual in this respect.

Conclusion

The issue of weak statehood lies at the core of the ASEAN states' security problems. Because all the ASEAN states (with the possible exception of Singapore) are to a greater or lesser extent weak, they are unable to resolve the wide range of territorial and other disputes which exist among them. Due to these continuing (though muted) intra-ASEAN disputes, ASEAN members cannot intensify significantly their current limited regional security regime. The weakness of ASEAN's regional neighbours (Vietnam, Cambodia, Laos and Myanmar) limits the usefulness of attempts to expand the existing regional regime to include them. The problem of weak states in Southeast Asia can probably only be resolved by a long-term process of continuing economic growth, social change and the institutionalization of more responsive political systems. In the short to medium term, however, this process may *weaken* rather than *strengthen* some states in the region.

But the weakness of states is not the only fundamental problem underlying the ASEAN states' security problems. Historical, ethnic and geographical factors have generated divergent external threat perceptions within ASEAN. Although there has been a degree of convergence in terms of their perceptions of China since the early 1990s, there is still no common strategic outlook amongst ASEAN members in relation to either that country or Japan.

These problems relating to weak states and lack of common threat perceptions within ASEAN have had two crucial consequences in security terms. In the first place, the inability of the ASEAN states to engage in effective, multilateral military cooperation means that they are all anxious for the US to remain involved in Southeast Asia as a 'regional balancer' against whatever new threats might arise as a result of the growing strength and confidence of the peri-regional powers (and particularly China). A senior Malaysian defence official's statement that Malaysia's commitment to the principles of the Non-Aligned Movement and ZOPFAN 'should not be seen as an obstacle' to seeking wide-ranging defence links with the West (*Straits Times Weekly Edition*, 2 October 1993) was a fairly explicit renunciation of the regionalist idea (encapsulated in ZOPFAN) that Southeast Asian countries should ideally seek to manage their own system of regional order.

The second consequence has been the reinforcement of a trend towards mutual interaction (rather than coordination) between the defence policies of the ASEAN states. The most widely underestimated influence on defence policies in the region is the competition and latent conflict which undoubtedly persists between various ASEAN members. 'Non-threat factors', notably military and national prestige in relation to ASEAN neighbours but also 'supplier pressures' from the defence industries of the US and Europe, have provided much of the impetus for this process. 'Threat factors' also play a part. Certain ASEAN governments base their defence planning and military force structures to a greater or lesser extent on the need to deter, or assert military power against, one or more of their ASEAN neighbours. This is particularly clear in the case of Singapore arming itself to deter Malaysian aggression or interference (Huxley, 1991), but tensions between various other combinations of ASEAN members also have important implications for the defence policies of the states involved. Whether or not Singapore and Malaysia are involved in an 'arms race' depends on how the term is defined, but a bilateral 'arms dynamic',[16] involving a fairly intense process of competitive military procurement, infrastructural development and operational planning, aimed at maintaining the military status quo between the two states, certainly does exist. Unless the mutual suspicions which continue to cloud intra-ASEAN relations (for instance, between Malaysia and Thailand) are resolved, the growing conventional warfare capabilities of the ASEAN states' armed forces may stimulate the expansion of this bilateral 'arms dynamic' to include other countries in the region.

While arming themselves and attempting to keep the US closely involved in regional security, the ASEAN governments have simultaneously attempted to play a central role in sponsoring a new regional security architecture involving the institutionalization of intra-ASEAN CSBMs, the expansion of the Association itself, and the establishment of a pan-East Asian security forum. This new approach potentially brings a greater sense of realism to ASEAN's security role, particularly in the sense that the very concept of the ASEAN Regional Forum (in contrast to ZOPFAN) implicitly recognizes the legitimacy of extra-regional powers' strategic involvement in Southeast Asia. The new approach also represents a logical and, arguably, necessary counterpart to the new economic architecture being established simultaneously through the ASEAN Free Trade Area, the East Asian Economic Caucus and the Asia-Pacific Economic Cooperation forum. The ARF — or whatever security-oriented forum eventually takes form in the region — certainly potentially complements APEC whereas ZOPFAN seems to contradict the intensification of Southeast Asia's trade and investment linkages with the wider East Asian, trans-Pacific, and global economies.

However, in view of the problems likely to be encountered in attempting both to intensify and to widen the existing regional security regime, these developments — at least as they are currently envisaged — seem unlikely to have more than a marginal impact on the security of ASEAN members, except in the long term. The proposed new arrangements include no effective mechanisms for arms control, beyond the tentative suggestion of a regional arms register. Even more importantly, the new architecture is hardly convincing as a means with which to contain China's growing power and assertiveness, which most (though not necessarily all) ASEAN members see as the principal threat to regional security in the late 1990s and beyond.

Notes

1. For Barry Buzan (1991, p. 218), a security regime is a group of states which 'cooperate to manage their disputes and avoid war by seeking to mute the security dilemma both by their own actions and by their assumptions about the behaviour of others'. This cooperation, according to Robert Jervis (1982, p. 173) (with whom the concept originated), is based on 'principles, rules and norms'. Karl Deutsch (1957, pp. 5-6) defined a 'security community', which is one step further away from international chaos in Buzan's view, as a grouping of states in which all disputes between members are resolved to such an extent that none fears, or prepares for, either political assault or military attack by any of the others.

2. It remains to be seen whether the ASEAN Free Trade Area (AFTA), launched in January 1993 with the intention of increasing intra-ASEAN trade, is able to maintain its relevance as 'ASEAN's integration into the global economy renders attention to tariffs (and their reduction) redundant' (Alburo 1995, p. 66).

3. Anne Booth (1993, p. 24) notes that between 1960 and 1980 Yugoslavia had one of the developing world's highest rates of per capita GDP growth. See Booth (1993, p. 24).

4. According to Buzan's definitions of 'weakness' and 'strength' as state characteristics, all ASEAN's members except Singapore could be classified as 'weak states' to a greater or lesser degree. The Singapore state's tight control over the media might also lead to doubts being cast on its 'strength'.

5. The Hon. Dato' Seri Mohd. Najib bin Tun Hj Abdul Razak, 'Towards a Comprehensive Regional Security Framework', Keynote Address to *Asia-Pacific Dialogue on Cooperative Peace and Security*, Subang, Malaysia, 9 June 1993, p. 8.

6. Ibid., p. 9.

7. Why the issue of ASEAN's expansion, which dominated the 1994 AMM's non-economic discussions, should have unexpectedly taken on such urgency as an issue for ASEAN is not entirely clear. However, the US' lifting of its trade embargo on Vietnam in February 1994 may have emboldened the existing ASEAN members to accelerate Vietnam's integration into the regional mainstream. The expansion issue may also have helped fill a vacuum in the 1994 AMM's political agenda: discussion of tensions between existing members was taboo, and ARF's first meeting, which immediately followed the AMM, was scheduled to discuss wider security issues.

8. Though Vietnam became a full member of ASEAN in 1995, it will be given extra time to comply with the tariff reduction programme required under the schedule for the implementation of the AFTA (Murray Hiebert, *Far Eastern Economic Review*, 10 August 1995, p. 15).

9. Prince Sihanouk (as he then was) declared in early 1993 that he opposed Cambodia eventually becoming an ASEAN member, apparently mainly

because of the economically exploitative activities of existing ASEAN members in his country. (*Straits Times*, 3 February 1993).

10. Speech by Surin Pitsuwan, Thailand's deputy minister of foreign affairs, 10 November 1994 (*Thailand Foreign Affairs Newsletter*, October-December 1994, p. 8).

11. In March 1993, a major Thai military exercise used a new Vietnamese invasion of Cambodia, with fighting spilling over into Thailand, as its scenario (*Straits Times*, 13 March 1993).

12. China and the former Soviet Union attended the July 1991 AMM and PMC as 'guests'.

13. See Joint Communique of the Twenty-fourth ASEAN Ministerial Meeting (*Indonesian News*, Vol. 19, No. 4, 15 August 1991, p. 3).

14. Washington has hinted that it would support the idea of APEC taking on a security role (Susumu Awanohara, *Far Eastern Economic Review*, 15 April 1993, p. 11). Even within ASEAN, former Thai premier Anand Panyarachun also backed this idea (*Straits Times*, 10 September 1992).

15. 'Chairman's Statement Reports Results of ASEAN Regional Security Forum', *Kyodo News Service*, 25 July 1994 (BBC *Summary of World Broadcasts*, FE/2059 B/1, 28 July 1994).

16. For a pertinent discussion of 'Arms Racing and the Arms Dynamic', see Buzan (1987, pp. 69-131).

References

Acharya, A. (1993), *A New Regional Order in South-East Asia: ASEAN in the Post-Cold War Era*, Adelphi Paper 279, International Institute for Strategic Studies, London.

Alburo, F.A. (1995), 'AFTA in the Light of New Economic Developments', *Southeast Asian Affairs 1995* (Singapore: Institute of Southeast Asian Studies [hereafter ISEAS], 1995).

Booth, A. (1992), 'Can Indonesia Survive As a Unitary State?', *Indonesia Circle*, No. 58, June, pp. 32-47.

Booth, A. (1993), 'Progress and Poverty in Southeast Asia', Paper presented to the *ESRC Pacific Rim Seminar Series*, Liverpool John Moores University, 27 May.

Broinowski, A. (ed.) (1982), *Understanding ASEAN*, Macmillan, London.

Buzan, B. (1987), *An Introduction to Strategic Studies: Military Technology and International Relations*, Macmillan, London.

Buzan, B. (1989), 'The Concept of National Security for Developing Countries', in Mohammed Ayoob and Chai-Anan Samudavanija (eds), *Leadership Perceptions and National Security: The Southeast Asian Experience*, ISEAS, Singapore, pp. 1-27.

Buzan, B. (1991a), *People, States and Fear: An Agenda for International Security Studies in the Post-Cold War Era*, 2nd ed., Harvester Wheatsheaf, Hemel Hempstead.

Buzan, B. (1991b), 'Is International Security Possible?', in Booth, K. (ed.), *New Thinking about Strategy and International Security*, Harper Collins, London, pp. 31-55.

Ching, F. (1994), 'Growing ASEAN Faces Strains', *Far Eastern Economic Review*, 29 December, p. 23.

Couchman, B. (1995), 'Rhetoric and Reality: The ASEAN Regional Forum' (unpublished paper).

Cronin, P.M. (1992), 'Pacific Rim Security: Beyond Bilateralism?', *The Pacific Review*, Vol. 5, No. 3, pp. 209-20.

David, H. (1995), *Die ASEAN nach dem Ende des Kalten Krieges. Spannungen und Kooperations-probleme*, Mitteilungen Nummer 244, Instituts für Asienkunde, Hamburg.

Deutsch, K. *et al.* (1957), *Political Community and the North Atlantic Area*, Princeton University Press, Princeton, NJ.

EIU (1995), *Country Report: Philippines*, 1st Quarter, Economic Intelligence Unit, London.

Findlay, T. (1990), *Asia/Pacific CSBMs: A Prospectus*, Working Paper 90, Peace Research Centre, Australian National University, Canberra.

Gainsborough, M. (1993), 'Vietnam and ASEAN: The Road to Membership?', *The Pacific Review*, Vol. 6, No. 4, pp. 381-7.

Ho Kwon Ping (1982), 'ASEAN: The Five Countries', in Broinowski, A. (ed.), *Understanding ASEAN*, Macmillan, London, pp. 196-237.

Huxley, T. (1985), 'ASEAN and Cambodia: the Hazards of Stalemate', *Asia Pacific Community*, No. 30, Fall, pp. 30-47.

Huxley, T. (1991), 'Singapore and Malaysia: A Precarious Balance?', *The Pacific Review*, Vol. 4, No. 3, pp. 204-13.

Huxley, T. (1993), *Insecurity in the ASEAN Region*, Royal United Services Institute for Defence Studies, London.

Huxley, T. (1994), 'The ASEAN States' Defence Policies: Influences and Outcomes', in McInnes, C. And Rolls, M. (eds), *Post-Cold War Security Issues in the Asia-Pacific Region*, Frank Cass, Ilford, pp. 136-55.

IISS (1993), 'Security Dilemmas in South-East Asia', *Strategic Survey 1992-1993*, International Institute for Strategic Studies, London.

Jervis, R. (1982), 'Security Regimes', *International Organization*, Vol. 36, No. 2, Spring, pp. 173-94.

Kahin, A.R. (1992), 'Crisis on the Periphery: the Rift Between Kuala Lumpur and Sabah', *Pacific Affairs*, Vol. 65, No. 1, pp. 30-49.

Karniol, R. (1995), 'New Channels of Asian Diplomacy Unfold', *Jane's Defence Weekly*, 24 June, pp. 27-31.

Kell, T. (1995), *The Roots of Acehnese Rebellion, 1989-1992*, Publication No. 74, Cornell Modern Indonesia Project, Ithaca, NY.

Leifer, M. (1983), *Indonesia's Foreign Policy*, George Allen & Unwin, London.

Leifer, M. (1989), *ASEAN and the Security of South-East Asia*, Routledge, London.

Leifer, M. (1992a), 'Debating Asian Security: Michael Leifer Responds to Geoffrey Wiseman', *The Pacific Review*, Vol. 5, No. 2, pp. 167-9.

Leifer, M. (1992b), 'Is ASEAN a Security Organisation?', in Sandhu, K.S. *et al.* (comps.), *The ASEAN Reader*, ISEAS, Singapore, pp. 379-81.

Leifer, M (1993), 'Regional Challenges and the Resilience of the State in Southeast Asia', *Nordic Newsletter of Asian Studies*, February, pp. 17-19.

Paribatra, S. (1994), 'From ASEAN Six to ASEAN Ten: Issues and Prospects', *Contemporary Southeast Asia*, Vol. 16, No. 3, December, pp. 243-58.

Schwarz, A. (1994), 'Bigger is Better', *Far Eastern Economic Review*, 28 July, p. 24.

Siemers, G. (1993), 'Myanmar 1992: Heading for "Guided Democracy"?', *Southeast Asian Affairs 1993*, ISEAS, Singapore, pp. 245-66.

Simon, S. (1988), *The Future of Asian-Pacific Security Cooperation*, Lexington Books, Lexington, MA.

Vatikiotis, M. (1991), 'A Bit More Backbone', *Far Eastern Economic Review*, 1 August, pp. 10-11.

Vatikiotis, M. (1992), 'Action at Last', *Far Eastern Economic Review*, 6 February, pp. 10-11.

Wiseman, G. (1992), 'Common Security in the Asia-Pacific Region', *The Pacific Review*, Vol. 5, No. 1, pp. 42-59.

3 'Greater China' and global-regional-local dynamics in the post-Cold War era

Ngai-Ling Sum

Introduction

The 'Greater China' bloc (i.e. Hong Kong-Macau, Taiwan and Southern China) emerged at the beginning of the post-Cold War era. This era is characterized by the demise of an international geo-politics dominated by military and political competition between the Soviet Union and the United States. International crises are no longer dominated and interpreted primarily with reference to Cold War geo-politics narrated in terms of the 'discourse of danger' (Campbell, 1992). Instead, there is talk of the rise of geo-economics (Hsiung, 1993, p. 5; Nester, 1993, pp. 42-3). This is rooted in the emergence of competition among state and non-state actors, such as transnational corporations (TNCs) and transnational banks (TNBs), in promoting and organizing production and finance on global, regional and local scales. This chapter argues that the Greater China bloc must be related to the temporal and spatial specificities of the post-Cold War era — an era which can no longer be sensibly interpreted in terms of the geo-politics/geo-economics dichotomy. For the distinctive features of this bloc are closely related to a multi-faceted, multi-layered coupling of geo-economics and geo-politics. In order to explicate these specificities/complexities in a systematic manner, this chapter situates the analysis, methodologically, in a structure-strategy-agency schema (Jessop, 1990; Sum, 1995).[1]

Structurally, the post-Cold War era is marked by the continued rise of economic superpowers such as Japan and Germany as well as the disintegration of the Soviet bloc. This has changed the security game from one of bipolarity to multipolarity. The multipolar world order involves a growing significance for Japan and China, the current and emerging regional hegemons respectively, which have joined global hegemons, such as the US, in redefining the geo-political and/or geo-economic interests and sentiments of the region — including above all those of the Greater China bloc. The coupling of geo-political and geo-economic strategies of the global and/or regional players involves a wide and often contradictory range of interests/identities for local social forces within Hong Kong and Taiwan. These forces are increasingly engaged in an identity struggle that is reflected in a 'multiple consciousness' for agents seeking to reposition themselves. Social and political alignments have gradually crystallized around these opposed meanings and consciousnesses and may spearhead new strategies in the post-Cold War world (dis)order. Before addressing these issues, however, let me start with the geo-political strategy of the US.

American security responsibilities have been redefined rather than abandoned in the newly emerging multipolar global system. Cold War mind-sets and strategies still prevail and the US is still inclined to act as a hegemonic power, especially in fast growing regions with emerging regional hegemons (Agnew and Corbridge, 1989; Dalby, 1990; Shelley, 1993). In this regard, US strategy assumes an intrinsic long-term strategic stake in regional stability in East Asia and the need to retain sufficient capabilities to induce caution in China as an emerging hegemonic power. In order to contain possible Chinese ambitions, US policy relies on building a network of bilateral security arrangements with smaller entities/states in the region, and for present purposes, we should emphasize the US' bilateral arrangements with two entities/states within the Greater China bloc, namely, Hong Kong and Taiwan.

More precisely, US strategies regarding China involve building a network of bilateral security arrangements with Hong Kong and Taiwan within the Greater China bloc (Pollock, 1992, p. 70). The two key strategies being pursued are: supporting Governor Patten, the representative of Britain in Hong Kong, in his 'democratization' package; and selling arms to Taiwan and the symbolic act of permitting Taiwan's President to visit the US. The articulation of US-British and US-Taiwan bilateralism is complicated by parallel nationalist and geo-economic strategies of China. The former constructs the 'unification' of China as an 'historical mission' and is reinforced, on a discursive level, by the imagined identity of Greater China (Anderson 1991). The latter re-defines and coordinates the internal complementarities between Hong Kong-Macau, Taiwan, and Southern China. The 'Open Door' policy of China since 1978 offers opportunities for consolidating a 'growth triangle' (Arndt, 1993, p. 272)[2] and is further strengthened by developments in post-1985 Japan, which now seeks to invest in cheap production sites in the region, and more specifically in Southern China. In the 1990s, Japanese foreign direct investment (FDI) has been deepened by entry into strategic alliances with Hong Kong and Taiwanese firms to penetrate the Chinese markets. Thus, social forces in Hong Kong and Taiwan are increasingly confronted with dilemma-full opportunities rooted in the interpenetration or coupling of geo-politics and geo-economics. The resulting dialectics are expressed in struggles over identities by individuals/groups within Hong Kong and Taiwan. Let us start by examining the geo-politics of America's regionally-focused Cold War strategy vis-à-vis Hong Kong and Taiwan in the first phase of the post-Cold War era.

The US' geo-political strategy: a regionally-focused Cold War mind-set

In the first phase of the post-Cold War era, the security agenda of the US has been redefined but still retains traces of the Cold War mind-sets. Thus, although the Soviet military threat is now seen as much reduced, there is a shift in the US security agenda from a 'threat-driven' to an 'insurance' concept of risk reduction in the region. The latter takes the form of marked fear about the growth/stability of China as an emerging regional hegemon in the next century.

A shift away from threat-driven strategy

With the ending of the Cold War, the shift away from the threat-driven strategy of military deployments is seen in the US military withdrawal from Southeast Asia. In the post-Cold War era, Russia's military presence in Asia-Pacific has diminished substantially. The old Soviet security alliances with Vietnam and India are now defunct. Russia no longer has any significant power projection capability in the region and its security priorities now stress pacifying border conflicts and protecting Russian ethnic minorities (Ziegler, 1994, p. 534). The successful thwarting of Soviet 'threats' in Asia, especially in the Southeast Asian straits, contributed to the US withdrawal from its Subic Bay and Clark Field bases in the Philippines in 1992. In this new era, the key challenges to the US concern its relations with Japan and China.

A movement towards an insurance strategy of risk reduction

In East Asia, the major players in the security game in the post-Cold War era are the US, Japan, China and the Soviet Union. The challenges to the US are its relation to Japan and China. Since Japan still lacks the military capabilities and will needed to threaten other countries' security, the US remains the prime strategic player in their regional partnership. In this regard, their relations are basically cooperative, despite the trade imbalance and economic friction. Indeed, some writers refer to the emergent bigemony (i.e. shared hegemony) between the US and Japan (Chan, 1993, p. 173) under the rubric of the G-7, the United Nations (UN) or other multilateral arrangements.[3] Moreover, from the perspective of the smaller entities/states in East Asia a US-Japan alliance, with an American rather than a Japanese military presence in the region, could serve to confine the Japanese to the role of regional economic hegemon and limit any military pretensions which Japan may have.

While US-Japan relations are basically cooperative, the US-China relationship is ambivalent and ambiguous. During the Cold War era, China was seen as a 'swing factor' in the tangle of US-Soviet conflict (Pollock, 1984, p. 174). This unique role of China has declined in the new global configuration of power (Hsiung, 1985, p. 116). In place of the US-Soviet military conflict, the post-Cold War world is characterized by the emergence of Germany and Japan as economic superpowers. Given that China can no longer enjoy the same swing role, there are certain signs and tendencies in post-Tiananmen Chinese foreign policy that may be interpreted as regional 'risks'. In the imagery of a redefined Cold War mind-set, these risks need to be 'insured' against in the post-Cold War era. They are: the nationalist and assertive character of Chinese strategic culture (Pollock, 1992, p. 76); the modernization of China's air and naval power (Hsiung, 1993, p. 83); the Sino-Russian military technology linkages (Godwin, 1994, pp. 178-80); the Beijing-Taipei 'mini-arms race' (Lin, 1993, pp. 793-9); China's claim of an 'historical border' in the South China Sea; and the promotion of China's diplomatic realignments with its major Asian neighbours.

First, when the People's Republic of China (PRC) emerged in the earliest days of the Cold War, its leaders brought with them traumatic memories of China's inability to determine its own fate in the preceding hundred years. China viewed itself as the victim of Western and Japanese imperialism (Godwin, 1994, p. 177). Nationalism, to a certain extent, is still part of China's vision of its role in the world in the post-Cold War era. This can be seen from its policies towards Hong Kong and Taiwan, and from China's response towards US arms sale to Taiwan in 1992. The signification of nationalism has become an important part of Chinese diplomacy and economic development. In this regard, it is seen to be more assertive than Japan and tends to favour strategic independence in its actions. These risks have been rendered more credible both by dynamic growth in collaboration with its neighbours and by China's appreciably upgraded efforts to enhance its military capabilities.

Second, given that China no longer enjoys the geo-political advantage of being a swing factor, it has been adjusting by upgrading its air and naval power since the mid-1980s (Hsiung, 1993, pp. 82-3). Between 1989 and 1992, Chinese military spending increased some fifty percent (Lin, 1993, p. 797; Dittmer, 1994, p. 108). In 1990, and with French assistance, China upgraded two Chinese Luda-class destroyers with air defence missiles and search radar. Between 1991 and 1992, Beijing purchased from the Russian Republic twenty-four high-performance SU-27 jet fighters and three IL-76TD military transport planes. Russia also considered helping China develop Yak-141 fighters capable of short take-offs and vertical landings. This is especially the case after the Gulf War allegedly demonstrated the effectiveness of high-technology weaponry. Thus China became an active shopper for aircraft carriers from the Ukraine and Russia, and according to the Russian Foreign Ministry, it would even transfer the manufacturing technology of SU-27 to Beijing by 1996. These are examples of China's military adjustment (Lin, 1993, pp. 797-8). China has also agreed to buy fifty T72 tanks and seventy BMP vehicles, two to four Kile-class submarines, and control aircraft and long-range early warning radar systems (Cheung, 1993).

Third, the above development might be interpreted as indicating the emergence of a more permanent and mutually beneficial Sino-Russian military technology relation of great concern for the US and its partners. For, whereas the Chinese military feels the need to move from a mass army to high-tech arms and equipment, and has acquired increased influence within the regime after the Tiananmen debacle, the shrinking of Russian military needs at the end of the Cold War, along with its underemployed defence industries, make the Russian elites eager to sell weaponry abroad (Godwin, 1994, pp. 178-9). Russian scientists are working with their Chinese counterparts to develop new defence technology. Indeed, more than 1,000 Russian defense-industrial exchanges exist. Closer ties in this area are naturally of great concern to the US and Japan, and could even provoke a major defence build-up in the latter (Chang and Deng, 1991, pp. 215-7; Chu, 1994, pp. 89-90).

Fourth, the modernization and build-up of advanced weaponry in China is also of great concern to another American partner in the region — Taiwan. Lin argues that from the perspective of the smaller entities/states in East Asia, a US-Japan alliance with an American rather than Japanese military presence in the region could serve to confine the Japanese to the role of regional economic hegemon and limit any military pretensions. Beijing has never made explicit that its military exercises are threatening to Taiwan, they have often coincided with its official denunciations of the Taiwanese independence movement and of Taipei's effort to expand its international presence (Lin, 1993, pp. 793-7). These operations occurred in areas close to Taiwan. On the other hand, Taiwan has made impressive progress in its defence capability, emphasizing improvement in quality over expansion in quantity. Such efforts continued and probably accelerated after the 1989 Tiananmen Incident. The US maintained arms sales to Taiwan and Taipei has become increasingly active in its own development of armaments. This mini-arms race in the post-Tiananmen period has heightened tensions in the region and this may have bearing upon American strategy vis-à-vis China.

Fifth, China has reiterated its claim to an historical border which encompasses the entire South China Sea. This claim maps an area of more than 800,000 square kilometres within its 'traditional maritime boundaries' and this has been 'illegally' delineated into the domain of other nations, including the Philippines, Malaysia, Vietnam, Indonesia and Brunei. China claims that these countries, which border the Spratly Islands, have drilled more than 120 oil wells within China's boundaries. This claim can be seen as a risk to regional security which is coupled to China's military build-up in recent years.

Sixth, in response to Western outrage over Tiananmen, China is actively promoting diplomatic realignments with its major Asian neighbours — Japan, Singapore, Vietnam, South Korea, and India. The promotion of closer ties with Japan and the Association of South East Asian Nations (ASEAN) in the region will not only boost Chinese diplomatic capital but also strengthen its position as an emerging regional hegemon. There are signs that China is performing such a role in the Asianization of regional security politics. In relation to North Korea, it appears that Beijing has applied some pressure to induce North Korea to accept International Atomic Energy Agency (IAEA) inspections of its nuclear plants (Burton, 1994) and for the two Koreas to conclude an historic agreement on mutual non-aggression on 12 December 1991. In relation to Cambodia, China helped to settle the twelve-year civil war through collaborative brokering with the ASEAN nations and the UN (Hsiung, 1993, p. 80).

The above perceptions of China's pursuit of strategic independence, and its search for an autonomous posture, may create a need for an insurance strategy to reduce risk. This risk-reduction strategy is to caution emerging regional actors/hegemons such as China. This can be done by building a network of bilateral alliances with the US' Cold War partners, such as Britain and Taiwan. Let us begin with the bilateral Anglo-American alliance/partnership.

The US' perception of risks in this regard is linked to the way in which the US regards democratization in Hong Kong as its preferred future for the PRC. This was evidenced in two ways. First, it formulated the US-Hong Kong Policy in September 1992. This states the principles for US policy after China resumes sovereignty over Hong Kong in 1997 and reasserts the importance of continuity in government programmes and intergovernmental agreements which involve Hong Kong. Second, it was prepared to take seriously Hong Kong's fears for itself about the implications of the US' China policy. This was evidenced by President Clinton's reception of Governor Chris Patten in April 1993. Shortly after arriving as Britain's representative in Hong Kong in September 1992, Patten introduced a democratization programme in his first Legislative Council Speech. This aims to restructure state-society relations in Hong Kong and this programme provoked strong critical reactions from the PRC. In search for international support, he was enthusiastically backed by Clinton and the US government (Yahuda, 1993, p. 705). The concerted action contrived a democratization drama in Hong Kong between 1992 and 1994. They managed to conduct a low-intensity discursive 'warfare,' termed 'the war of words' by local journalists, against the emerging regional hegemon — China. Strategically, if Hong Kong can be sustained as a democratic hub after 1997, it may become a political lever that can contribute to the growth of a centrifugal sub-regionalism in China (Segal, 1993, p. 38). This tendency for sub-regionalism is also evident in the establishment of a Special Economic Zone in Guangdong. Guangdong is seen as being a relatively powerful centrifugal sub-regional force because of its high growth rate, which was twice the national average (Segal, 1994b, p. 19). The maintenance of Hong Kong as a democratic hub within a tendentially centrifugal Guangdong may weaken and induce caution in China as an emerging regional hegemon in the 'new world order'.

Parallel to this Anglo-American bilateralism is the maintenance-renewal of the US-Taiwan alliance in order to induce greater caution on the part of China. This is seen in continued US arms leases/sales to Taiwan. For instance, President George Bush, on 19 July 1992, approved the lease of three Knox-class anti-submarine frigates to Taiwan for five years. Later, in the heat of the presidential campaign, President Bush approved the sale of 150, F-16 aircraft (Hsuing, 1994, p. 227). In addition, US Congressmen and US-based lobbyists and organizations active on Taiwan's behalf continued to support its independence movement. In March 1992, Senators Pell, Kennedy and Lieberman introduced a resolution to the effect that the authorities in Taiwan should permit the return to Taiwan of all current and former citizens who are committed to 'peaceful' change and that Taiwan's future should be left to the people of Taiwan to determine. As for the actions of the Taiwanese-based organizations in the US, the Formosan Association for Public Affairs (FAPA), which had close associations with the pro-independence Democratic Progressive Party (DPP), stepped up its lobbying activities in Congress. The US-Taiwan bilateral relationship improved further when Clinton granted President Lee Teng-hui's visit to the US in June 1995. The maintenance and deepening of US-Taiwan bilateralism through arms sales, the support for its democracy and independence movements, and the granting of the 'unofficial' visit of Taiwanese politicians to the US, may constitute part of the US' insurance strategy in inducing caution on China through the deployment of Taiwan as a leverage on China's plan for 'national reunification'.

China's reunification and geo-economic strategies: the construction and coordination of the Greater China bloc

The coupling of the American, the British (Hong Kong) and the Taiwanese geo-political strategies is made more complex by the parallel geo-economic strategies of China and Japan. China's geo-economic strategy for Hong Kong-Macau and Taiwan is structured around the idea of Greater China. The construction of this bloc is related to two sets of policies. The first relates to a national reunification policy which builds on the concept of 'one country, two systems'. The second is based on an Open Door policy which enables China to envision economic development by encouraging local incentives, especially in the Southern provinces (Guangdong and Fujian) close to Hong Kong and Taiwan. In the case of the former, the tendency to foster internal complementarities of the bloc is further strengthened by developments in post-1985 Japan as its firms look for cheap production sites in regions such as Southern China. In the 1990s, Japanese FDI has sought to penetrate the Chinese markets by entering into strategic alliances with Hong Kong and Taiwanese firms. Let us start by examining the national reunification policy in China.

The national reunification policy

The Chinese leadership has perceived national reunification as an historical mission since the 1980s. It was first formulated under the model of one country, two systems in 1984. It means that there is only 'one China' and Taiwan is a part of China. Any other conception such as 'two Chinas' (i.e. Taiwan's independence) would be unacceptable to Beijing. 'Two systems' means socialism in the Mainland and capitalism in Hong Kong-Macau-Taiwan, with the latter becoming special administrative regions (SARs) of China. As SARs, the Hong Kong and Taiwan governments would have a high degree of autonomy in administrative, legislative, and judicial matters. The national reunification policy resulted in the signing of the Sino-British Joint Declaration and the promulgation of the Basic Law in which China will resume the sovereignty of Hong Kong after 1997. Beijing's model is also extended to Macau and from the viewpoint of the former the Macau case is largely in order. In the case of Taiwan, it would be allowed to retain its present political and judicial systems, its economic and social structure, its armed forces, and independent trade and cultural relations with other countries. After reunification, Taiwan would be represented in the central government. All of these proposals were reaffirmed in *The Taiwan Question and Reunification of China* White Paper, published by the PRC State Council on 31 August 1993.

In relation to China's reunification discourse and process, China shied away from the rhetoric of 'liberation of Taiwan' after 1979. Instead, the rhetoric emphasizes a 'peaceful negotiation', which involves a two-step approach. The first is signified as 'people-to-people diplomacy', i.e. the promotion of China-Taiwan linkages through the 'three communications' policy (trade, postage and transport communication) and 'four exchanges' (academic, cultural, sporting and technological). Taiwan responded with its 'three nos' policy (no compromise, no negotiation, and no contact with the Chinese Communist Party). This implied that the Taiwanese government would only permit 'indirect trade' between the two states through an intermediary like Hong Kong. The second step was for China to push for reunification talks at the end of the 1980s. In response to the demand in Taiwan for legal protection of Taiwan's Mainland investments, both sides agreed to talks in Singapore. A quasi-cabinet-level Commission on Mainland Affairs was established by Taiwan, and a semi-official Straits Exchange Foundation (SEF) was formed in 1991; both were responsible for negotiation on practical aspects with Beijing. The Association for Relations across the Taiwan Straits (ARATS) is charged by Beijing with dealing with matters arising from people-to-people relations, including tourism, trade, legal affairs, cultural affairs and general affairs (Clough, 1993, p. 134). It was described as a 'bridge' across the Strait that would ensure 'smooth' relations among the people and pave the way for reunification. On 27-28 April 1992, a milestone conference took place in Singapore between the SEF and ARATS from China. A number of agreements on document verification and registered mail were signed. However, there are still some bottlenecks in the China-Taiwan relationship, notably the protection of Taiwanese investment in China, the rejoining of the UN by Taiwan, the development of an independence movement in Taiwan, and the internationalization of Taiwan's diplomatic contacts.

The Open Door policy

Parallel to the national reunification policy was China's Open Door policy. Since 1978 this has taken the form of decentralization and coastal strategies. The decentralization strategy was spearheaded by coastal provinces such as

Guangdong and Fujian — the two most economically open of Chinese provinces. For example, Guangdong demanded more power and special policies from the central government. In negotiation with the central government, the following measures were gradually introduced in the two provinces. First, they were given substantial legal and administrative power in managing the four special economic zones (SEZs), three of which were located in Guangdong (Shenzhen, Zhuhai, and Shantou) and one in Fujian (Xiamen). Under administrative bodies that were set up by the provinces, the objectives of the SEZs are: to develop economic links between Hong Kong (Zhenzhen), Macau (Zhuhai), Taiwan (Xiamen) and overseas Chinese communities (Shantou), with a view to the reunification of China; and to serve as 'windows' for learning advanced technology and managerial skills as well as attracting foreign investment.

These reforms made Guangdong and Fujian provinces the most open arenas for FDI in China in the 1980s. Since the establishment of the four SEZs, China has designated a number of other open areas for FDI. These include fourteen coastal cities and three coastal areas (e.g. Pearl River Delta). Foreign investment in these different types of open areas enjoy varying incentives, e.g. the income tax rate is fifteen per cent in the SEZs and twenty-four per cent in coastal areas. Given the head-start of Guangdong, in that it has the biggest concentration of open areas, it remains in a favourable position for FDI. In addition, the reform programme has offered Guangdong provincial and local governments exclusive fiscal incentives to develop an outward-looking economy. According to a contract between Guangdong and the central government, the former was allowed to retain seventy per cent of its export earnings above the 1978 export level (US$ 1.4 billion), while other provinces (except Fujian) were entitled to retain only thirty per cent for centrally managed goods and forty per cent for locally managed goods. The provincial and local governments in Guangdong and Fujian thus had great incentives to actively seek export-oriented FDI from Hong Kong and, later on, Taiwan.

In response to the above opportunities emerging in Guangdong and Fujian, the rise of Western protectionism, and the increase in its own domestic costs for land and labour, Hong Kong's FDI in Guangdong has grown rapidly. It is now the biggest investor by far in the province; eighty per cent of the FDI in Guangdong has come from Hong Kong. Pearl River Delta is now a major production base for its more labour-intensive products. It is estimated that almost 20,000 Hong Kong manufacturing enterprises, mostly in textiles and clothing, and toys and consumer electronics, have moved to this region to take advantage of the low, labour and rent costs there. Together they employ about three million workers. Hong Kong has also diversified into sectors such as tourism and real estate (Chen, 1993, pp. 36-8).

Unlike Hong Kong, the Taiwanese government in the early 1980s saw few advantages, and serious risks, in trade between Taiwan and the Mainland. However, the opening of China made the Chinese market increasingly attractive to business people in Taiwan. Some of them urged the government to cease restrictions on trade and expressed concern that they were losing out in the rapidly growing China market to their Japanese and South Korean competitors. The Taiwanese government bowed to growing popular pressure by allowing indirect links with China, beginning with the decision in November 1987 that Taiwanese citizens would be allowed to 'visit relatives' in China (Clark, 1993, p. 120). The legalization of travel sharply accelerated the growth in trade between the two areas. In 1988, the Chinese State Council promulgated a set of twenty-two measures to encourage investment from Taiwan. As a result, some five million Taiwanese have visited China and some 10,000 small and medium-sized Taiwanese firms have moved their labour-intensive production processes there, with investment of US$ 11 billion between 1987 and 1993.

China's Open Door policy is reinforced by economic changes in Japan after 1985. In response to the deteriorating trade relationship with Japan, the US forced the appreciation of the yen relative to the dollar under the Plaza Accord in 1985. Saddled with uncompetitive prices in export markets, Japan is seeking to coordinate the region by increasing its investment and trade ties with the newly industrializing countries (NICs), ASEAN countries and the Greater China bloc. Typically, Japanese FDI tends to foster a distinct sub-regional division of labour which is simultaneously giving rise to a new division of knowledge (Morris-Suzuki, 1992, p. 147). Japanese FDI is focused primarily on the manufacturing sector and on the production of particular manufactured components, finished goods and producer services. While Taiwan has high level and sophisticated manufacturing bases for chemicals, textiles, and electronics components (Chen, 1993, pp. 33-4; Kwan, 1994, p. 96), simple consumer electronics are produced in Southern China. There is an increasing tendency for Japanese FDI to move into the service sectors such as finance, commerce, telecommunications, and technological support services. This pattern suggests how Japanese FDI has given rise to a new regional division of knowledge in which Japan is a base for high-technology industries, and research and development; Taiwan produces sophisticated components; Hong Kong is important for producer services and finance; and Southern China engages in low-wage production (Sum, 1996). In the 1990s, Japanese FDI coordinates with Hong Kong and Taiwanese firms to penetrate the Chinese markets and other regions beyond Southern China (e.g. Shanghai-Pudong area for the development of high technology).

Coordination of the Greater China bloc

Given the above structural and strategic changes in the region, most of the Taiwanese/Japanese FDI targeted on Guangdong and Fujian provinces has passed through Hong Kong, which has consolidated itself as a gateway city (Ash and Keuh, 1993, p. 721). In this regard it acts in conjunction with Southern China and Taiwan as the nodal point of a multi-spatial production site. Let us illustrate this with reference to the case of international subcontracting. International subcontracting between Hong Kong, Southern China and the rest of the world involves at least two nexus. The Hong Kong-foreign buyers nexus involves international commercial subcontracting; and the Hong Kong-China/Hong Kong-Taiwan-China nexus involves international industrial, and in some cases commercial, subcontracting. The confluence of these nexus in Hong Kong implies that producers there have a dual role: as subcontractors (of foreign firms) and as subcontracting managers (between overseas and Chinese subcontractors). As such, producers come to assume an industrial-cum-mercantile role in providing production and circulation services (Chan and Kwok, 1991, pp. 201-3; Leung, 1993, pp. 281-91; Sit, 1989, pp. 5-8; and Sung, 1991, Ch.2). In addition to assuming the industrial-cum-mercantile role, good relations with local/central officials are essential for a smooth operation in China. In this regard, it involves linkages/networking with the bureaucratic sphere. It is this entire process which I refer to as subcontracting management that can be analyzed in four major modalities: sourcing management, production management, authority management, and distribution management. How these modalities are mediated is through pre-existing social and institutional networks, e.g. familial linkages, clans, and trading companies (Leung, 1993, pp. 281-91; Smart and Smart, 1991, pp. 216-33).

In sourcing management, Hong Kong/Taiwanese producers, with their overseas contacts, seek to transfer their more labour-intensive sub-processes to China. With the opening of China and the establishment of indirect links between China and Taiwan, the sourcing of Chinese partners takes the form of trial and error, repeated contacts with familial networks in China, clans contacts, and formal trade fairs as well as Chinese quasi-state trading companies in Hong Kong. On establishing contacts, they may enter into agreements with private/state-owned factories in China. State-owned firms, especially the large and medium-sized ones, enjoy substantial allocative advantages in investment, bank loans, foreign exchange quotas and utility supplies. The linkage between Hong Kong, Taiwanese and Chinese firms may gradually consolidate into longer-lasting ties such as joint ventures and strategic alliances. The sourcing and consolidation of alliances need to draw on more complex services related to business consultancy, legal services on production-sharing contracts, and licensing and accounting expertise on mergers, takeovers, and franchising in Hong Kong.

As a result of establishing the sourcing networks, the Hong Kong/Taiwanese firms then engage in cross-border production management. This involves coordinating and supervising the more skill-intensive sub-processes in Hong Kong/Taiwan with the more labour-intensive ones in China. This means that production managers from Hong Kong and Taiwan have to offer value-adding services such as pre-production planning in merchandising, preparing production schedules and tighter monitoring so that the various sub-processes can be welded together just-in-time and just-in-place across boundaries. Ensuring smooth production often involves Hong Kong/Taiwanese personnel staying in China almost permanently, overseeing activities such as engineering, quality control and accounting. This will also require frequent visits and attention from Hong

Kong/Taiwan-based managers to ensure that the operations are conforming to specification (Chan, Sculli and Si, 1991, p. 189).

Essential to cross-border production is the building and maintaining of good relations with local and/or central officials in China. This kind of institutionalized networking with state officials is important because the state still controls enormous resources such as land, labour, capital and regulations. Ad hoc relaxation and tightening of registration and licensing requirements, environmental protection and safety standards, land use and labour regulations, and accounting procedures and tax codes, for example, can alter the cost of production. In this regard, establishing contacts with state officials, which I term authority management, contributes towards consolidating contacts with state organizations and officials. This kind of public-private network can be cemented through regular gifts, bribes, donations to ancestral towns/universities, and so forth. Once contacts have been established and regularized, they enable the Hong Kong and Taiwanese counterparts to gain access to extra information (e.g. interpretation of laws and procedures, and contacts in parallel networks) and/or speedy documentation (e.g. work permits for migrant labour, factory licences, and export and import documents) in the state-related domain.

Apart from production and authority management in the multi-spatial production process, circulation services are needed for distribution management. Finished goods need to be exported and distributed to overseas markets to meet consumer demand. This requires the management of multi-spatial procedures of import/export licensing, customs liaison, arranging shipments, etc., so that goods can be delivered just-in-time and just-in-place for overseas buyers. Again, this involves a network of service-based firms in Hong Kong and China, as well as the trading and customs authorities in China and elsewhere. In essence, this cross-border private-public network can be, in the ideal case, cemented by the three 'T's': time, trust, and truth. They form the basic ingredients for the production and reproduction of this private-public network. It is through the production and reproduction of this strategic network that Hong Kong is crystallizing its position as a gateway region,[4] in providing producer and financial services, and that Taiwan is distilling its own position as the source of investment and technology on the material level.

These developments on the material level are reinforced by an imagined identity of Greater China on the discursive level. There is an increasing body of literature using Greater China to summarize the vibrancy of economic interactions in the economically, culturally, and linguistically compatible area of Taiwan, Hong Kong, Macau, and the Mainland's Guangdong and Fujian provinces. Most of this literature forecasts an optimistic future for economic growth in this region (Cheng, 1992; Fang, 1992; Fu, 1992). Ethnic Chinese business people and interested Chinese intellectuals envision a Greater China of a much larger territorial scope and maintain that the formation of an economic Greater China of sorts is the first step towards national reunification (Zha, 1994, p. 41). This form of 'pragmatic nationalism' (Sum, 1995) is used to redefine and coordinate the

64

internal complementarity of the region in relation to China and its competitiveness in the changing global economy.

For China, Hong Kong is defined as a strategic gateway for Beijing to implement its policies to attract *huaqiao* (patriotic) investments into the 'motherland' of China. Thus, the construction of the identity of 'patriotic ethnic Chinese investors' links nationalism with economics and not politics. This discursive construction enables China to secure Taiwanese and Hong Kong investment/technology without having to engage directly in the thorny problem of the relationship between nationalism and politics, at least in the short-term. As for Taiwan, the new economic relation with China in the 1990s is redefined under the rubrics of 'flexible diplomacy' and 'economic reunification'. These enable Taiwan to join major international/regional organizations (e.g. Olympics and Asian Development Bank) under the name of 'Chinese Taipei' and also to orchestrate unofficial contacts between Taipei and Beijing.

Nevertheless, these redefinitions of economic relationships in Greater China are, in the main, endorsed by Taipei and Beijing authorities (Zha, 1994, p. 51). This does not imply, however, that various forces in or beyond this private-public network (e.g. international or regional capital, and the Chinese, Taiwanese, and Hong Kong democracy and independent movements) are not faced with dilemmas rooted in this particular global, regional, and local interface. The following section analyzes these dilemmas in terms of moments of identity struggle within the Greater China bloc.

Moments of identity struggle in Hong Kong and Taiwan

Social and economic forces (as opposed to official diplomatic agents) are faced with awkward choices opened by the emerging geo-political/geo-economic/nationalist interface. Here I will concentrate on Hong Kong's and Taiwan's dilemmas as expressed in the form of identity struggle. I noted above a change of US strategy towards an insurance concept of risk reduction by building a network of bilateral alliances with Britain and Taiwan that might caution China against acting in a manner inimical to US interests. The Anglo-American and the US-Taiwan partnerships strengthened Britain's claim for democratization in Hong Kong as well as the DPP's claim in Taiwan. Likewise, I also suggested that this Anglo-American geo-political strategy is made more complex by the existence of a parallel geo-economic/nationalist development related to the economic dynamism of a regional bloc, and is reinforced, on the discursive level, by an imagined identity of Greater China. Hong Kong is defined as a strategic gateway for Beijing and Taiwan to implement their policies to attract *huaqiao* investments to the motherland. The construction of patriotic ethnic Chinese investors links nationalism with economics, which I have termed 'pragmatic nationalism' (Sum, 1995). Forces within/outside this network are faced with dilemmas rooted in this three-way interface. The dialectic is expressed in the form of two main sets of competing discursive formations in Hong Kong which can be described as democratization vis-à-vis pragmatic nationalism. In the case of Taiwan, it can be epitomized as the contradictory articulation of democratization vis-à-vis pragmatic nationalism, economic reunification versus liberal indigenism, and one China against two Chinas, with their respective identities and security implications. Let us start with the case of Hong Kong.

Moments of identity struggle in Hong Kong

In Hong Kong, Govenor Patten's democratization package was initially presented in his first policy speech in the Legislative Council in October 1992. In the language/mind-set of the Cold War, he re-presented democracy as universal and claimed that democratization could protect Hong Kong against the onslaught of communism and authoritarianism after 1997. In his speech, he sought to redefine the state-society relations (Sum, 1995), which had the effect of repositioning all subjects in the following ways. First, he chose Hong Kong people as the starting point and constructed 'citizen participation' as a principal entry point into the struggle over Hong Kong's future identity (Patten, 1992, pp. 30-38). This struggle for citizen participation was defined as an essential precondition for maintaining Hong Kong's prosperity in the future (Patten, 1992, p. 30). Second, he also (re-)constructed Britain as a 'moral' actor in 'protecting' Hong Kong against the encroachment of China through democratization. Given the 'moral' nature of this act, a Pax Britannica-type 'exit in glory' (Segal, 1994a, pp. 36-7) was not only possible but desirable. Third, the Chinese Government was presented as the 'democratic other' constraining the 'political progress' in Hong Kong. Given this application of the Cold War mind-set to Hong Kong, any counter-arguments/attacks by his critics were thereby interpreted as 'undemocratic,' 'pro-China' and 'conspiratorial' in spirit, if not in action. Patten's discursive formation of an imagined identity for Hong Kong had the potential of consolidating a social basis of support. Individuals and groups, directly or indirectly, related to the democracy movement in Hong Kong come out in full or partial support of his package (Sum, 1995).[5]

However, Patten's democratization package in Hong Kong was met with strong responses from Chinese officials. The mass media characterized this period as one of a war of words. The PRC constructed an alternative genre to counteract Patten's Cold War rhetoric. China's reaction can be analyzed in terms of a two-part construction that clustered around 'violation' and pragmatic nationalism. China's violation discourse derived its authority from an insistence on Britain's moral duty to abide by its agreements, as well as to the principles and spirit of international and constitutional documents, such as the Sino-British Joint Declaration and the Basic Law. Departure from these principles and spirit was defined by the PRC as a violation, a 'unilateral termination of talks', and an 'indecency', which may not be beneficial to the prosperity and stability of Hong Kong.

66

The rhetoric of anti-colonialism is common in nationalist discourse in the non-European world (Chatterjee, 1993, p. 18). However, the PRC's anti-colonialism was also contingently articulated here to a narrative of pragmatism. The resulting discursive formation was — and remains — pragmatic nationalism. It revolves around two main elements, viz., historical shame and a pragmatic vision of Hong Kong's future. The construction of China's 'historical shame' derived from its defeat in the Opium Wars and the inequality involved in the Sino-British treaties which ceded Hong Kong Island and other territories from 1842 onwards. As a nationalist discourse, it privileges shame related to colonialism and is used to justify unification of the Chinese nation by 'mapping' the Hong Kong Chinese as part of the 'Chinese in China' and not as subjects of a colonial power. It is through the deployment of China's historical shame that China could invoke nationalism as a reaction to colonialism and use the Chinese in China to cultivate loyalty and patriotism in Hong Kong.

However, nationalist rhetoric assumes an unorthodox form in that it is not generated, in the first instance, from within Hong Kong. Instead it is created by a sovereign power which is re-calling the inclusion of Hong Kong in its historic territory and aims to integrate it more fully into its economic orbit. It takes the form of a top-down nationalism which is quite different from messianic missions for self-determination imagined by domestic intellectuals, as happened, for example, in India. To put it differently, although nationalism, as defined by the PRC, is certainly articulated to anti-colonialism, it is also de-coupled from (Hong Kong's alleged right to) self-determination. In place of the latter we find a contingent articulation to Deng's pragmatism and a strong desire to regain Hong Kong as a strategic gateway for the Greater China bloc.

Together these discursive formations create not only a terrain of struggle but they also have the potential for consolidating two new, but not unchanging, social bases of support in Hong Kong. Each social basis of support is drawn from across different classes and ethnic/racial groups, and together they are oriented to two imagined identities. On the one hand, Patten's discursive approach clearly privileges the politico-ideological plane of identity formation. In addition, his position as the Governor of Hong Kong means he can facilitate access to political positions, and to individuals prepared to re-negotiate their identities on short-term pragmatic grounds — at least up to 1997. In this regard, Patten has managed to consolidate support from groups related to the democracy movement, some top-ranking civil servants, and certain British *Hong* (conglomerate). On the other hand, the PRC tends to (re-)state the discourse of pragmatic nationalism, which privileges the economic-historical-cultural dimensions. China managed to consolidate support from many Chinese businessmen, nationalist-oriented groups and trade unions (Sum, 1995, pp. 88-94). Let us now turn to the identity struggle in Taiwan.

As a result of pressure both within Taiwan and from the US, Chiang Ching-kuo lifted the martial law and removed the ban on organizing new political parties in 1987. The hegemony of the *Kuomingtang* (KMT), which were almost exclusively composed of 'Mainlanders', was challenged by the 'Islander' dominated opposition DPP in the elections of 1986, 1989, 1992 and 1994. Even though the KMT won strong majorities in the elections, it has become internally divided with the growing power of Islander legislators demanding constitutional reform as a way of establishing an 'independent Taiwan', a direction that would depart from the reunification plan of China. However, the Mainlander faction, which is mainly supported by Chinese capitalists, privileges a form of pragmatic nationalism that prioritizes the role of economic reunification and the identity of one China encoded in pragmatism as well as the 'fear of military invasion by China'.

While China wishes to incorporate Taiwan by means of economic integration, the KMT wishes to use economic integration to defer and halt the threat of political unification with China (Hsiao and So, 1994, p. 141). This was encoded in the *Guidelines for National Unification*, adopted in March 1991. These guidelines emphasized two major ideas: there is one Chinese territory, but two political entities; and unification is relegated to the very distant future. Thus, the KMT prioritizes process variables/steps as opposed to forms of reunification. For example, negotiations on the 'three links' policy (air, sea, and mail links) are possible if China recognizes Taiwan on 'a basis of equality' (Lee, 1990), so that 'channels of communication' can be established. It is through these channels of communication that reunification can occur through a three-phase process starting with exchange and reciprocity, followed by mutual trust and cooperation, and finally consultation and unification (National Unification Council, 1991). These procedural steps tend to create a fuzzy kind of one China identity, which forms a distant object of gazing that helps to consolidate support from the Mainlander KMT, the pragmatic capitalists and even certain factions of the middle class in Taiwan up to 1993.

The one China discourse is challenged by the DPP construction, which re-presents the 'future' of Taiwan by prioritizing 'self-determination' as a means, and 'independent sovereign Taiwan' as an end. In contrast to the 'old guard' KMT construction, they isolate the identity of China from that of Taiwan by naming it as 'one China and one Taiwan'. This rhetorical construction drives a wedge between the two entities across the Strait and creates a separatist moment for Taiwan. It also maps this separatist identity to that of democracy by deploying symbols such as 'a new constitution', which is 'to be decided by all inhabitants of Taiwan' through 'a plebiscite'. Encoded in these symbols is the call to link the separatist movement to an imagined identity derived from Cold War rhetoric (c.f. Chomsky, 1991, pp. 9-19). This identity is based on a re-presentation of democracy as universal, the associated claim that this democracy can protect individuals against the onslaught of communism, and its ability to create independence. This discursive construction of liberal indigenism has consolidated a social basis of support stemming from the ethnic Islanders, the more 'radical' factions of the middle class as well as students.

Up to 1993, then, the ethnic competition between the Mainlander KMT and the Islander DPP created two competing discursive formations in Taiwan: '(economic) reunification' (*tong*) and 'democratic independence' (*du*). The former can be described as a form of pragmatic nationalism that supports economic integration with China, whereas the latter is a variant of liberal indigenism that links democracy with ethnic separatist movements in Taiwan. The construction of these two imagined identities marked a moment of identity struggle which invites social and political forces to reposition themselves. The DPP moderated its call for independence in the 1992 election, and in 1993, president Lee pushed his Taiwanization of the KMT leadership by replacing Hau Pei-tsun, who was a leader of the Mainlander faction, by Lien Chan, who was a Taiwanese scholar. The new Lee-Lien leadership constructs the identity of the 'Republic of China in Taiwan,' which has become more concrete and vocal at the international level. This is evidenced in Lee's 'cheque-book' and 'academic' diplomacy. For example, in June 1995, he offered a donation of US$ 10 billion for the re-entry of Taiwan as a political entity into the UN, and in the same month, he was granted an 'unofficial' visit to the US through the 'invitation' of Cornell University. As for the Mainlander faction, it split from the KMT and formed the Chinese New Party (CNP) in August 1993. The latter accused the present KMT leadership (i.e. President Lee and his faction) of adopting an unrealistic three nos policy and, at the same time, of fostering a 'quiet' withdrawal from the one China policy, thereby favouring the Taiwanization of the political future. The formation of the CNP demonstrated the ethnic insecurity of the Mainlanders when faced with the growing power of the Islanders within the KMT and the DPP. It continues to prioritize the one China identity that is based on direct/official dialogue with Beijing, direct cross-Strait communications, economic and trade ties, and the creation of a 'Greater China Economic Sphere'.

The struggle over, and re-negotiation of, identities in Hong Kong and Taiwan sketched above are reflected in the emergence and consolidation of different social bases in each (sub-)state. These bases are by no means static and unchanging. Even at the time of writing individuals and collective forces in each bloc are taking steps to redefine and reposition themselves discursively. They have variously adopted the following strategies in the politics of identity: emphasizing notions similar to those in the PRC's pragmatic nationalism; accommodation in the hope of making short-term gains in economic linkages with China; re-focusing the discourse on new issues/identities (e.g. welfare policy or the rhetoric of Republic of China in Taiwan); re-naming groups/organizations to highlight a change in their political profile and electoral strength; forming new groups to highlight new platforms; and adopting strategies such as internationalization and/or indigenization. The above responses involve a multiplicity of discourses in and through which groups and individuals redefine and re-present their identities

69

in the hope of forming allies in and across the two social bases of support. In this particular conjuncture, where geo-politics and geo-economics interact with struggles over national identities, the process of re-negotiating identities has become a new field of struggle and collaboration. This in turn confronts a wide range of forces in Hong Kong and Taiwan, such as groups in the democracy movement, British Hongs, Chinese capitalists, civil servants, workers, CNP, and Islander KMT, with dilemmas regarding their future identities and interests.

Conclusion

The first phase of the post-Cold War world has not engendered the demise of an international geo-politics dominated by the balance-of-power strategy of the Cold War hegemon. Instead, there is a coupling of geo-politics and geo-economics at the global, macro-regional, national, and local levels. The Cold War strategy and mind-set still pervade foreign, political and economic policy-making, especially in the policy orientation of established global players towards newly emerging regional hegemons. The rhetoric of democratization and independence, which are promoted by Governor Patten in Hong Kong and the DPP in Taiwan respectively, and are supported by the US, is derived from the Cold War mind-set. It is used, strategically, as a lever against China as an emerging regional hegemon in the new world order. The articulation of Britain's democratization rhetoric and the DPP's talk of independence from the US' geo-political strategy is complicated by a parallel geo-economic development related to the economic dynamism of the Greater China bloc and is reinforced, on the discursive level, by an imagined identity of Greater China. The dialectical interface of global, regional, and local forces expresses itself in struggles over identity, in which there exists a multiple consciousness derived from competing discursive formations — pragmatic nationalism versus democratization, economic reunification versus liberal indigenism, and the one China policy against the two Chinas policy. These sets of discursive formations have the potential for consolidating new, but not unchanging, social bases of support in Hong Kong and Taiwan. These struggles are increasingly mediated and affected by the strategies adopted by agents in reconstructing meanings and identities. In the short term, this results in a multiplicity of meanings which enable individuals and groups to form new allies and, in the long term, may significantly change the structure of political opportunities.

Acknowledgements

I am grateful to the Harold Hyam Wingate Foundation for its financial support during my research on these issues and the writing of this paper. I am also grateful to Bob Jessop for his help in editing the final version.

Notes

1. Jessop's (1990) strategic-relational approach attempts to transcend the structure-agency dichotomy. He regards strategies as mediating the reciprocal relations between structures and agencies. Structures can be analyzed in terms of their strategic selectivity insofar as some structural forms are more suited than others for the purpose of realizing particular strategies. Strategies also occupy and thereby help to constitute a terrain of struggle in which competing agents attempt to change the present structures. The present paper seeks to locate the dialectical interface of Hong Kong as a gateway region of the Greater China bloc in this schema.

2. 'Growth triangle' refers to the open regionalism of cross-border economic interdependence. 'Greater China' involves the economic coordination between Hong Kong, Taiwan, Macau and China. Singapore, Malaysia and Indonesia forms another 'growth triangle' in the Asia-Pacific region.

3. Whereas the US continues to be the principal military power, Japan has increasingly become a primary source of technology and capital for its neighbours. Japan also absorbs the bulk of its neighbours' exports of foodstuffs and raw materials, and, in turn, is the chief supplier of their manufactured goods. However, the US still has a stronger cultural and ideological influence than Japan, even in former Japanese colonies such as South Korea and Taiwan.

4. According to Cohen (1990) and Shelley (1994), a 'gateway region' is an area located near the boundary between major geostrategic realms, often containing a nation or an ethnic group that has not yet achieved political independence.

5. In general, most groups in the democracy movement support Patten's package. However, more liberal-oriented groups such as the United Democrats of Hong Kong think that his package is not democratic enough, whereas more centralist groups such as the Meeting Point are more sympathetic to Chinese nationalism in particular, and socialism in general.

References

Agnew, J.A. and Corbridge, S. (1989), 'The New Geopolitics: The Dynamics of Geopolitical Disorder', in Johnston R. J. and Taylor, P. J. (eds), *A World in Crisis: Geographical Perspectives*, Blackwell, Oxford, pp. 266-288.

Anderson, B. (1991), *Imagined Communities: Reflection on the Origin and Spread of Nationalism*, Verso, London.

Arndt, H. W. (1993), 'Anatomy of Regionalism', *Journal of Asian Economics*, Vol. 4, No. 2, pp. 271-82.

Ash, R. and Kueh, Y.Y. (1993), 'The Economic Integration within Greater China: Trade and Investment Flows between China, Hong Kong and Taiwan', *The China Quarterly*, December, No. 136, pp. 711-45.

Burton, J. (1994), 'Asian Relations on the Line over North Korea', *Financial Times*, 12 June, p. 9.

Campbell, D. (1992), *Writing Security*, Manchester University Press, Manchester.

Chan, J. C. M., Sculli, D. and Si, K. (1991), ,The Cost of Manufacturing Toys in the Shenzhen Special Economic Zone in China', *International Journal of Production Economics*, Vol. 25, pp. 181-190.

Chan, S. (1993), 'U.S. Power and Policy: Choices in the Pacific Region', in Hsiung, J. C. (ed.), *Asia Pacific in the World Politics*, Lynne Rienner Publisher, Boulder, pp. 161-76.

Chan, T. M. H. and Kwok, R. Y. W. (1991), 'Economic Development in the Shenzhen Special Economic Zones: Appendage to Hong Kong?', *Southeast Asian Journal of Social Science*, Vol. 19, Nos. 1-2, pp. 180-205.

Chang, P. H. and Deng, Z. (1991), 'China and Southeast Asia: Overseeing the Regional Balance', in Myers, D. J. (ed.), *Regional Hegemons: Threat Perception and Strategic Response*, Westview, Boulder, pp. 215-217.

Chatterjee, P. (1993), *Nationalist Thought and the Colonial World*, Zed Books, London.

Chen, X-M. (1993), 'China's Growing Integration with the Asia-Pacific Economy', in Dirlik, A. (ed.), *What is in a Rim? Critical Perspectives on the Pacific Region Idea*, Westview, Boudler, pp. 89-120.

Cheng, C-Y. (1992), 'Greater China Common Market', *World Journal*, 26 July, pp. C2-4 (in Chinese).

Cheung, T. M. (1993), 'China's Buying Spree: Russia Gears Up to Upgrade Peking's Weaponry', *Far Eastern Economic Review*, 8 July, p. 26.

Chomsky, (1991), *Deterring Democracy*, Vintage, London.

Chu, S. (1994), 'The Russian-US Military Balance in the Post Cold War Asia-Pacific Region and the 'China Threat'', *Journal of Northeast Asian Studies*, Vol. XIII, No. 1, pp. 77-95.

Chun, A. (1994), 'From Nationalism to Nationalizing: Cultural Imagination and State Formation in Postwar Taiwan', *The Australian Journal of Chinese Affairs*, January, No. 31, pp. 49-72.

Clark, C. (1993), 'Taiwan in Post-Cold War Asia Pacific', in Hsiung, J. C. (ed.), *Asia Pacific in the New World Politics*, Lynne Rienner, Boulder, pp. 113-34.

Clough, R. N. (1993), *Reaching Across the Taiwan Strait: People-to-People Diplomacy*, Westview, Boulder.

Dalby, S. (1990), *Creating the Second Cold War: The Discourse of Politics*, Pinter, London.

Dittmer, (1994), 'China and Russia: New Beginnings', in Kim, S. S. (ed.), *China and the World: Chinese Foreign Relations in the Post-Cold War Era*, Westview, Boulder, pp. 94-113.

Fang, S. (1992), 'A Proposal for Establishing a Mainland-Taiwan-Hong Kong Economic Commission', *Jingji Ribao*, Beijing, 24 June, p. 4 (in Chinese).

Fu, L. (1992), 'Hong Kong-Macao and Both Sides of the Taiwan Strait: a Chinese Economic Sphere', *Journal of Beijing University*, Social Science Edition, Vol. 5, pp. 85-92 (in Chinese).

Godwin, (1994), 'Force and Diplomacy: Chinese Security Policy in the Post-Cold War Era', in Kim, S. S. (ed.), *China and the World: Chinese Foreign Relations in the Post-Cold War Era*, Westview, Boulder, pp. 171-86.

Hsiao, M. and So, A. (1994), 'Ascent Through National Integration: the Chinese Triangle of Mainland-Taiwan-Hong Kong', in Palat, R. A. (ed.), *Pacific-Asia and the Future of the World System*, Greenwood, Westport, pp. 133-50.

Hsiung, J. C. (1985), *Beyond China's Independent Foreign Policy*, Praeger, New York.

Hsiung, J. C. (ed.) (1993), *Asia Pacific in World Politics*, Lynne Rienner, Boulder.

Jessop, B. (1990), *State Theory*, Polity, Cambridge.

Kwan, (1994), *Economic Interdependence in the Asia-Pacific Region*, Routledge, London.

Lee, T-H. (1990), 'Presidential Inaugural Address in the Executive Yuan,' 20 May, Executive Yuan Archive, Taipei.

Leung, C. K. (1993), 'Personal Contacts, Subcontracting Linkages, and Development in Honk Kong-Zhujiang Delta Region', *Annals of the Association of American Geographers*, Vol. 82, No. 2, pp. 272-302.

Lin, C-P. (1993), 'Beijing and Taipei: Interactions in the Post-Tiananmen Period', *The China Quarterly*, December, No. 136, pp. 770-804.

Morris-Suzuki, T. (1992), 'New International Division of Labour in East Asia', in Tokunaga, S. (ed.), *Japan's Foreign Investment and Asian Economic Interdependence*, Tokyo University Press, Tokyo, pp. 143-56.

National Unification Council (1991), *Guidelines for National Unification*, Taipei, February.

Nester, W. (1993), *American Power, the New World Order and the Japanese Challenge*, St. Martin's, New York.

Overholt, W. H. (1993), *China: the Next Economic Superpower*, Weidenfelf and Nicolson, London.

Patten, C. (1992), *Our Next Five Years: the Agenda for Hong Kong*, Address by the Governor at the Opening of the 1992-93 Session of the Legislative Council, Hong Kong Government.

Pollock, J. (1984), 'China and the Global Strategic Balance', in Harding, H. (ed.), *China's Foreign Relations in the 1990s*, Yale University Press, New Haven, pp. 165-87.

Pollock, J. (1992), 'The United States in East Asia: Holding the Ring', in IISS, *Asia's International Role in the Post-Cold War Era: Part 1, Adelphi Paper*, No. 275, Brassey for the International Institute for Strategic Studies, London, pp. 69-82.

PRC State Council (1993), *The Taiwan Question and the Reunification of China*, White paper, 31 August, Beijing.

Segal, G. (1993), *The Fate of Hong Kong*, Simon and Schuster, London.

Segal, G. (1994a), 'A Clearer Fate of Hong Kong', *The World Today*, Vol. 50, No. 2, pp. 36-39.

Segal, G. (1994b), *China Changes Shape: Regionalism and Foreign Policy*, Adelphi Paper, No. 287, International Institute for Strategic Studies, London.

Shelley, F. M. (1993), 'Political Geography, the New World Order and the City', *Urban Geography*, Vol. 14, No. 6, pp. 557-67.

Sit, V. F. S. (1989), 'Industrial Out-Processing — Hong Kong's New Relationship with the Pearl River Delta', *Asian Profile*, Vol. 17, No. 1, pp. 1-13.

Smart, J. and Smart, A. (1991), 'Personal Relations and Divergent Economies: A Case Study of Hong Kong Investment in South China', *International Journal of Urban and Regional Research*, Vol. 15, No. 2, pp. 216-33.

Sum, N. L. (1995), 'More than a 'War of Words': Identity Politics and the Struggle for Dominance during the Recent 'Political Reform' Period in Hong Kong', *Economy and Society*, Vol. 24, No. 1, pp. 69-100.

Sum, N. L. (1996), 'Strategies of East Asian Regionalism and Construction of NIC Identities', in Gamble, A. and Payne, A. (eds.), *Regionalism and World Order*, Macmillan, Basingstoke.

Sung, Y. W. (1991), *The China-Hong Kong Connection*, Cambridge University Press, Cambridge.

Wang, Z. (1994), 'Reform and Opening to the Outside World and Economic Development in Guangdong Province', *Social Science in China*, Vol. 3, pp. 33-44.

Yahuda, M. (1993), 'The Foreign Relations of Greater China', *The China Quarterly*, Vol. 136, pp. 687-710.

Zha, D. (1994), 'A 'Greater China'? The Political Economy of Chinese National Reunification', *Journal of Contemporary China*, Vol. 5, Spring, pp. 40-63.

Ziegler, C. (1994), 'Russia in the Asia-Pacific: A Major Power or Minor Participant?', *Asian Survey*, Vol. 34, No. 6, pp. 529-111

4 Inter-region tension and China's reforms

Terry Cannon and Le-Yin Zhang

Introduction

Since the mid-1980s, increasing tension between various levels of China's hierarchy of government have become evident, including those between central government (CG) and provincial governments (PG), between provinces themselves, and also between larger-scale regions (as in the 'East-West Divide'). It is also evident that attempts by the CG to encourage inter-provincial co-operation in the 1980s foundered, despite a continuous stream of initiatives to promote macro-regions such as the Shanghai Economic Region. The terms 'region' and 'regional' are not perfect in describing the antagonistic qualities of these tensions. But they convey the sense that there are significant issues that lie beyond conventional political and economic analysis, much of which tends to treat the country as a single entity. This chapter sets out to analyze various types of regional tension arising in association with the economic reforms, and illustrates the need to approach China's political economy in a much less spatially-aggregated manner than is normally permitted by economics and political theory. Related approaches are of growing significance in the literature on China's economic reforms (see Chung, 1995 for a survey), and is evident in several recent English-language studies (e.g. Goodman, 1989; Jia and Lin, 1994; Goodman and Segal, 1994), and the authors' own work (e.g. Cannon, 1989, 1990; Kirkby and Cannon, 1989; Zhang, 1994).

After the policy focus of the Communist Party of China (CPC) and the government shifted to economic construction in 1979, regional tensions were apparent especially in conflicts arising from the newly-acquired economic self-interest of governments at province-level and below. It appeared in many forms, from differences over interpretation of policy to open disagreement with CG over major policy issues; from passive non-compliance or non-co-operation to active bargaining, competition and dispute; from vocal complaint to militia-aided action.

We do not argue that regional tensions are only a phenomenon of the economic reform period, but that they are sufficiently different and of greater seriousness than earlier conflicts that they warrant our attention. In fact the tensions are perceived within China to have grown to such an extent that it is widely accepted that they could affect the ultimate success or failure of China's economic reform. Some analysts even assert that they could culminate in the disintegration of the People's Republic of China and the end of the Communist role in the country (Cheng, 1992 pp. 211-227). They also must have related impacts on China's neighbours, trading partners and investors. These external actors are significantly concentrated in Pacific Asia, and so these issues that potentially destabilize China have very great significance for the wider region as well.

A close scrutiny of the factors and forces that surround regional tensions, and of the policy response emerging in China is therefore an urgent task. A recent policy response seems at least partly designed to address these issues. In January 1994, a set of new economic reforms was introduced whose implementation is expected to occupy centre stage for the next seven years. They are intended to bring about a market economy in China, though it is unclear how well they can address the issue of regional tensions.

The plan of the chapter is as follows: first, various forms of regional tensions will be described and the underlying causes identified; then there is a review of the discussion about these problems within China, in the context of their arguments about what the appropriate policy responses should be; next, some attention is given to the 1994 reform measures; and finally some concluding suggestions are made about future prospects for regional relations.

Regional tensions and their underlying causes

In this section we first explore the most significant forms in which regional tensions have arisen. During the economic reforms, most types of stress have originated from the increased power of local governments (in relation to the central authorities). The reforms have invoked significant changes in the economic behaviour of PGs and other local economic actors. These have been induced by shifts in the political and economic relationship of CG with provinces. In other words, provinces and other local authorities have in many places emerged as a new type of entrepreneur, reacting in new ways to changes in the economic environment set by the CG. Local authorities have responded to a new situation by attempting to maximize their local advantages, even if this is at the expense of the CG or neighbours. The basis for this is generated by the continued exitence of local government ownership or control of enterprises as a legacy of the state-ownership and planning system (Grannick, 1990). Thus inter-provincial relations are largely determined by the impact of CG policies on provincial behaviour (even when such policies were not necessarily intended to have an impact on provincial activity).

Under the economic reforms, some of the changes in provincial-level behaviour led to increased antagonism with neighbouring provinces, and to serious rivalries between larger groups of provinces, some of which consider themselves disadvantaged by CG policies. By the same token, relations between CG and economically-successful provinces are strained because the latter resist attempts by CG to obtain a greater share of their revenue. Thus during the reforms the response of lower-level authorities to changes in their economic environment have varied according to numerous factors: the level of submission of taxes to, or receipt of subsidies from the CG; the scale and character of economic activity in the province; the granting of policy privileges (and their timing) such as for enterprise zones.[1] In general, local responses to greater autonomy have been significant and rapid. Conversely, attempts by the CG to shift provinces into greater accord with its own intentions, or the strengthening of macro-economic controls, are slow and difficult: provinces are very resistant to what they perceive as hinderance on their own legitimate activities. In other words, attempts to recentralize are much more difficult than devolution and decentralization.

As a result, the reforms have had effects that are in direct contradiction with their intended aims of promoting a greater role for market relations. The CG promotion of the coast in support of that region's assumed comparative advantage has provoked provinces in the interior to various forms of protectionism in order to reduce the disadvantage they have perceived for themselves. Moreover, the increased autonomy granted to provinces and to state-owned enterprises (SOEs) (especially after the 1984 'urban reforms') has led to widespread use of protectionism by many provinces to maximize local value-added production and maintain (or increase) their local revenue base.

Paradoxically, the reform policies have also induced provincial and local authorities to reinforce their self-interest by maintaining a link between enterprises and local government. This means that instead of encouraging the increased separation of state-owned enterprises (SOEs) from their local government patrons, these connections are maintained and even extended to new enterprises begun by local governments (either alone or in joint ventures with foreign investors). This conflicts with the CG's intention that the reforms increase the exposure of SOEs to market forces, and to reduce the overall role of local administration in economic activities.

In addition, the enhanced autonomy and associated self-interest in economic activity of many PGs and local administrations reduced the incentive to engage in the inter-provincial co-operation and larger-scale economic regions that the CG favours and which were intended to overcome the 'cell-like' economy of independent and self-reliant provinces instigated under central planning.[2] This disincentive to inter-provincial collaboration affects both richer provinces (who want to avoid dilution of their wealth) and many poorer ones (which see protectionism and retention of raw materials as advantageous).

The difficulty is to evaluate how much these anti-marketization consequences of the increase in provincial autonomy have undermined the 'efficiency' of the reforms, or been detrimental to the overall potential of the economy. A related concern in China is that it seems certain that the inability to control local investment has been a crucial component fuelling inflation. Inflation has had a disproportionately adverse impact on poorer sections of the population and has led to increased social tension. However, economic growth has remained high throughout the periods when protectionism has been at its strongest. It is difficult to imagine how, if economic growth is the main criteria of success, a more fully marketized economy could have improved on what has already been happening.

It is therefore worth exploring an alternative interpretation of the role of local administrations, provincial enterprise activity and self-interest during the reform period. We argue that there is merit in evaluating the positive impacts of protectionism and the non-marketization outcomes of the reforms. These may not have restrained economic growth in the manner that neo-liberal economic theory suggests. Moreover, it can be argued that local entrepreneurial activity and even protectionism have contributed to a spread of development to some areas and rural communities in China that otherwise might not have benefitted under a fully marketized economy.[3] Clearly the spread is not uniform, and some regions have been able to benefit much more than others, but it is also possible that the full pursuit of regional comparative advantage might not have produced such a spatially extensive pattern of development.[4] It is therefore questionable as to how much new attempts at reform that are insisting on full marketization will benefit the economy.

Inter-provincial tensions

A number of expressions of inter-provincial tension can be identified, of which the most important and palpable expression is economic protectionism. This involves a local authority trying to promote its self-interest by employing administrative means to obstruct, restrict and block trade with other provinces and regions, and eroding extra-provincial economic ties in the exchange of resources and technology. Three major types of such behaviour have been identified:

Obstructing flow of goods and materials Four kinds of goods are involved: i) raw or semi-raw material and energy resources, ii) manufactured goods, iii) exportable products, iv) foodstuffs. The first category of products are relatively lower-priced in comparison with the second, and yield low tax-plus-profit value. They are also in short supply, despite their low price (which is a remnant of the planning system). It therefore makes superficial economic sense for a province to try to retain the first category of products and turn them into manufactured goods, and not to supply them to outside processors many of which were accustomed to being allocated them under the planned economy.

With the second group of products, barriers to inward transfers may be put up to protect infant industries within a province. There is an incentive to retain and process the third category of products, since exporters are allowed to retain a proportion of foreign exchange earnings. The attempt to retain foodstuffs within producing provinces has led some PGs into conflicts with neighbouring provinces and their own farmers because they tend to want to retain staple food products within their territories. This is because there are large non-agricultural populations to feed in the cities, most of whom still rely mainly on state-procured foods obtained through rations or subsidised prices. As a result, some PGs are loath to let their own farmers seek higher prices elsewhere, since the surplus available for procurement is reduced (Delfs, 1991, pp. 26-28).

An extraordinary array of measures have been employed to implement protectionist policies, ranging from prejudice and tariffs to the use of armed militia, in order to restrict the flow of goods to and from other provinces or force outright prohibition. For example, in 1988, Hunan officials installed inspection stations along their rail lines and restricted shipments of foodgrains and pork to Guangdong. They wanted to retain their access to sufficient grain at the lower procurement prices they wanted to pay to secure food for the subsidised wage-earners in the cities, and this meant preventing price rises consequent on exports going out in search of higher prices. The Xinjiang government restricted the importation of some 48 commodities originating in other provinces. Hubei, Jilin and Liaoning also engaged in similar activities. Taxes have been imposed on 'outside' goods, and sanctions levelled against those who utilized 'outside' goods and supplies. On the other hand, incentives are offered in the form of low interest loans and generous profit retention formulae to those engaging in the production, purchase, or sale of local products. Some communities even printed their own currency (in form of special coupons) to force local residents to purchase local products.[5]

Contention for state funds and duplication of projects Provinces have all rushed to build projects that are likely to yield high profit-plus-tax returns so that overlapping investment, superfluous construction and repeated projects have become commonplace. There are examples of the 'automobile assembly-line war', the 'colour TV assembly-line war', and the 'refrigerator assembly-line war'. Such conflicts reduce the opportunity for economies of scale and hamper efficiency in resource allocation (*Guangming Daily*, 9/3/1994). On the other hand, provinces competed with each other for state-funded projects, regardless of the suitability of their circumstances.

Lack of co-operation between provinces The centre has sought to encourage inter-province and inter-region economic and technical cooperation without much success. The outstanding example is the Shanghai Economic Region. This was one of the economic zones that both the 6th (1981-85) and 7th (1986-90) Five-Year Plans (FYP) designated to foster collaboration between Shanghai and its neighbours (Cannon, 1990). In order to promote economic integration within the region a Planning Office, under the State Council but based in Shanghai, was established in early 1983. The zone expanded from consisting of only ten cities in

1982 to include five provinces (Jiangsu, Zhejiang, Anhui, Jiangxi, Fujian) as well as Shanghai by 1985. In its heyday in 1985, it included a population of 220 million (21.8 per cent of the national total).

The Planning Office undertook a large number of planning exercises, covering almost every field, some extending to the year 2000. In particular, co-operative development of electricity and coal industries were planned. In fact, Shanghai invested billions of Renminbi (Rmb) in other provinces's coal mines and raw material industries in exchange of promise of supplies. But few results were delivered, and the Planning Office was disbanded in 1988. One of the explanations for the failure of the Zone was that it was sponsored by the central government as a device to help the development of some less developed provinces such as Jiangxi and Anhui. This was not attractive to some of the more developed provinces.[6]

The underlying causes

Such activities are surely only symptoms of some deep-seated problems. So far a wide range of factors, or combinations of factors, have been suggested (Yang Wandong, 1991), including:

Government policies A number are held to be responsible. Firstly, the government's regional policy underwent a major shift in the late 1970s from a partial commitment to reducing regional disparity to an emphasis on 'efficiency' (comparative advantage). In particular, the 7th FYP adopted a policy that assigned lower priority in economic growth to central and western regions in favour of the coastal region (see Figure 4.1). As a consequence, state investment was dramatically reduced in inland areas (Cannon, 1990; Yang Dali, 1990). This put the relatively less-developed west and central regions at a disadvantage, causing strong resentment among many of their provinces' governments (Xu Changming, 1989).

Secondly, the open policy has strongly favoured coastal areas, with special incentives for foreign investment in these regions. Moreover, to help these provinces to develop a so-called export-oriented economy, they were also given more favourable treatment in foreign exchange retention and foreign loan quotas, and in revenue-sharing and investment allocation. Two southern provinces (Guangdong and Fujian) were given particular advantages very early in the open policy. In fact, the reform process itself was pushed much faster and further in the coastal regions than inland. Such discriminatory policies have distorted the pattern of comparative advantage (the coast has benefitted from investment, and not simply its supposed inherent advantages) between regions and has subsequently produced antagonism and inter-region tensions. In fact, inland provinces often take these as justification for the protection of their local economy.

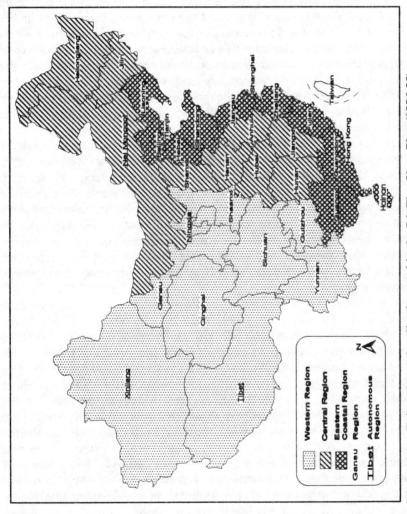

Figure 4.1　Tripartite regionalization used in the 7th Five-Year Plan (1986-90)

81

The resentment at the preference given to the coast has rumbled on since the second half of the 1980s, and became a significant issue at the National Peoples' Congress in April 1993.[7] In his speech President Jiang Zemin expressed concern to 'solve the widening gap in economic development between the east and west, and between the rich and the poor' (*Beijing Daily*, 14-20/6/1993).

Systemic faults There are a number of aspects to this. The first involves the tax system and fiscal regime, in which the role of local government is significant. There were various changes to the fiscal regime in the 1980s, which in general meant that local governments were allowed to retain either a percentage of locally-collected revenue, or were responsible for handing over a fixed contracted amount. Crucially, they were also allowed to keep an even larger share of any increase in revenue arising from economic growth in the years after the contract was fixed.[8] This greatly encouraged local government interest in the economic performance of enterprises. Such interest was reinforced by the fact that they are allowed to use a so-called extra-budgetary fund, whose main source is transfers taken from enterprises.[9] But at the same time, local authorities had to finance an increasing burden of spending responsibility, which increased their need to generate revenues (Wong, 1991).

Therefore, local authorities have a vested interest in both boosting the profits of local enterprises and undercollecting normal taxes (which are supposed to be shared with the CG) so as to avail themselves of the opportunity of extracting other funds from enterprises to which the CG has less access. This provided motivation both to protect local producers against outside competition, and to try and reduce revenue contributions towards the central treasury. The fiscal contract system, which gave local authorities the power to determine de facto tax rates for enterprises and products, further expanded their capacity to engage in discrimination and protectionism, as well as further sharpening their sense of local self-interest.

Also, in the late 1980s, contractual arrangements were made between each province and the CG to cover not only fiscal but also other relations between them. These covered the amount allowed in retention of foreign exchange earnings, allocation of credit and investment funds, scarce material supplies. This give rise to the so-called comprehensive contract system (*dai bao gong tizhi*). This system therefore also gave local authorities the power to decide de facto localized exchange rates, and to influence interest rates and price structure. In the meantime, there was also a retreat from earlier efforts (begun in the 1984 'Urban Reforms') to shift the previous revenue system (in which profits were transferred to the CG) to a tax-based system for state enterprises. A contract system was introduced in state-owned enterprises to decide annually the amount of tax-plus-profit remittance that individual enterprises have to turn into state revenue. Local authorities were made responsible for implementing this system. By these two arrangements, the redistributive and administrative role once played by central government was transferred to provincial governments. The degree to which local enterprises depended on local governments increased substantially.

In combination, these systemic changes transformed the role of local government from the implementor of central planning to that of an independent economic entity, whose interest is identified with the growth of the local economy. To make the matter even worse for the CG, there was a general lack of regulatory framework and the necessary enforcement mechanism to codify their conduct. As a consequence, regional authorities were both motivated and equipped to interfere in the economy unlawfully, without restriction and penalty. In effect they enjoyed the benefits of local control without having to endure many responsibilities.

Adverse market conditions The ill-developed market structure and structural imbalance in supply and demand for some commodities provided the basis for much protectionism. Markets for raw and semi-finished industrial materials, and for factors of production such as capital and land, are still fragmented. Enterprises therefore have to turn to local authorities for support (for raw material supplies, capital, land) from time to time, and there is thus an incentive for local protectionism. But by the same token there is also inter-locality competition to construct processing industries (with resulting duplication) and related general neglect of basic industries. And so there is a structural oversupply of processed goods, and a shortage of raw and semi-finished materials. Such problems reflect the CG's staggered price reforms which have affected various sectors differently. The study of the 'wool war' in the second half of 1980s illustrated that very well (Watson et al., 1989).

The interaction of politics and the economic reforms

What most analysts of China have failed to discuss is that many of these contradictory outcomes of policies were themselves consequences of the wider political process surrounding reforms in China in the 1980s. In fact, we would argue that regional tensions are only part of a series of power struggles between various sections of Chinese society, and that, as such, they are inevitably affected by other power struggles.

The most significant power struggle is between the CPC and the Chinese population as its subject. By the late 1970s the Chinese leadership, particularly Deng Xiaoping, had realized that their legitimacy in claiming power would only be justified if they could offer a better life to their subjects. It is precisely for this reason that the CPC chose, at the outset of the reform and open policy period, to place the highest priority on economic growth.

There are many ramifications of this priority. For instance, the balance of power between ministries underwent a readjustment. More significantly, within the party and the government, economic performance has become an important criterion for promotion, so that local officials have a strong incentive to encourage local economic growth. On the other hand, the CPC and the central government were reluctant to discipline local leaders for fear of possible adverse effects on the latters' enthusiasm for promoting economic growth. As a consequence, the centre has often turned a blind eye to some of the illicit 'creative' practices by local government in the 1980s. For instance, the 'three light tactics' devised by Guangdong province was much publicized in both the provincial and national press and met with implicit central government approval prior to the turn of the decade, although this is a primary example of policy violations by local governments.[10] Another example concerns the compromise effect of such political choice on personnel policy: Lei Yu, the man held mainly responsible for the Hainan Scandal, was not seriously punished, but transferred to be a deputy mayor of Guangzhou.[11] It is no coincidence that this same man was quoted as saying in 1991 that 'our cadres [leaders] cannot blindly follow Beijing's orders'(*Shijie ribao*, 8/5/1991). In a word, the need to win the political power struggle for the CPC has to some extent tied the hands of the CPC and the central government in dealing with both corruption and ruthless or ambitious local officials.[12]

Moreover, the hand of local officials was further strengthened by changes in the appointment system. Given China's size and diversity, it has been a tradition that the centre maintains its control through its appointment (or dismissal) of provincial leaders.[13] Since the early 1980s, however, the CPC and the CG have gradually introduced electoral reforms so that representative election is now playing an increasingly important role in the appointment of officials at province level and below (Wang Huning, 1988). Such change was promoted by the desire of Deng Xiaoping and the party's reform wing to create a bureaucracy that would be more responsive to the economic reforms. But the consequence is that local electorates now have some influence over the election of officials.

This impact has been most significant in elections of lower level officials. But as early as 1986, several party-nominated candidates were defeated at the deputy-governor level. By 1992-93, such defeats were recorded, according to Fewsmith, even in elections for provincial governors (Fewsmith, 1994). The implication of this change is that officials with better economic performance will have more chance of being elected. An example is that Lei Yu, despite (or because of?) his record, was able to win election as a vice-governor of Guangxi province in 1991 and in early 1993 was elected over the party's choice as a delegate from Guangxi to the Eighth National People's Congress (Fewsmith, 1994, p. 250).

What is remarkable is that, in the 1980s, the change in political prioritization and the introduction of reform in the appointment system combined to produce a political environment where local officials who helped economic growth in their region, regardless of the means, are cherished and promoted.

Finally, for centuries the relations between the centre and provinces have been characterized by political calculation and intense power struggle. While the provinces needed the centre for their mandate to govern, the centre needed the provinces for local control of population, and crucially for revenue collection. This was also largely true in the People's Republic of China before the reform. Moreover, under the central planning system, the provinces needed the centre for resources in major capital investment projects and deficit goods, while the centre needed the provinces for both surplus goods and revenue.

In the 1980s, however, the centre and provinces got increasingly disenchanted with each other. This was because the declining role for planning and reduction in centrally-distributed financial and material resources meant the centre was no longer able to play its redistributive role. In addition, recognizing that their loss would be another province's gain, the provinces became increasingly unwilling to surrender resources to the central government. As a result, tension between the two has also grown, expressed by the Chinese as so-called regionalism. This is defined as the inclination by officials to identify with and be loyal to geographically limited administrative units rather than the nation-state. This has the following expressions:

1. An increasingly independent disposition on the part of provincial government. For example, localities openly disregard growth targets set by the central government during retrenchment and readjustment periods.[14]

2. Difficulties for the central government to implement territory planning. In the 7th FYP, the government's basic aim was to 'speed up development in the east coast region, concentrate on building the energy and raw and semi-finished materials industries in the central region, and make active preparations for further development in western region' (*Beijing Review*, 28/4/1986, p. 11; see also Cannon, 1990, for a summary of the regional content of the plan). But there was strong opposition to this hierarchy by provincial governments in the central and western regions, as there had been to earlier versions of this type of policy (Falkenheim, 1988). In fact, the ferocity of the opposition was such that the planning outline for the 1990s Ten-Year Development Programme, and the 8th FYP (1991-1995) did not refer to the three-region division, although the 7th FYP clearly indicated that its three-region strategy was to be applied in the 1990s as well (Wei Houkai, 1993 p. 36).[15]

3. Difficulty for the central government to enforce macro-economic discipline. In order to finance their desired projects, local governments sponsored high-interest fund-raising. This sparked a drastic drop in savings in state bank deposit accounts and caused difficulties in the sale of state bonds. On the other hand, local tax reduction and exemption and profit release for enterprises has lead to a dramatic decline in state budgetary revenue (Wei Houkai, 1993 p. 8.).

To sum up, inter-regional tension is related to a host of political and economic factors. To remedy the situation would require systemic changes in several areas. The resulting situation can be characterized as one in which 'the centre pretends to rule and the provinces pretend to be ruled'. To an extent this captures the outcome of the reforms for the CG-PG bargaining position at the beginning of the

1990s. But it is not accurate for all provinces, and fails to express the diversity of provincial attitudes and needs (especially those of budget deficit provinces).

Central and local responses to regional tensions up to 1993

In this section we analyze the responses of central and local governments to the situation of regional conflicts in the period from the mid-1980s up to the new reforms of 1994.

The political setting

As inter-region and local-central tensions intensified throughout the second half of the 1980s and early 1990s, responses from academics and government departments also grew. To better understand these responses, however, requires an understanding of some aspects of Chinese politics. The Tiananmen Incident and the collapse of communism in Central and Eastern Europe and the events that followed have influenced politics in a number of important ways. There was an attempt to regain political credibility by resurrecting some of the most dated political models such as Lei Feng, who had been heavily promoted during the Cultural Revolution.[16] Such tactics were ineffective and rejected by the general public. There were soon renewed attempts to push ahead with economic reform. Nevertheless, until 1992, the conservative wing was apparently in the dominant position. Fearing the impact of this, in January and February 1992 Deng Xiaoping went on a special tour to the south of the country and encouraged local authorities to press ahead with reform and opening-up to the outside world. As evidence of the intense intra-party struggle, the news of his tour and speeches was suppressed, and appeared on television two months afterwards.[17] When the news did break, however, local authorities all over China responded enthusiastically, in deeds as well as in words.

By October 1992, when the 14th Party Congress was convened, the reform wing represented by Deng Xiaoping was already back in control of the political situation. More importantly, the party had reached a political consensus about a number of key issues. First, the leaders became more aware of danger from outside and from the provinces. They realized that there was substantial opposition among the masses, and that intra-party factionalism might jeopardize the party's position in the Chinese society. Second, the entire party leadership understood that the different outcomes of events in 1989 in China and Eastern Europe were largely to be explained by the differences in economic performance. For this reason, the party had renewed its faith in economic growth and arrived at a stronger sense of political purpose in promoting economic development.

In order to promote long-term economic development and continue its modernization programme, the party decided finally to abandon central planning and let the market play the central role in resource allocation. It was argued that what really counts in judging whether a system is capitalist or socialist is not whether central planning plays any role or how significant the public ownership is, but how fast the system is able to promote the development of the productive forces.

Intellectual and policy responses up to 1993

By the early 1980s, influential economists were able to argue that pursuing a more spatially-balanced economic development had been at the expense of economic efficiency and comparative advantage (Yang Dali 1990, p. 241). The regional development strategy outlined in the 7th FYP was therefore very much a reflection of contemporary orthodox thinking. It was welcomed by academics who argued that investment and construction should be arranged to achieve greater economic efficiency, with the coast given priority in the immediate future, although efforts should be made to reduce regional disparity as economic development progressed (Shao Henping, 1990).

However, for a number of reasons serious criticism started to emerge in the late 1980s. First, the impact of the policy became clearer as the 7th FYP proceeded. For instance, capital investment, funded by the state, was dramatically reduced in the central and western regions but increased in the coastal region. Second, with the introduction of the comprehensive contract system, inter-region tension in practice increased. Third, there was an important change in the political climate. In January 1987, Zhao Ziyang was replaced by Li Peng as the premier and there was growing criticism of rising inflation and the previous reform measures associated with Zhao.

The criticisms of regional policy pointed out that its three-region representation was crude. It failed to represent both intra-region and South-North differentials in China's economic geography, and the dualism (of traditional agriculture and modern industry) in the economic structure. Second, it was argued that the three-region division did not reflect existing economic regionalization and a rational regional division of labour and co-operation. Third, this regional division was blamed for seriously hampering the development of resource-related industries in the west and giving rise to a growing similarity in industrial structure between regions. Fourth, it was seen as over-simplistic to assume that technology transfer would automatically take place in the desired direction to reduce regional disparity. Finally, the policy offered little in the way of positive measures to encourage the development of other regions (Wei Houkai, 1988; Yang Wandong, 1991).

In addition, two practical problems were attracting attention: one was the immense size of the agricultural labour surplus in the countryside, which had partly been absorbed by an increasing number of township and village enterprises (TVEs) but which was increasing more rapidly than new employment opportunities; another was the need to import foreign technology to upgrade Chinese industry.

Following the Tiananmen Incident in June 1989 and the subsequent ousting of Zhao Ziyang, there were many articles published in the press criticizing the regional development policy and other reform measures adopted under Zhao (Fewsmith, 1994 p. 229). A distinctive feature of such debates was the growing inclusion of arguments about political and security issues. Opponents, who were often associated with institutions in the interior, started to emphasize that regional development policy should take into account impacts on inter-region relations. In particularly this meant those between the Han majority and minority nationalities. This suggests that the uneven regional development policy was seen by some to threaten the social stability in these frontier areas (Xia Yongxiang, 1992).

Conversely, while accepting the social and security implications of regional development policy, the mainstream commentators stressed the political significance of ensuring further national economic growth. For them this dictated the need to continue to emphasize efficiency, rather than shift emphasis to reducing regional disparity. The latter group supported this with the argument that regional disparity in China so far is not substantial in comparison with other comparable countries such as India (Yang Kaizhong, 1993). These arguments and counter-arguments were summed up rather neatly by one commentator, who proposed the following guideline for the government on regional development policy:

> The essence of regional development policy is a trade-off between 'balance' and 'growth'; ... the tilt towards 'balance' should not exceed the level where the overall development and growth prospects of the national economy is hindered; on the other hand, the tilt towards 'growth' should not exceed the tolerance limit of poor regions so that social and ethnic conflicts can be kept at bay (Jiang Qinghai, 1991, p. 10, our translation).

Another major development during the period was the arrival at a consensus that inter-region relationships based on sacrifice by one region for the good of others is socially and politically unsustainable. Commentators increasingly talked of compensation measures to reduce inter-region tension. In a report by the Chinese Society of Regional Economy, which undertook a study for the government on regional development policy in the 8th FYP and the 1990s, it was suggested that the state should further develop its regional compensation policy, improve its existing policy of 'aid to poor areas', strengthen policies for minority nationalities, and continue fiscal subsidies to compensate regional interests. The report also suggested that inland regions should be compensated for having been allowed to open up later than the coast (Regional Development Policy Project Group, 1991).

Partly as a result of the discussion on the 8th FYP, economic protectionism become a major issue in 1990. There were numerous articles analyzing its causes, consequences and countermeasures. The attention was concentrated on the economic side: on the formation of a unified national market, on efficiency of resource allocation and structural adjustment, on enterprises' market-orientation development, and finally on central government's regulatory power over the national economy (Li Shihua, 1991; Re Yihong and Du Bengao, 1991; Yang Jialin and Wang Xun, 1991).

But there was also some discussion of the political implications. In fact, as early as 1988, Wang Huning (a professor of international politics at Fudan University, Shanghai, and identified by Fewsmith as a conservative) had realized that inter-region tension would have repercussions on local-central relations. His paper noted that so far the reforms had transformed the role of local authorities and provided them with economic and political motivation for pursuing their own interest. Inter-region tension, which could result from the introduction of the comprehensive contracting system, would affect local-central relation. In the worst scenario, it could lead to the loss of control by the central government both economically and politically (Wang Huning, 1988). In the United States, a group of Chinese scholars launched a research project on local-central relationships, since they felt that this topic 'can best capture the changing nature of the Chinese polity' (Jia Hao and Lin Zhimin, 1994).

The central government responded by stressing the need to create an 'appropriate relationship between the centre and local authorities', by criticizing the 'regional barriers and market blockades, and self-integrated [i.e. closed] systems' and by emphasizing national economic unity, regional economic co-operation and assistance to poor areas in the 8th FYP and the Ten Year Programme (Goodman, 1991, p. 3.). Moreover, laws were passed explicitly to prohibit such wrongdoing by local authorities and to encourage inter-provincial co-operation.

The outline of the 8th FYP was approved by the National Congress in April 1991, and reflected much of these criticisms. Notably, the notion of the three regions was dropped. The outline criticized the phenomena of regional compartments and market blockades, and called for national market unity, regional economic cooperation and aid to the poorer areas.

That does not mean, however, that economic protectionism ceased. In fact, it took place with even greater intensity. This was very much fuelled by the economic retrenchment policy that the central government pursued from late 1988 to 1991, as the market for consumer goods, particularly durable electronics, slumped. The tightened financial market resulted in massive inter-enterprise debts, which were made worse by local governments' attempt to limit repayment to outsider creditors. Responding to Deng's call for bolder actions, the government opened a large number of inland cities and ports to foreign investment. The influx of foreign investment between 1992-1993 was spectacular. At the same time, local authorities launched a new wave of capital investment. As a result, new inflationary pressure built up in the second half of 1992 and the first half of 1993. The centre attempted to restrain the economy by introducing the 16 Point Program, overseen by Zhu Rongji. The programme was short-lived, due to practical sabotage and vocal opposition of local authorities.

This failure was perhaps a stimulus behind the central government's campaign from mid-1993 onwards to deal with local governments. The start of this campaign was signalled by the extraordinary reaction to a report by two Chinese economists. In June 1993, the foreign press noticed a report apparently circulated through the Chinese Academy of Science which was seen as the first writing apparently from official Chinese sources that referred explicitly to the possible chaos to follow in China if a strong man (implying Deng Xiaoping) dies. But in China, the paper 'A report on the Chinese Nation-state's capacity' was attracting attention for quite another reason. It graphically painted the dangerous state of China's fiscal and financial situation. In fact, the report was not entirely official, and was authored by Wang Shaoguang and Hu Angang, who had either studied or worked at Yale University.[18] One of their main arguments was to establish a new tax system that clearly assigned a share of revenue of different types of taxes between the centre and provinces. Immediately following its appearance in mid-June 1993, it was taken up by the Chinese press, and was being read by top leaders in the Central Committee of the CPC (CCCPC). In July, to the apparent surprise of the authors and the Finance Ministry, top leaders of CCCPC announced at the National Finance Works Conference that the tax assignment system would be implemented from 1st January 1994 without undergoing a trial procedure.[19]

In effect, the Hu-Wang report was an opportunity seized by the CG to launch its new reforms. In July 1993, the group that worked on the Chinese Economic System Reform produced an outline identifying four broad causes for the reappearance of inflation. Three of these related to the fiscal and administrative relationship between the central and local governments. Accordingly, the plan suggested tax reform and strengthening fiscal capability as the top priority of the medium-term reform.

To summarize, between mid-1980s and 1993, particularly since 1989, there was a general process of politicization in China. Within the party, the political prioritization of economic development was reinforced. But the party was faced with a new political challenge, namely to maintain control over local governments. To meet both of these needs, a new radicalism has been adopted, which abandons the party's formal commitment to socialism in any substantive form. The new strategy is to promote the role of market; to strengthen central government control capacity by gaining financially at the expense of local authorities; and to separate enterprises from local governments. A significant by-product of this is supposed to be greater control of provincial investment, seen as a major source of inflation.

The 1994 reforms

By 1993, a range of political factors combined with the experience of the economic reforms in reducing CG control over the economy and local government, produced a situation in which drastic fiscal reform was advocated along with the proposed expansion of the market economy. To effect this, new reforms were introduced early 1994 in six different areas. These relate to: *gong shang shui* (industry and commerce taxes),[20] central-provincial fiscal relations, management of foreign exchange, banking, the price mechanism, and state-owned enterprises. Such wide-ranging and co-ordinated reforms are unprecedented. The policies were designed by the Financial and Economic Leadership Group (FELG) of the Central Committee of the CPC. The group is controlled by Jiang Zemin, then party General Secretary and subsequently also state President. The deputy heads are Li Peng, the premier and a renowned conservative, and Zhu Rongji, the first vice-premier and a pragmatic reformer. The new reforms have not been in operation for long enough to evaluate their impact on regional relations, though a few of the intentions are apparent, which are discussed here.

The tax and fiscal reforms will substantially alter relations between enterprise, individuals and governments. To start with, the contact between enterprises and local authorities will be reduced. This should happen on a number of fronts: first, the establishment of a separate state tax administrative body will largely remove local government's power to grant tax exemption and reduction on central and shared taxes. Second, ending the practice of state-enterprises signing contracts with the state for the amount of tax they pay should reduce local government influence over state-owned enterprises by cutting out their supervisory role in the making of such contracts. Third, VAT will become the main tax, and will be assigned 75 per cent to CG and 25 per cent to provinces. The fact that PGs will receive only 25 per cent of VAT will reduce the incentive for local government to be involved in enterprises' operation.

On the other hand, the fact that (enterprise) income tax from local industry will go entirely to local government means that local authorities will probably become less interested in maintaining loss-making enterprises. With the entirety of 'business' (i.e. service sector) tax going to them, however, tertiary activities will probably become very attractive to local authorities. Local authorities are expected to make major efforts in collecting individual income tax. Finally, the reform will end the fiscal contract system so that the complex system of bargaining relations between central and provincial government will be removed.

The banking reform measures will have important implications. First, central funds will be concentrated on implementing industrial and regional policy. This is supposedly to improve the structural readjustment and the regional inequalities. A new role has also been found for the State Planning Commission, by making it into the designator of policy-related projects. It is however not clear how the provinces are to play a role in controlling overall investment scale.

The enterprise reform will have to break new ground. It has been widely held since 1984 that reactivating enterprises, especially state-owned large and medium enterprises, is the crux of economic system reform. But reform in this field has not touched deep-rooted systemic problems. So far, enterprise reform has been moving along the line that enterprises be given more management autonomy, reformed management methods, be detached from government, and that property rights should be separated from management rights. During this process, enterprises were made to pay income tax rather than submit profit; central planning was reduced to a minimum; a contract system was introduced between enterprises and the government over performance targets and so on. Yet enterprises are still not independent of government; property rights and responsibilities are not clearly defined; management mechanisms are still inefficient. It is now realized that the various targets will be unattainable without giving a new form to enterprises. Thus the focus of the new reform is the introduction of the so-called *shindai qiye zhidu* (Modern Enterprise System).

It seems to us that this enterprise reform relies heavily on the ability of the state sector to attract private capital. By making the government only one of the investors and by adopting a policy of private limited-liability companies for most enterprises, the government hopes to be no longer indefinitely responsible for enterprises' losses. But this will depend very much on whether a substantial amount of private capital can be attracted into such enterprises. Otherwise, the government will still be the sole or main investor, so that it will be tempted to come to the aid of ailing enterprises. The successful transformation of SOEs will also depend on the development of a social security system, which has to provide not only for large-scale redundancies and unemployment, but also to replace the welfare benefits granted to state employees.

In addition to the six reforms mentioned above, the FELG had also designed reforms for investment procedures and foreign trade. These have not yet been implemented, and whether this is because of political difficulties needs further investigation. The proposals for investment have potentially profound implications for regional tensions, and are briefly introduced here.

Under the previous regime for capital investment, there were two categories: budgetary and extra-budgetary investment. The former was usually financed by the central government. Although formally enterprises have to pay back bank loans granted by CG, enterprises were allowed to make the repayment out of pre-tax profit so that in reality the enterprises and their local governments did not have to bear any responsibility for such investment. As a result, there was a virtually insatiable appetite among local officials for centrally-funded capital investment projects. Inter-provincial competition for such investment was fierce.

On the other hand, extra-budgetary investment by local governments expanded rapidly during the reforms. Such investment was often made in factories that produce high profit-plus-tax goods (e.g. tobacco and alcohol). Duplicated construction of such enterprises led to the widespread operation of small-sized, inefficient factories. To sustain such projects, local governments had to employ protectionism. The proposed reform will seek to deal with this problem on two fronts: by amending the investment and finance mechanism, and by reform of the banking system. The basic intention is to make banks operate on more of a commercial basis, and to insist that capital borrowed for projects is the responsibility of the borrower, and accountable by the agency that makes the loan. The new system will also increase the responsibility of provinces in regulating overall investment size and structure, will step up the management and regulation of total investment, and strengthen investment structure control.

It is also mentioned that a regional economic policy should be implemented to support underdeveloped regions to undertake investments that are encouraged by the state. The state will also raise the share of policy-related loans going to these regions, which will also be given priority in hosting capital investment projects when other conditions are the same. Moreover, the state will offer economic incentives to encourage more developed regions to invest in less developed regions (FELG, 1994, pp. 137-43.).

Conclusion and prospect

To sum up the discussion in the last section, it seems that the thrust of the reforms is on two fronts: first, redistribute power and financial resources from local authorities to central government and enterprises; second, detach enterprises from government. Apart from changes in the tax and fiscal system, the device for implementing the first point is an emphasis on the role of the market. The so-called modern enterprise system is adopted to implement the latter. The signs are that the central government is much better motivated in promoting the former than the latter.

Some Chinese academics and officials expressed their belief that inter-province co-operation and alliance is not a direction that the central government would like to promote, as these may develop to such an extent that the central government will have to deal with a handful of powerful regional blocks rather than the 30 provinces. In fact it has been suggested by some of our informants that a degree of inter-regional conflict and tension is preferable to close co-operation within a number of enclosed regional units.

The main thrust of Wang and Hu's approach was to stress the need to strengthen the central government's role in China's transition to a market economy. It was selfish local governments that were directly under fire. But in both the decision of the CCCPC and the subsequent publicity, heavy emphasis is put on the establishment of a market economy. Given that the report received such careful attention from the government, it would be difficult to believe that such a shift is not well-thought out. In fact, we would argue that the shift of emphasis to the market economy is a means of evading the real emphasis, which is to increase CG control over local governments.

The emphasis of the new reform measures was designed mainly to deal with central-local tension rather than inter-regional tension. The idea is to let the market displace the role of provincial government. In advocating the role of the market, the central government would remove one of the most powerful foundations on which regionalism expresses itself. However, insofar as inter-region tension is related to provincial-central relations, changes in the latter will inevitably influence the former, but with less predictable results. It was

93

apparent that various provinces responded differently to the reform measures, and that each sees in them what they want to see. Thus in Guangdong province, academics talked of a conspiracy of those whose interest is tied to the state sector to shift policy preference away from Guangdong to state-sector dominated provinces like Shanghai. In contrast, the new fiscal system was broadly welcomed by Shanghai officials as it will allow them to reduce the metropolis's contribution towards central treasury. In other words, the current changes in relations between the centre and provinces is not enough to convince all provinces that there are no longer any grounds for inter-regional conflicts.

Another important policy initiative during this period is the up-grading of China's 'Aid to the Poor program'. Started in 1985, it initially targeted 100 million poverty-stricken people (Lyons, 1992). In early 1994, a new phase of 'aid to the poor program' was launched, aiming to eliminate absolute poverty (defined as per capita annual income below 500 yuan at 1990 price) for 80 million people by the end of this century (*Renmin ribao*, 25/7/1994). In the National Aid to the Poor and Development Works Conference, where this programme was launched in early 1994, Premier Li Peng emphasized that the implementation of this is a strategic measure designed to gradually reduce the gap between the west and the east (*Jingji ribao*, 4/3/1994).

Our analysis suggests that it is dangerous simply to adopt a pro-market, neo-liberal approach to solving such issues as those involved in reforming the enterprises and widening competition. In the context of the division of power between CG and PG, and the activities of new economic actors which have arisen in the reforms, there is neither the full potential nor the virtue of doing so. The policies required are extremely difficult to implement and unpredictable in their outcome. Therefore it may be preferable to develop policies that build on the positive attributes of the curious hybrid economy that has emerged in the country, and to promote inter-provincial co-operation without attempting to dismantle immediately the understandable desires (especially of poorer areas) to protect and enhance their own development. There is considerable value in having the protection of the local state as entrepreneur, even if it is not possible for all regions to benefit equally. The unique economy that has emerged in China is probably producing a wider spread of development than that experienced in other countries, and a more equitable distribution of income than if it were a more fully marketized economy.

This is not to ignore the fact that income distribution is getting wider, and that social and political tensions are rising. Nor is it to claim that the situation is ideal as a model for development. But what is the context? In East Asia the economic success of Japan and the Newly Industrialising Countries (NICs) has been claimed by neo-liberal economists as evidence of the value of a hands-off approach to the economy. This claim has been justifiably challenged by several studies that have emphasised the significance of the state in organising the structure of finance and of the enterprises themselves, and their connection with government departments (leaving aside the labour regime and suppression of unions and bargaining rights).

Two arguments follow about China. Firstly, much of the economic growth of the last fifteen years can be ascribed to the entrepreneurial activity of local authorities, and that it is part of a *commercializing* economy rather than the extension of the market. In other words, like Japan, South Korea and Taiwan, the Chinese 'miracle' is related to an administrative and macro-economic framework, rather than the free play of market forces. Secondly, policies that seek to increase the role of markets and reduce the control of local governments as economic actors are couched in terms of returning fiscal advantage and macro-economic control to the CG. While this may reduce some inefficiencies of the existing system, it may also substitute new and unpredicted ones. There is no guarantee that the CG will be able to increase its revenues against the behaviour of recalcitrant provinces, and no certainty that it will be able (or will really want) to deal with regional poverty.

Notes

1. The reactions of provinces which are recipients of CG subsidies for their budgetary spending has generally been less entrepreneurial than that of the tax-submitting provinces. Ironically, although the reforms were intended to reduce the reliance of provinces on CG for subsidies, the number of provinces in receipt of budget support increased during the 1980s.
2. The notion of the cellular economy was developed by Donnithorne (1972) as a way of describing the attempts under central planning in combination with strategic military planning to create a set of relatively self-contained regional economies each with the capacity to produce basic goods (producer goods and associated raw materials and some consumer goods) independently of other regions.
3. Hubbard (1995) argues like Granick (1990) that the benefits of the local entrepreneurial economy are a result of the ownership patterns derived from the state-owned enterprise system, but that they are temporary gains vulnerable to erosion by the further and more complete emergence of competition and market forces.
4. It is evident that other forms of protectionism also exist. For example, Cheng (1992 p. 220) reports that 'Boundary disputes over trade, taxation and public order are increasing among the provinces, autonomous regions, and counties. In recent years, there have been over 800 disputes involving 39 per cent of the 66 boundaries in China.'
5. These details are from Cheng (1992) p. 217, but the existence of such behaviour is described in the writing of Chinese academics and officials, and is evidenced by frequent government attempts to curtail such activities. Some of the Chinese discussion from the mid to late 1980s is given in

95

English translation in a special issue of *Chinese Economic Studies*, 1993, Vol. 26, No. 5.

6. Information from authors' interviews with ex-officials of the Planning Officer in May 1994. Government officials in Shanghai were optimistic in 1994 about a new Shanghai Economic Region being established which would succeed because it was a response by rich neighbouring local authorities and entrepreneurs to commercial opportunities, and would deliberately exclude poor parts of neighbouring provinces.

7. The report of the issue in an official weekly magazine puts the controversy in a positive light in terms of suggesting that 'many deputies to the Eigth National People's Congress suggested that the vast central and western regions...should narrow economic gaps with the eastern coastal areas by...entering into cooperation with the coastal areas and introducing more foreign funds.' (Han Baocheng, 1993, pp. 23-6).

8. The contracts and the ratios involved in them were usually negotiated (in great secrecy) on a one-to-one basis between provinces and CG. This process was institutionalized in the mid-1980s by the so-called regional fiscal contract system. For details of changes in the fiscal regimes, see Oksenberg and Tong (1991) and also Dai, Y-C and Xu, Y-P (1992).

9. According to the World Bank (1990, pp. 85-6), extra-budgetary funds consist for the most part (80 per cent) of the retained earnings of State-Owned Enterprises. Anecdotal evidence indicates that local authorities are able to gain access to these funds either by coercion (e.g. compulsory levies) or persuasion (e.g. voluntary contributions). Expenditure items seem to range widely, from capital investments to social welfare, infrastructure development and benefits for employees.

10. The 'three lights tactics' likens central government policy to traffic light at road junctions. Local government should find a way around when obstructed by a red light triggered from Beijing, to hurry up when confronted by a yellow light, and speed up when green light is in sight. The essence of the tactics is: keep going in all cases. See Sun Liren and Dai Yuanchen (1990, p. 19).

11. In fact some in Guangdong consider that he was in fact promoted, given that his transfer was to a post at the level of vice-governor of a province, and the post in Hainan was at district head level. The Hainan Scandal was one of the most notorious examples of 'corruption' in the 1980s, which came to light in 1985. The local government, then under the jurisdiction of Guangdong province, imported 2.86 million colour televisions, 252,000 video recorders, 122,000 motorcycles and 10,000 cars and minibuses, and then arranged for most of them to be resold onto the mainland for double or triple the price (Riskin, 1987, p. 336).

12. There are however signs in 1995 that the issue of corruption has been shifted into a more significant part of the political arena, with the investigation of several senior officials and suicides of others. In January the wife of the

retired party general secretary of Guizhou province was executed for fraud, and Lui Zhengwei himself committed suicide a few months later. He was also a retired member of the CCCPC. In April Wang Baosen (a vice-mayor of Beijing) committed suicide after allegations of serious corruption.) Subsequently Chen Xitong (ex party general secretary for Beijing) has been under investigation (*Beijing Review*, Vol.38,30, 24-30 July 1995, p. 5). The official weekly comments that the CPC faces a severe challenge as to whether it can effectively curb corruption at the same time as extending the market economy.

13. Tong (1989) provided a valuable analysis of the processes and criterion involved in his study of the fortunes of provincial First Party Secretaries (FPSs). He compared the period before (1971-82) and after (1983-86) fiscal reform and found that in the first period the FPSs of provinces which remitted revenue were more likely to be sacked (Table 2, p. 10), while in the second period not a single FPS had been purged. However, his focus on the year 1982 as a relevant divide over fiscal policy may be less relevant than the year 1979, and the significance of party factionalism in the pre and post reform era. From his own data (Table 2) it can be seen that only one FPS was sacked after 1978.

More recently, the Governor of Heilongjiang province was sacked by the CPC leadership in April 1994, during a tour by Zhu Rongji to reinforce the CG desire to get provinces to toe the line (*China Now,* 1994, No. 149, p. 6.). The key to understanding the conflict and the varying impact of CG direction is how the bargaining and negotiation process between CG and PGs has altered under the reforms, and in which direction and in whose favour the tendency is moving. In fact Heilongjiang's economy is still dominated by SOEs in heavy industry sectors, and is dependent on CG subsidies.

14. For example, the central government set a target of 9 per cent economic growth for 1994. But in the coastal region the local governments own growth target often approaches 20 per cent. See *Inside China Mainland,* Vol. 16, No. 6, June 1994, p. 4.

15. The Ten-Year Development Programme and the 8th FYP are summarized in English in *Beijing Review* 1991, Vol.34,15, 15-21 April, pp. I-XXIV Supplement. The CPC Central Committee's proposals for both plans did not mention the three-region division, although it stated that China will carry on its economic development strategy for coastal regions and promote their export-oriented economy.

16. For an analysis of the immediate attempts to exercise greater central control, see 'Postscript' in Cannon and Jenkins (1990).

17. For details of the propaganda battle see *China News Analysis,* No. 1458, 15 April 1992.

18. An earlier English version of Wang Shaoguang's ideas is his chapter in Jia Hao and Lin Zhimin (eds) 1994. The report has been published in Chinese

as *China's State Capacity Report*, Shenyang: Liaoning People's publishing House, 1993. A revised Chinese version (in traditional characters) has been published in Hong Kong: Wang and Hu (1994).

19. According to another source, approved by the State Council, the Ministry of Finance did carry out a trial of such a tax system since in nine provinces, autonomous regions and separately planned cities, started from June 1992. See Gao Shusheng (1993).

20. In China, according to the administrative bodies that organize the collection of taxes, three broad categories of taxes are distinguished: *gong shang shui* (by State Tax Administration Bureau), agricultural taxes (Ministry of Finance), and customs tax (State Customs Administration Bureau).

References

Beijing Review (1986), 'The Seventh Five Year Plan of the People's Republic of China for Economic and Social Development (1986-1990), Excerpts', Vol. 29, No. 17, 28th April, p. 11.

Beijing Review (1993), No. 24, 14-20 June, p. 4.

Cannon, T. (1989), 'National Minorities and the Internal Frontier', in Goodman, D.S.G. (ed.), *China's Regional Development*, Routledge, London.

Cannon, T. (1990), 'Spatial Inequality and Regional Policy', in Cannon, T. and Jenkins, A. (eds), *The Geography of Contemporary China: the impact of Deng Xiaoping's Decade*, Routledge, London, pp. 28-60.

Cannon, T. and Jenkins, A. (eds) (1990), *The Geography of Contemporary China: the Impact of Deng Xiaoping's Decade*, Routledge, London.

Cheng, M. H. (1992), 'China's Future: Regionalism, Federation, or Disintegration', *Studies in Comparative Communism*, Vol XXV, No. 3, September.

Chung, J. H. (1995), 'Studies of Central-Provincial Relations in the People's Republic of China: a Mid-Term report', *The China Quarterly*, No. 142, pp. 487-509.

Dai, Y-C and Xu, Y-P (1992), 'Caizheng tizhi gaige yu zhongyan tifang caizheng guanxi bianhua' ('Fiscal System Reforms and Changes in the Central-Local Fiscal Relations'), *Jingji xuejia* (Economist), pp. 5-14.

Delfs, R. (1991), *Far Eastern Economic Review*, 4 April, pp. 26-8.

Donnithorne, A. (1972), 'China's Cellular Economy: Some Economic Trends Since the Cultural Revolution', *The China Quarterly*, No. 52, pp. 605-19.

Falkenheim, W.C. (1988), 'The Political Economy of Regional Reform: an Overview', in Reynolds, B.L. (ed.), *Chinese Economic Policy: Economic Reforms in Midstream*, Paragon House, New York, pp. 285-307.

FELG (1994), *Dangjian jixiang zhongda jingji tizhi gaige dianshi xilie jiangzuo zhuanji* (The Current Important Economic Reforms), Finance and Economy Leadership Group, Office of the CCCPC, Beijing.

Fewsmith, J. (1994), *Dilemmas of Reform in China: Political Conflict and Economic Debate*, M. E. Sharpe, New York.

Gao Shusheng (1993), 'Fenfen yangyan fenshuizhi' ('Tax assignment system in the centre of attention'), *Jingji ribao* (Economic Daily), 16 November.

Goodman, D.S.G. (ed.) (1989), *China's Regional Development*, Routledge, London.

Goodman, D.S. G. (1991), '*The People's Republic of China in 1991: Provinces Confronting the State*', Working Paper No. 3, Asia Research Centre, Murdoch University of Western Australia.

Goodman, D.S.G. and Segal, G. (eds) (1994), *China Deconstructs: Politics, Trade and Regionalism*, Routledge, London.

Granick, David (1990), *Chinese State Enterprises - a Regional Property Rights Analysis,* University of Chicago Press, Chicago.

Guangming Daily, 9th March 1994, p. 3.

Han Baocheng (1993), 'Development Strategies for Central and Western Regions', *Beijing Review,* Vol.36, No. 16, 19-25 April, pp. 23-6.

Hubbard, Michael (1995), 'Bureaucrats and Markets in China: the Rise and Fall of Entrepreneurial Local Government', *Governance,* July, pp. 335-53.

Jia Hao and Lin Zhimin (eds) (1994), *Changing Central-Local Relations in China: Reform and State Capacity,* Westview Press, Boulder.

Jiang Qinghai (1991), 'Zhongguo quyu jingji zhengce mushi de zhuanbian yu chongxin xuanzhai' ('The changes in China's regional economic policy pattern and re-orientation'), *Jingji kexue* (Economic Science), No. 5, pp. 9-10.

Jingji ribao (Economic Daily), 4 March 1994, p. 2.

Kirkby, R. and Cannon, T. (1989), 'Introduction', in Goodman, D.S.G. (ed.) (1989), *China's Regional Development*, Routledge, London.

Li Shihua (1991), 'Difang baohu zhuyi pouxi' ('An anatomy of local protectionism'), *Jingji lilun yu jingji guanli* (Economic theories and economic management), No. 1, pp. 67-9.

Lyons, T.P. (1992), 'China's War on Poverty: a Case Study of Fujian Province, 1985-1990', USC Seminar Series, No. 7, Hong Kong Institute of Asia-Pacific Studies, The Chinese University of Hong Kong.

Oksenberg, M. and Tong, J. (1991), 'The Evolution of Central-Provincial Fiscal Relations in China 1971-1986: the Formal System', *The China Quarterly,* No. 125, pp. 1-32.

Re Yihong and Du Bengao (1991), 'Diqu fengsuo de chengyin weihai ji duice' ('Causes, danger and counter-measures for regional blockage'), *Jingji wenti tansuo* (Exploring Economic Issues), No. 3, pp. 24-6.

Regional Development Policy Project Group of the Chinese Society of Regional Economics (1991) 'Pawu shiji de Zhongguo quyu jingji zhance' ('Regional economic policy for China in the 8th Five-Year Plan period'), *Zhongguo gongye jingji yanjiu* (Chinese Industrial Economic Research), No. 1, pp. 48-53.

Renmin ribao (People's Daily), Overseas edition, 25 July 1994, p. 1.

Riskin, Carl, (1987), *China's Political Economy: the Quest for Development Since 1949*, Oxford University Press, Oxford.

Shao Henping (1990), 'Lun jingji fazhuan yu diqu junhenghua' ('On economic development and inter-region balance'), *Jingji kexue* (Economic Science), No. 3.

Shijie ribao (World Daily), 8 May 1991, p. 10. cited in Cheng, M. H. (1992), 'China's Future: Regionalism, Federation, or Disintegration', *Studies in Comparative Communism*, Vol XXV, No. 3, September, p. 215.

Sun Liren and Dai Yuanchen, 'Woguo zhuhou jingji de xingcheng jiqi biduan he gengyuan' ('The formation, shortcomings and causes of China's princedom economy'), *Jingji yanjiu* (Economic Research), No. 3, 1990, p. 19.

Tong, James (1989), 'Fiscal Reform, Elite Turnover and Central-Provincial Relations in Post-Mao China', *The Australian Journal of Chinese Affairs*, No. 22, July, pp. 1-30.

Wang Huning (1988), 'Zhongguo bianhuazhong de zhongyang he difang zhengfu de guanxi: zhengzhi de hanyi' ('The changing relationship between China's central and local governments: connotations of politics'), *Fudan xuebao (She hui kexue ban)* (Fudan University Bulletin (Social Science Edition)), No. 5, pp. 1-8, 30.

Wang Shaoguang and Hu Angang (1994), *Zhongguo guojia nengli baogao* (A Report on the Capacity of the Chinese Nation-state), Oxford University Press, Hong Kong.

Watson, A, Findlay, C and Du Yintang (1989), 'Who Won the 'Wool War'?: A Case Study of Rural Product Marketing in China', *The China Quarterly*, No. 118, pp. 213-41.

Wei Houkai (1988), 'Quyu kaifa lilun yan jiu' ('Studies on regional development theories'), *Diyu yanjiu yu kaifa* (Regional Studies and Openness to Outside), No. 1, 1988.

Wei Houkai (1993), 'Quyu jingji de xin fazhuanguan' ('New point of view of regional economic development'), *Zhongguo gongye jingji janjiu* (Chinese Industrial Economic Research), No. 5.

Wong, C. P. W. (1991), 'Central-Local Relations in an Era of Fiscal Decline - the Paradox of Fiscal Decentralization in Post-Mao China', *The China Quarterly*, No. 128, pp. 691-714.

World Bank (1990), '*China: Revenue Mobilization and Tax Policy*', World Bank, Washington D.C, pp. 85-6.

Xia Yongxiang (1992*), 'Lun woguo dongxi diqujian de junheng yu feijunheng fazhan de xuanze'* ('On China's choice of east-west even and uneven development'), *Jingji kexue* (Economic Science), No. 2, pp. 9-12.

Xu Changming (1989), 'Guan yu qing xie shi qu yu jing ji zheng ce de si kao' ('Thoughts on the tilting regional economic policy'), *Jingji wenti tansuo* (Exploring Economic Issues), No. 1, quoted in Yang Wandong (1991), 'Jinnian le woguo quyu jingji wenti taolun zongshu' ('A review of the discussions on

China's regional economic issues in recent years'), *Jingji lilun yu jingji guanli* (Economic Theories and Economic Management), No. 2, p. 78.

Yang Dali (1990), 'Patterns of China's Regional Development Strategy', *The China Quarterly*, No. 122, pp. 230-57.

Yang Jialin and Wang Xun (1991), 'Lun di fang bao hu zhu yi' ('On local protectionism'), *Jingji kexue* (Economic Science), No. 3, pp. 63-6.

Yang Kaizhong (1993), 'Yanhai yu neidi jingji xiediao fazhan zhanlue xuanze' ('The strategic choice of co-ordinating economic development in coastal and inland regions'), *Zhongguo gongye jingji yanjiu* (Chinese Industrial Economic Research), No. 1, pp. 31-6.

Yang Wandong (1991), 'Jinnian le woguo quyu jingji wenti taolun zongshu' ('A review of the discussions on China's regional economic issues in recent years'), *Jingji lilun yu jingji guanli* (Economic Theories and Economic Management), No. 2, pp. 74-9.

Zhang Le-Yin (1994), 'Location-Specific Advantages and Manufacturing Direct Foreign Investment in South China', *World Development*, Vol.22, No. 1, pp. 45-53.

5 Regional disparities and inter-governmental fiscal relations in Indonesia

Anne Booth

Historical background

Indonesia is, by any standard, an improbable country. The Dutch liked to superimpose the map of their enormous Asian colony on that of Europe, so that Aceh projected out into the Atlantic Ocean, while the border of West Irian fell somewhere to the east of the Black Sea. No doubt this tickled the vanity of Dutch colonial administrators whose own country was about the same size as the present Indonesian provinces of Central Java and Yogyakarta. The various pieces of what became Indonesia were assembled through the nineteenth century as a result of a series of deals with, and preemptive strikes against, the British, and other European powers. There can be little doubt that fear of the colonial ambitions of other Western powers was the major reason for Dutch territorial acquisitions in what had become known by the early twentieth century as the 'Outer Islands'. As Ricklefs (1981, p. 125) has argued, 'the Dutch felt obliged to establish their claims to the outer islands of the archipelago in order to prevent some other Western power from intervening there, even where the Dutch initially had no great interest themselves'. Another reason for the acquisition of further territory was to secure the areas already held. As Dutch naval and military technology became more sophisticated, native rulers found it wiser to desist from unequal armed struggle and submit to what was usually indirect control from a colonial authority based in distant Java, who in turn answered to a monarch and parliament on the other side of the world.

Outside Java, the Dutch were usually reluctant to interfere with local customs and styles of government except insofar as they prevented the development of Western plantations and the exploitation of natural resources. Where Islam had not already spread among local populations, they did encourage the work of both Protestant and Catholic missions, and it was the Moslem and Christian religions that provided the main links between the diverse ethnic groups of the archipelago.

But the role of these two foreign monotheistic creeds could hardly be compared with that of indigenous Hinduism in the Indian sub-continent in bonding together peoples of diverse linguistic and ethnic backgrounds. To the extent that such bonds were created in the final decades of Dutch colonial rule they sprang from a third foreign creed, the ideology of nationalism. Gradually the idea spread among educated Indonesians that the Dutch colonial regime, and the political and social repression and economic exploitation with which it was associated, could be replaced by an independent Indonesian nation.

Due to the concentration of educated Indonesians in Java, and because many parts of the Outer Islands remained largely untouched by Western notions of modernization right up until 1945, the independence movement was inevitably Java-based and oriented to Javanese cultural norms. Robert van Niel has written that Sukarno always believed that nationalism was to be the chief ideology of the independence struggle, encompassing other creeds including Marxism and Islam. 'National unity through harmony and tolerance was at the centre of his thinking, and reflects values basic to the Javanese tradition of which he was very much part. This unity was to be conceptualized and personified in the leader. He believed that Islam would be forced into a consensus with this strongly national force and was prepared to be adamant on this need for unity' (van Niel, 1979, p. 149).

Nevertheless, if indeed Indonesian nationalism was so dominated by Javanese values, why did so many non-Javanese decide in 1945 to throw in their lot with the new Indonesian nation? Even the religious leaders of the fiercely independent and Islamic Achinese, who had fought a long and bitter war with the Dutch and were soon to challenge again the power of the central government in Jakarta, never wavered in loyalty to Sukarno, and their desire to be part of the state of Indonesia (Morris, 1985, p. 91). The loyalty of so many outside Java to the nationalistic ideals of Sukarno, Hatta and the other leaders of the independence movement reflected both their disillusion with Dutch colonialism, especially after its ignominious defeat at the hands of the Japanese in 1942, and their desire to be part of a large, and potentially powerful new nation. No matter if the concept of Indonesia was itself an artifact of Western colonial rule,[1] or if 'its geographical spread, archipelagic character, ethnic complexity and economic diversity hardly made it a natural candidate for independent nationhood' (Legge, 1990, p. 127). The very improbability of such a huge and heterogeneous collection of islands forming itself into a single country became a source of national pride, as it remains to many Indonesians to this day.

Having chosen to form one nation, why did the founding fathers of Indonesia opt for a unitary state? Why did they not follow the federal model of the United States, by far the most powerful country in the immediate post-war world, which had used its enormous economic bargaining power to force the Dutch into finally conceding independence in 1949. Certainly there were, as Feith (1962, p. 72) argued, some convinced advocates of a federal structure within the Republican leadership, 'and Prime Minister Hatta appeared at times to be one of them'. But the Dutch stratagem of creating a federal Indonesian state in 1945-46 effectively

103

discredited the concept of federalism in the eyes of the nationalist leadership. In his book on *Central Authority and Regional Autonomy in Indonesia*, Legge (1961, p. 7) pointed out that 'in developing their proposals for a federal Indonesia after 1945 the Dutch were not building on prewar foundations'. In spite of some devolution of powers to the provincial administrations in Java after 1922, the colonial government had certainly never been federal in concept or in practice, and there can be little doubt that 'divide-and-rule tactics did in fact enter strongly' into the 1945 decision to convert the archipelago into a federation (Taylor, 1960, p. 330).

By far the largest of the federal units created by the Dutch was the state of East Indonesia, and by the end of 1947, responsibility for finance, justice, general economic affairs, police, education, information, health, social affairs, industry, shipping, forestry, irrigation and agrarian affairs had all been delegated to the regional government, although in practice, as Kahin (1952, p. 360) stressed, the exercise of all these powers was greatly vitiated by the numerous general and specific powers reserved to the central government in Batavia.

It was not by accident that Eastern Indonesia was chosen as the model for the Dutch experiment in federalism. As Kahin (1952) showed in his classic study, the Dutch found it easier to deal with the nationalist movement there than in Java or Sumatra. Although many traditional leaders in Sulawesi supported the Republic, the Dutch were able to muster sufficient force to overcome their resistance. Many of the rajahs, karaengs and other native rulers in southern Sulawesi were removed and replaced with more pliant people. So cynical were the means used by the Dutch to establish their federal state in Eastern Indonesia and elsewhere that the nationalists, not surprisingly, equated federalism with collaboration. As Feith (1962, p. 71) argued, when the form of the independent state came to be finalized in 1949, the issue was not one of a federal versus a unitary constitutional form. Rather, it became one of support for an independent republic versus cooperation with Dutch policies of divide-and-rule. However, Feith also pointed out that the appeal of the anti-federalist case was 'undoubtedly greatest in Java'. This was because the federal units established by the Dutch in Java were transparently artificial, and also because the independence struggle generally had come to take on a deeper importance in Java than elsewhere.

Outside Java there can be little doubt that support for the independent republic was overwhelmingly strong in 1949. Feith distinguished only three groups of potential dissidents. The first, and most obvious, were those ethnic Indonesians who had fought for the Royal Dutch Indies Army (KNIL). Second, there were those who by reason of their Dutch education and their adoption of Christianity, felt themselves to be culturally more Dutch than Indonesian: certainly there were many Ambonese and Minahasans in this category, although by no means all Christians outside Java felt alienated from the new republic. Last, there were those traditional rulers in various parts of Sumatra, Kalimantan and Sulawesi who had supported the Dutch mainly because they feared for their future if egalitarian nationalism triumphed. None of these groups were sufficiently powerful to pose any threat to the new state. Many Ambonese departed for the Netherlands and a miserable future on the margins of Dutch society. In 1950, Indonesian nationalism was triumphant, and its 'power as a cohesive force binding the archipelago together was at its zenith' (Feith, 1962, p. 74).

However, triumphant nationalism by itself could not solve the many economic and social problems which the new republic faced. The attainment of independence triggered a rise in expectations among almost all Indonesians. The better educated thought that they would inherit not just the jobs of their Dutch colonial masters but also their living standards. Many millions more expected a dramatic rise in their economic and social fortunes. Few grasped that their country was one of the poorest in the world, and quite unable to offer the majority of its citizens even a decent subsistence. Nor did they grasp that their country was quite incapable of offering the kind of lifestyle that the Europeans had enjoyed in colonial times, or that citizens of Western countries appeared to enjoy in the foreign, and especially American, media, which was becoming increasingly available, at least in the larger cities. Those nationalists who were concerned about economic issues at all considered the country's poverty to be due to colonial exploitation, and expected that political independence would allow the vast resources of the archipelago to be used for a rapid improvement in living standards.

Sadly, this rapid improvement did not happen. Instead, the infant republic lurched from one political crisis to another. Between December 1949 and March 1957, there were seven different administrations: some lasted only a few months and none survived more than two years. Certainly there were able and conscientious people in several of the cabinets in the early 1950s; men like Sumitro Djojohadikusumo and Sjarifuddin Prawiranegara were as competent as any of the economists who came to prominence after 1965, and as Glassburner (1971, p. 82) argued, both were 'essentially pragmatic' in their desire to make the system work. But neither held office for long enough, or were given sufficient scope by their cabinet colleagues, to implement unpopular policies and make them stick until the benefits became perceptible to a long-suffering population; they were, in Glassburner's words, confined to 'tinkering round the edges'. Neither of these men held office in the most durable administration of the constitutional democracy period, the first cabinet of Ali Sastroamidjojo, which lasted almost two years. During this period, any attempt at fiscal stringency was abandoned, and in the first nine months the government debt trebled and foreign reserves dwindled to zero. The Minister of Economic Affairs, Iskaq Tjokrohadisurjo, found that issuing licences to indigenous 'businessmen' was a lucrative way of getting funds for the PNI — *Partai Nasional Indonesia* (Indonesian National Party) — and although he was eventually replaced, the reputation of government programmes designed to assist indigenous entrepreneurs was severely compromised. At the same time, the increasingly unrealistic exchange rate was acting as a tax on export producers outside Java, and there was increasing recourse to smuggling.

The Harahap cabinet, which replaced that of Ali in July 1955, saw the return of Sumitro to the finance portfolio, and the implementation of measures designed to depersonalize the licensing system and stabilize prices. But the cabinet was only interim and after the elections of September 1955, a deal was struck between the PNI and the NU — *Nahdatul Ulama* (Islamic Scholars Party) — allowing Ali to form his second cabinet with Mohammad Roem as his deputy. From the outset the cabinet was perceived as weak, and it was, as Feith has pointed out, during this period that many of the ethnic and regional tensions, which had been simmering since 1949, came to a head.

> Over the whole period which followed the formation of the unitary state there was a crescendo of demands from the provinces and regions. Provincial spokesmen denounced 'Jakarta' for not giving them enough autonomy. They castigated it for its cumbersome administrative procedures, for the fact that governmental leaders in the regions had often to fly to Jakarta for approval of quite minor decisions of policy. They criticised the central government for the supervision which it exercised over their affairs through its pamong pradja representatives, governors, residents, regents and so on ... Above all they reproached the center for not giving them enough money (Feith, 1962, pp. 487-8).

From a strictly economic point of view, much of this discontent was caused by the fact that, by the early 1950s, Java was producing only a small fraction of the nation's exports, but was consuming the bulk of the imports. This led to constant complaints by the exporting regions, that although they were the main generators of the nation's wealth, they were neglected when decisions were made on its expenditure. The whole issue of regional finance had been subject to detailed investigation in the mid-1950s by a committee headed by M. Nasroen, a senior civil servant in the Department of the Interior, and many of the findings of this committee had been incorporated in Law No. 32 of 1956, concerning financial relations between the centre and the autonomous regions. This law did in fact make some important concessions to the regions in that it allowed the proceeds of both income taxes and foreign trade taxes to be shared between the provinces, where the tax revenues originated, and the centre. Unfortunately, as Legge (1961, p. 193) has pointed out, implementation of this law was slow. In particular little progress was made in laying down rules for the sharing of the most important taxes between the centre and the regions.

By early 1956, there was growing evidence that the main exporting regions were fed up with vacillation and delays at the centre and were increasingly prepared to take matters into their own hands. Stories began to circulate of the growing barter trade that was occurring in North Sulawesi, in which locally produced copra was being traded for imported food, cars and machinery of various kinds, with the obvious cooperation of local civilian and military authorities. By the middle of 1956, it was clear that large-scale smuggling activities had spread to North Sumatra. Ships were calling in to small ports and loading rubber, coffee and other commodities under obvious army protection. The authority of the central government was being severely tested. In late 1956 and early 1957, a series of army-led rebellions broke out in various parts of Sumatra, Sulawesi and Kalimantan, and in March 1957, the second Ali cabinet finally collapsed. President Sukarno declared a state of siege and war, and a non-party cabinet was formed under Dr Juanda. Juanda attempted to arrive at an overall settlement with the dissident regions and could perhaps have succeeded had Indonesia not failed to win a two-thirds majority in the UN General Assembly vote on the future of West Irian. This led to the take-over of all Dutch assets in Indonesia and chaos in the estates, manufacturing, shipping and financial sectors. The virtual collapse of the inter-island shipping system placed more strain on the regions and led to the departure from Jakarta of several senior Masjumi politicians, including two former prime ministers and the head of the central bank. On 15 February 1958, the Revolutionary Government of the Republic of Indonesia was proclaimed in Padang.

There is very little evidence to suggest that the dissidents in Padang, or indeed in other parts of the country, were trying to secede and establish independent states. What they wanted was to bring about the collapse of a government in Jakarta they disliked and to impose one which would implement policies they considered in the regions' interests. Such policies included not just a more equitable sharing of the nation's wealth between the resource-rich Outer Islands and the poor inner core of Java, Bali and Nusatenggara. In the case of Aceh, the rebels wanted separate provincial status and more religious autonomy (both subsequently granted), while in South Sulawesi there was anger on the part of traditionalists that they were being pushed aside, in both the national and the provincial power structures, in favour of people from other regions, who had better education and were more deft in dealing with modern military and bureaucratic systems.

By the early 1960s, the army had demonstrated its capacity to impose the writ of the central government in most parts of the archipelago. As Mackie (1980, p. 674) pointed out, regional discontent did not disappear in Indonesia with the collapse of the parliamentary system and the advent of Guided Democracy. Indeed, increasing inflation and a hugely overvalued exchange rate led to increased smuggling, much of it carried on with army connivance. But increasingly the dissident regions found that they could make common cause with the anti-Communist military (in whose senior ranks there were after all a fair sprinkling of non-Javanese) in their continuing struggles with the centre. As Mackie (1980, p. 674) summed up the situation, 'a politics of manipulation and compromise replaced the earlier confrontational pattern'. A system of 'de facto federalism' came to apply, where compromise and ad hoc action affected economic as well as political aspects of the relationship between the centre and the regions. Bargains over the imposition of illegal taxes and imposts, and the sharing of revenues from smuggling were struck between local officials, the military and civilian representatives of the central government, with the last being usually by far the weakest partner. The centre indeed had little option but to turn a blind eye to much of what was going on because it had no effective means of enforcing central government laws and regulations, even where its official representatives in the form of governors, bupatis, and camats might have wished to do so.

New order regional development policies

Little changed in the immediate aftermath of the 1965 coup and the accession to power of the triumvirate led by General Soeharto. It is easy to forget in 1995 just how weak Soeharto appeared to many observers in the years 1966-69. Many expected him to be toppled by rival elements within the military, and although western aid donors were quick to come to the assistance of such an obviously anti-Communist regime, there was a reluctance to be too closely associated with any particular leader. As we know now, Soeharto's tactical astuteness, and his amazing capacity to see opposition emerging and defuse it before it could damage the fragile fabric of the post-Sukarno state system, proved triumphant. By 1969, inflation was reduced to single digit figures, the economy had returned to a stable growth trajectory and Soeharto felt strong enough to embark on the first of the New Order Five Year Plans. The large amounts of foreign aid which were promised, combined with the growing revenues from oil, greatly increased the financial power of the centre and what Mackie (1980, p. 676) termed 'an inexorable trend towards recentralisation of power' set in. It has continued unabated to the present day.

The rapid growth in oil revenues, which accrued to the central government budget through the 1970s from increased production, and after 1974 from the dramatic increase in the world price for oil, greatly increased the power of the central government vis-à-vis the regions. Beginning in 1969, the central government began a series of programmes whose purpose was to enable provincial, district (*kabupaten*) and village administrations to carry out much needed rehabilitation of infrastructure (roads, bridges, irrigation facilities, villages halls, etc.), using earmarked grants from the centre. These programmes, which became known by the acronym INPRES — *Instruksi Presiden* (Presidential Instruction) — were important not just because they demonstrated the concern of the centre for the parlous state of local infrastructure, especially in rural areas. They were also important because of the way that the grants were allocated.[2] Clear guidelines were drawn up on allocation procedures and, with very few exceptions, these were adhered to. The various levels of government thus knew how much they could expect from year to year, and could begin to make rolling plans for infrastructure development over several years secure in the knowledge that the funds would be available. After the first oil shocks, new INPRES programmes were initiated that were directed to specific types of infrastructure; the largest was the INPRES SEKOLAH DASAR, which provided funding for the construction of a simple three-roomed school house in every village unit in the country. A parallel programme provided funds for the construction of primary health care centres. Again, clear guidelines were laid down on the allocation of funds, and the construction of facilities to minimize corruption and waste.

As these programmes accelerated, together with the growth in expenditure on development projects implemented by agencies of the central government, people everywhere in the archipelago began to see some evidence that the oil wealth accruing to the government was being used on facilities that would directly benefit them and their families. The road that was sealed for the first time in living memory, the new school, the new health clinic, the improved irrigation system, all these were convincing evidence that *pembangunan* (economic development) meant improved access to public amenities, which in turn could lead to increased earning opportunities, and higher family incomes and living standards. By the latter part of the 1970s, it was impossible to doubt that incomes and living standards were improving, especially in Java where the great majority of the rural poor were concentrated (Booth, 1992). But it was not only true that the proportion of the population whose expenditures were below a stipulated poverty line was falling over time. In addition, infant mortality rates were dropping, and school enrollments as a proportion of children in the seven to fifteen age groups were growing. By the late 1980s, the goal of universal primary education was effectively reached and educational planners were talking of achieving universal education to age fifteen by early in the twenty-first century.

These were remarkable achievements for a country as backward as Indonesia was in the mid-1960s. They were made possible not just because the government had considerable oil revenues at its disposal; other OPEC (Organization of Petroleum Exporting Countries) economies with large populations, such as Nigeria, were not as successful in using their oil revenues in ways which led to improved incomes and living standards for the majority of the population. In Indonesia the growth in oil revenues was accompanied by an undeniable improvement in the implementation capacity and administrative efficiency of government agencies at all levels. This in turn was due to a slow but relentless tightening of central authority over both the military and civilian bureaucracies, so that policy-making everywhere in the country could proceed on the assumption that orders from the centre would not be ignored, contradicted or subverted by officials further down the line. Those officials, either civilian or military, who for whatever reason were dilatory in carrying out central programmes, were removed from office. While corruption continued, it became clear that there were limits, and officials who transgressed those limits would not be tolerated.

This tightening of central control through the 1970s was greatly facilitated by the continual improvement in transport links. Not only did air links make it possible for people to travel from one end of the archipelago to the other within twenty-four hours, but the advent of modern telecommunications infrastructure made contact by phone, telex and more recently fax, quick and reliable. The ideology of accelerated economic development could thus be disseminated through frequent travel of officials to and from Jakarta for numerous meetings, briefings, workshops and upgrading courses. These had the additional benefit of enhancing the prestige of the regional civil service in the eyes of the local community by associating them more closely with the national development effort. At the same time, improved road and sea transport led to a marked acceleration in mobility of the population at large, not just within, but also between, islands. Those who moved from Java to other parts of the archipelago under the official transmigration scheme often passed news of employment opportunities in their new locality back to friends and relations in Java, who could then move quickly and cheaply to join them.

There can be little doubt that these expanded opportunities for travel contributed to a dramatic widening of horizons for many Indonesians in the 1970s, both officials and non-officials alike. New opportunities for migration and employment compensated to a considerable extent for any frustration which the virtual ban on political activity (except for the short and heavily stage-managed election campaigns) may have caused either the civilian and military bureaucracies or the general public. The effective 'depoliticization' of Indonesian life in the 1970s, particularly in rural areas, meant that any exploitation of lingering resentment over Javanese domination or excessive centralization was almost impossible to exploit by opposition elements, even where those elements could command a sizeable following. The eruptions of popular unrest that did occur, most dramatically in March 1974 in the wake of the visit of the then Japanese prime minister, Mr Tanaka, to Jakarta, were confined to urban areas and were quickly brought under control with minimal effect on the rest of the population. By the end of the decade, President Soeharto's position appeared invulnerable and the power of the centre vis-à-vis the regions had never been stronger.

It is perhaps surprising that the oil boom of the 1970s did not bring with it any demand on the part of the producing provinces to retain a larger share of the profits. In fact most of the oil came from two provinces, Riau in Central Sumatra and East Kalimantan. Both were small and isolated, conspicuously lacking in strong regional identities or in much tradition of regional nationalism. In both provinces, but especially in East Kalimantan, a large number of migrants from other parts of the country were drawn into the oil and logging sectors and related activities, and in both provinces ethnic Javanese held key positions in the civilian and military bureaucracies. Although there is debate about the extent to which the oil boom 'spilled over' to the local populations in both these provinces, there were sufficient signs of improvement in infrastructure and living standards to convince the majority of the indigenous populations that they were benefiting from the exploitation of their provinces' natural resources, even if those benefits were modest in comparison with the total value of their oil exports, an issue to which I will return below.[3]

As world oil prices began to fall in the early 1980s, the Indonesian government was forced into making cuts in its budgetary expenditures to compensate for

110

falling oil revenues. In the early 1980s, fiscal austerity particularly affected the routine budget (excluding the debt service component), which meant that salaries and perquisites of the military and civilian bureaucracies were frozen in nominal terms, while other types of routine expenditure (for example, on the maintenance of buildings and equipment) were drastically curtailed. But in the fiscal year 1986-87, foreign debt service obligations increased substantially in rupiah terms as a result of the rupiah devaluation and the yen revaluation. In order to maintain the budget balance the government had little choice but to make deep cuts in the development budget, which in one year fell from eleven to eight per cent of GDP (Gross Domestic Product) (Asher and Booth, 1992, Table 2.6). Although these cuts affected the departmental development budgets (especially industry, energy, transmigration and the environment) more drastically than the regional development grants, these latter also declined in real terms, and by 1989-90 they were only 3.4 per cent of total budgetary expenditures, compared with 7.2 per cent two years earlier (Asher and Booth, 1992, Table 2.11).

By and large, both central and regional governments accepted the decline in real resources available to them through the 1980s as the inevitable consequence of the fiscal austerity necessitated by the decline in oil prices.[4] Severe social unrest was minimized because, in contrast to countries such as Mexico, Venezuela and Nigeria, Indonesia had not used its oil revenues to subsidize prices of basic needs, so that budgetary cutbacks did not involve massive increases in prices of staple foods or other essential services. In fact the rapid growth in food grain production, which occurred over the decade 1975-85, meant that Indonesia had become virtually self-sufficient in rice by the time that the deep budget cuts had to be made; the problem was actually to keep rice prices from falling too sharply as a result of the bumper harvests of the mid-1980s. Certainly prices of some petroleum products such as kerosene have had to be increased, and public transport and electricity tariffs raised, but the increases have been quite modest and overall rates of inflation have been lower in the second half of the 1980s than at any time since the years 1968-72. In spite of falling rates of economic growth between 1981-88, real per capita consumption expenditures continued to grow and numbers below the official poverty line continued to fall. By the late 1980s, Indonesia was in fact being hailed by the World Bank as a successful example of 'painless' structural adjustment.

The period of the Fifth Five Year Plan (1989-94) saw a considerable growth in INPRES expenditures relative to total government expenditure, which in turn grew relative to GDP; by 1993-94, they accounted for over eighteen per cent of the development budget, and seven per cent of total budgetary expenditures (Figure 5.1). Most categories of INPRES expenditures shared in the growth over these five years, although the fastest growth was experienced by the INPRES JALAN, which was targeted towards the rehabilitation and extension of the road network (Table 5.1). In 1994-95, a new INPRES programme was introduced which was targeted particularly towards those villages that were considered to have been 'left behind', i.e. not to have benefited from the rapid economic growth of the past two

111

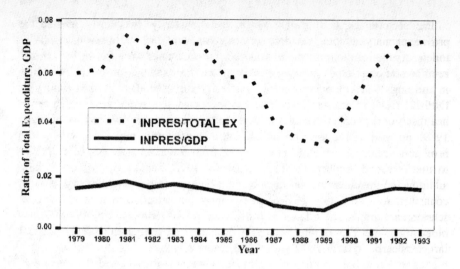

Figure 5.1   Ratios of INPRES to total expenditure and GDP, 1979-93

decades.[5] This new programme reflected growing official concern with spatial inequalities in economic development, an issue to which I return below. First, I address the issue of INPRES allocation criteria in greater detail.

Criteria for allocating INPRES funds

The first two INPRES programmes comprised block grants to villages and districts (*kabupaten*). The village grants, which began in 1969-70, were lump-sum allocations to each village-level unit in the country, to be used to pay for construction materials needed for local development projects; the labour was provided by the local population. At the district level the INPRES grants were allocated primarily on a per capita basis, although some small isolated districts outside Java were given extra grants to compensate for their high construction costs, relative to the national average. In 1974-75, block development grants to the provinces were also initiated (van Leeuwen, 1975). These replaced the old system whereby the provinces had received a share of their export tax revenues, a system which obviously favoured the export-producing provinces outside Java, although not the oil-producing provinces as oil exports were taxed according to different criteria from other exports. To begin with, the provincial INPRES allocations tended to favour the populated provinces in Java and Sumatra, but by the mid-1980s, the allocation criteria had changed to a system which gave every province a lump-sum grant, almost regardless of population, geographic size or any other characteristic.

112

The 'sectoral INPRES' grants, which developed in the 1970s, were intended to provide primary schools, health clinics, markets and other facilities such as public toilets. A small programme was also initiated to encourage soil conservation and re-afforestation. The allocation procedures for these programmes varied, although in the mid-1980s the allocation of funds in the two largest programmes, the INPRES SD (for primary school buildings) and INPRES KESEHATAN (for health clinics), were biased towards the smaller provinces outside Java (Booth, 1989, pp. 197-201). The very high per capita allocations to small, remote provinces such as Central Kalimantan and East Timor were no doubt due in part to the very high construction costs in these areas, compared to Java. But in addition the government was keen to be seen to be assisting those parts of the country that were lagging in terms of access to social infrastructure, such as schools and clinics. In per capita terms, total INPRES allocations (including both block grants and sectoral allocations) were much higher in smaller provinces than larger ones in the mid-1980s, although there was apparently little attempt to give higher allocations to poorer provinces. Small but relatively rich provinces in terms of per capita GDP in Sumatra and Kalimantan received higher total INPRES grants than small but relatively poor provinces in Eastern Indonesia.

Using data on total INPRES allocations per capita by province for 1985-86, Ravallion (1988) adapted the modelling techniques developed by Behrman and Sah (1984) in their study of aid allocation criteria, in order to identify the social preferences implicit in the Indonesian government's INPRES allocation criteria. Ravallion found only a modest tendency for poorer provinces (income proxied by average per capita consumption expenditures) to receive higher INPRES allocations than richer ones; his analysis confirmed that the smaller the population, and the lower the population densities, the higher the provincial INPRES allocation relative to total consumption expenditures. Table 5.2 gives the results of re-estimating Ravallion's model using data on INPRES allocations for 1993-94. Three separate results are shown: the first includes both the block grants to provinces, districts and villages; the second includes the INPRES JALAN allocations; and the third includes both block and INPRES JALAN grants (data on the INPRES SEKOLAH DASAR and the other INPRES allocations are not available broken down by province for 1993-94).

The most striking result from these equations is that the index of aversion to absolute inequality is found to be considerably higher than the 0.05 which Ravallion estimated from the 1985-86 data. For the INPRES JALAN grants, the index was 2.4, while for block grants it was 1.8. In other words, the considerable increase in INPRES grants which occurred over the Fifth Plan period was biased towards poorer provinces. The estimates reported in Table 5.2 confirm the results of previous studies that grants as a proportion of household incomes are higher in the smaller and less densely populated provinces. The positive and significant sign on the poverty variable suggests that INPRES allocations in 1993-94 were higher in the provinces with higher proportions of the population under the official (Central Bureau of Statistics) poverty line. This was especially the case for the block INPRES grants to the provinces, districts and villages.

Own-revenue growth

In addition to grants from the centre, provinces and sub-provincial levels of government in Indonesia now raise considerable funds from their own sources of revenue. Historically, most analysts have argued that the Indonesian fiscal system has been highly centralized, that regional and local government have had few autonomous revenue sources of their own, and those that they have been given earn little revenue and are income inelastic (Paauw, 1960; Booth, 1977; Devas, 1989). In the latter part of the 1980s, Devas (1989, p. 55) made the following argument about local taxation reform in Indonesia:

> there would seem to be two main objectives for any reform of local taxation. The first is the need to simplify and streamline the system of local taxation, which at present appears to have 'nuisance value' out of all proportion to the revenues generated ... The second objective would be to increase local tax revenues, in order to reduce the dependence of local government on central government grants. This is particularly important now, with the government's significantly reduced revenues from oil.

At the provincial level, the two most important sources of tax revenue are the motor vehicle registration tax, and the tax on change of ownership of motor vehicles. At the district level, a range of taxes are collected; the most important one is the hotel and restaurant tax, which in some tourist destinations yields substantial revenues. Indonesia is in fact unusual among developing countries in assigning motor vehicle taxes to a sub-national level of government. Not surprisingly, given the concentration of motor vehicles in the capital city, the Jakarta Special Region (which has provincial status) receives by far the most revenue from motor vehicle taxes in per capita terms (Mahadi, Schroeder and Wang, 1993, Table 1). Given the high income elasticity of demand for motor vehicles in Indonesia, it is to be expected that revenues from motor vehicle taxes would have grown more rapidly than GDP; in the years from 1977-78 to 1988-89, the elasticity of revenue growth with respect to GDP was estimated by Mahadi, Schroeder and Wang to be 1.25. Largely because of the importance of motor vehicle taxes, all but three provinces in Indonesia in 1991-92 managed to collect more own-revenues at the provincial level than at the district (*kabupaten*) level. In twelve provinces, own-revenue collections at the provincial level were more than forty per cent higher than at the district level.[6]

For Indonesia as a whole, own-revenue collections at the provincial level were much higher than the INPRES grants to the provinces, although this was not true at the district level (Table 5.3). But the data for the whole country disguise substantial regional variations. In Western Indonesia (Sumatra, Java and Bali), own-revenue collections at the provincial level were substantially higher in 1991-92 than the INPRES grants to the provinces (Table 5.3). Own-revenue collections at the district level were also higher than the INPRES grants to the district, although the difference was not as great. In Eastern Indonesia by contrast, own-revenue collection at the provincial level was much less than the INPRES grant, although at the district level the two were broadly similar.

Cross-sectional analysis of the data on provincial and district own-revenue collections in 1991-92 shows that revenue buoyancy with respect to GDP (total and non-oil) and with respect to per capita consumption expenditures are all higher for provincial than for district revenues (Table 5.4). This confirms the finding of many researchers that revenues available to the district level governments in Indonesia are inherently less elastic than those available to the provinces. But the districts do have another important source of revenue in the form of the Land and Property Tax (PBB). Previously known as the IPEDA, this tax has been substantially reformed over the last decade, with a consequent growth in revenues, especially from urban property, and from the mining sector (Kelly, 1993). In 1987, the PBB provided almost thirty per cent of non-grant revenue to urban and rural district governments (*kotamadya* and *kabupaten*), and 10.3 per cent of total revenues (Kelly, 1993, Table 1). Although it is legally a central government tax which is assigned to the district level, and the assessment remains the responsibility of the Department of Finance, the PBB is an important part of local government finance in Indonesia. In 1991-92, the elasticity of revenues (from the urban and rural components) with respect to non-oil GDP was 1.06, and with respect to per capita consumption expenditures, 1.91 (Table 5.4).

In spite of the rapid growth in provincial and district own-revenues (PAD) since the early 1980s, total collections remain very low relative to central government domestic revenues. Ranis and Stewart (1994, Table 1) argue that total local government revenues from their own sources fell as a proportion of central and local government revenues between 1974-75 and 1983-84, although they increased again thereafter, mainly because of the effect of declining oil revenues on central government receipts. According to their estimates, by 1988-89, total local government revenues amounted to 8.4 per cent of government revenues at all levels. The figures contained in the Sixth Plan, and used in Tables 5.3 and 5.4 (which refer to own-revenues accruing to provinces and districts only), indicate that provincial and district own-revenues were around 5.6 per cent of central government revenues from domestic sources (excluding foreign aid and borrowing) in both 1986-87 and 1991-92.

Total provincial and district revenues increased slightly as a proportion of GDP between 1986-87 and 1991-92 (from 0.88 per cent to 1.02 per cent). But these averages disguise substantial variation by province (Table 5.5). Only in ten of the twenty-seven provinces did own-revenue collections at the provincial and district levels amount to more than one per cent of provincial GDP in 1991-92. Not surprisingly, given the importance of taxes such as the motor vehicle tax in total provincial revenues, by far the highest PAD/GDP ratio was in Jakarta, followed by

115

Bali where the hotel tax is a very important source of revenue to those districts with large international hotels. It is interesting that several very poor provinces such as East Nusatenggara and East Timor, without the obvious advantages of Bali or Jakarta, also manage to achieve a high PAD/GDP ratio. This would suggest that the government grant system should be structured in such a way as to reward those poor provinces which achieve a high revenue/GDP ratio. I return to this point below.

Spatial inequalities in Indonesian economic development

The findings that the targeting of INPRES grants towards poorer provinces appears to have become more pronounced in recent years, and that there is considerable variation in the PAD/GDP ratios between provinces, are especially important when viewed in the light of recent evidence on the development gap between regions in Indonesia. Table 5.6 summarizes the most recent evidence. Eastern Indonesia (defined here to include the four provinces on the island of Sulawesi, as well as East and West Nusatenggara, East Timor and Maluku) contained 12.1 per cent of the country's population in 1993 (some 22.9 million people), and 11.7 per cent of the labour force, but in 1991 produced only 6.4 per cent of GDP. This can be contrasted with the four mineral-rich provinces, which produced 18.1 per cent of GDP, but contained only 5.7 per cent of the population, or Jakarta, which produced 11.6 per cent of GDP, with only 4.6 per cent of the population. The disparities become even more pronounced when we look at GDP broken down by sector. Eastern Indonesia produced around 12 per cent of total agricultural GDP, but only 2 per cent of manufacturing GDP in 1990 (Table 5.7). Apart from agriculture, the only other sector where the share of national output was close to the share of population was government and defence. In other productive sectors, such as public utilities, construction, trade, financial services and other non-government services, Eastern Indonesia's share was well below the national average.

Eastern Indonesia's labour force is more concentrated in agriculture than the national average, and less concentrated in manufacturing and in trade (Table 5.8). The agricultural labour force in Eastern Indonesia accounted for almost fifteen per cent of the national agricultural labour force, although the region only accounted for 11.7 per cent of total national agricultural output. In other words, although the regional economy is dominated by agriculture to a greater extent than the national economy, agricultural productivity (output per worker) is lower than the national average.[7] Manufacturing productivity is also lower than the national average, although it must be stressed that this is also the case in Java and Bali. In both of these regions, manufacturing absorbs more labour, proportionately to output, than in Jakarta, the mining provinces and other parts of the country.

It is clear that Eastern Indonesia has benefited little from any of the three main forms of industrialization that have occurred in Indonesia over the past twenty-five years. Import-substituting industrialization has been mainly based in Java, and especially in Jakarta and West Java, in order to benefit from the large market concentrated on that island. The recent growth of labour-intensive, export-oriented industry has also been based in Java, to take advantage of both superior infrastructure and abundant reserves of cheap labour. Resource-based industrialization has for obvious reasons been concentrated in those provinces which are well-endowed with oil, gas and minerals. Given its lack of natural resources, its poor infrastructure and its relatively dispersed population, the prospects for rapid industrial growth in Eastern Indonesia, and indeed in other relatively isolated provinces such as West, Central and South Kalimantan, are hardly encouraging.[8] Even the prospects for the kind of rapid agricultural growth that took place in Java, Bali and Sumatra in the 1970s and 1980s do not seem good. Rural infrastructure such as roads and irrigation is undeveloped, unfavourable biophysical conditions such as low rainfall and poor soils prevail over most of the region, and there is a dearth of new agricultural technologies appropriate to the local situation. Although some agro-industry, based for example on fishing, livestock or fruit and vegetable growing, may be commercially viable, it is hardly likely to provide a basis for the kind of rapid export-oriented manufacturing growth now underway in Java, Bali and parts of Sumatra. Indeed, it might appear that the best hope for the more isolated provinces outside Java is to become an exporter of labour, with inward remittances accounting for a growing proportion of regional income.

I have argued that the considerable growth in INPRES expenditures over the past five years does appear to have been biased towards the less populated and less prosperous provinces. In 1993-94, the four provinces of West and East Nusatenggara, Timor Timur and Maluku had the highest incidence of poverty in Indonesia (Table 5.6). They accounted for only 2.3 per cent of total GDP but received 10.9 per cent of INPRES expenditures (Table 5.9). They also accounted for 2.3 per cent of PBB revenues (urban and rural sectors only) and 3.8 per cent of district own-revenues. The three provinces of South, Central and West Kalimantan also had a high incidence of poverty relative to the national average; they too received a high share of INPRES allocations relative to their populations. But are these infrastructure grants sufficient to make up for the neglect that Eastern Indonesia has suffered for many decades in the provision of infrastructure? In 1991, Western Indonesia still accounted for over seventy per cent of all asphalt roads in the country, and over ninety per cent of all cars and buses were registered in Western Indonesia (Table 5.10). Western Indonesia also accounted for over ninety per cent of electricity production. As long as infrastructural imbalances of these orders of magnitude remain, the longer run development prospects for Eastern Indonesia must remain uncertain.

Poor little rich provinces: the special problems of the mining four

Although Indonesia is the third poorest of the ASEAN (Association of South East Asian Nations) countries in terms of GDP per capita, after the Philippines and Vietnam, some regions in Indonesia are among the wealthiest in the Southeast Asian region. Indeed the province of East Kalimantan in 1985 had a per capita GDP exceeding that of Bangkok and Central Malaysia. If we rank the forty-eight regions of Indonesia, Malaysia, the Philippines and Thailand for which data are available by per capita regional GDP (US$) in 1985, we find eight Indonesian provinces among the richest twenty regions: East Kalimantan, Riau, Aceh, Jakarta, South Sumatra, Irian Jaya, Central Kalimantan and Bali (Table 5.11). However, all these regions, except Jakarta, ranked much lower in terms of per capita consumption expenditures, the main determinant of living standards, than they did in terms of per capita GDP.

The extreme case was Irian Jaya, ranked sixth in terms of per capita GDP in Indonesia in 1985, and fourteenth in the ASEAN region, but was one of the poorest regions in terms of per capita consumption expenditures, even poorer than Bicol in the Philippines or East Timor in Indonesia. Indeed, the most recent evidence (*Household Expenditure Survey, 1993*) indicates that the incidence of poverty in rural Irian Jaya is now higher than in any other province in Indonesia, except for West Kalimantan and East Timor (Central Bureau of Statistics, 1994a, Table 3.3). The reason for this high incidence of poverty in spite of high per capita GDP was that the gap between exports from and imports into the province amounted to over sixty per cent of GDP in 1983-84, and has fallen only quite slowly to around thirty-seven per cent of GDP in 1991. In net terms Irian Jaya remitted almost half of its total regional product to other parts of the archipelago and abroad over the 1980s (Central Bureau of Statistics, 1994b, Tables 28-31).

In some other resource rich provinces the gap between exports and imports has been even larger than in Irian Jaya; in Aceh, for example, it has amounted to over sixty per cent of GDP for all years between 1983 and 1990. Although Aceh is still a prosperous province in the Indonesian context, it is relatively poor in the context of neighbouring Malaysia; in 1987, about seventy-five per cent of the population of Aceh had per capita consumption expenditures below the Peninsular Malaysia poverty line, compared with only 17.3 per cent in Peninsular Malaysia. Although per capita GDP in Aceh is still below that of Malaysia, the gap is not nearly as wide as that in consumption standards and poverty incidence; it seems obvious that if a higher proportion of the revenues from gas exploitation were allowed to stay in the province, living standards in Aceh would be that much closer to those of Malaysia. A similar argument can be made in the context of East Kalimantan, where between fifty and seventy per cent of total regional GDP has been remitted from the province between 1983 and 1990. As a result, consumption expenditures are much lower and poverty incidence much higher than in the contiguous Malaysian state of Sabah, in spite of the fact that, at least in 1987, per capita GDP was only slightly lower in East Kalimantan than in Sabah (Table 5.12).

These differences probably would not matter very much if the indigenous people in Aceh, East Kalimantan or indeed in the other resource rich regions of the country were ignorant of living standards in neighbouring countries, and happy to acquiesce in the centre's control over their natural resource wealth. Unfortunately for the Indonesian government, it cannot assume that this is the case. Even if the population of Aceh are well-off in comparison with much of the rest of Indonesia, their social and economic backwardness compared with their Malaysian neighbours (with whom many Achinese have close family links) must be an increasing source of irritation to people in that province. In the context of Irian Jaya, experienced observers argue that popular sympathy for the secessionist aims of the OPM (Free Papau Organization) is quite limited, and there is little reason to think that the great majority of the population in Aceh want a complete break with the rest of Indonesia. What appears to characterize the unrest in both provinces at the moment is a fear that immigrants from other parts of the country will dominate the local economy, frustration that the indigenous people have so little say in the disposition of their resource wealth, and, consequently, a desire for greater control over their own futures.

Policy options

How is the central government likely to react to these fears, frustrations and aspirations? Before answering this question, let us look for a moment at the direction in which Indonesian economic development is likely to progress over the next decade and beyond. There can be little doubt that manufacturing industry and the modern service sector (including tourism and financial services) will take over as the engine of growth for the economy as a whole, and especially in the densely populated inner core of Java and Bali. Labour-intensive exports will almost certainly account for a growing share of total export earnings. Thus after almost a century of Outer Island dominance of the export economy, it is probable that by the early years of the twenty-first century, Java and Bali will again account for more than half of total export earnings.[9] Populations in the large conurbations in Java will continue to grow rapidly, mainly as a result of in-migration, while those in the rural hinterland will probably decline. Indeed, the Sixth Five Year Plan predicts that more than 100 per cent of total population growth in Java between 1994 and 1999 will take place in cities of more than 250,000 (Booth, 1994, Table 10). Although natural resource exploitation will continue to be an important component of several regional economies outside Java, such activities will continue to be located in capital-intensive enclaves. It seems unlikely that employment opportunities outside agriculture in many parts of Sumatra, Kalimantan and Eastern Indonesia will grow rapidly enough to absorb the growth in population in these regions. Thus the agricultural labour force will continue to grow, and have to be accommodated either on existing land, or on marginal land newly brought under cultivation.

The prospect of continual growth in rural populations outside Java is especially worrying because, by and large, technical change in smallholder agriculture in Indonesia has been confined to the food-grain sector (especially rice and corn) and is thus concentrated in Java, Bali and the well-irrigated parts of Sumatra and Sulawesi (Tabor, 1992). In spite of considerable government efforts to raise yields in the smallholder tree-crop sector (especially rubber, coconuts and coffee), the results have been disappointing, and the great majority of farmers are using much the same cultivation technologies and obtaining much the same yields as did their fathers and grandfathers. The danger is that, over time, growing rural populations in many parts of the Outer Islands will be trapped in technologically stagnant agriculture, producing the same type of agricultural 'involution' as characterized rural Java in the half century or so from 1920 to 1970. Under these circumstances it is probable that the gap in income and living standards between Java and many parts of the Outer Islands will continue to widen. To the extent that this gap is accompanied by continuing centralization of natural resource revenues, the potential for growing resentment and unrest is obvious.

So what can the central government do? It seems to me that there are basically three options to be considered. The first is to stick with the status quo, to make only marginal changes in the financial relations between the centre and the regions, and certainly to make no change in the system of appointment of governors, bupatis, etc. The second is to deal with regional problems on an ad hoc basis; problems in Irian Jaya could for example be addressed through special development grants which remedy, at least to some extent, the extreme imbalance between the province's resource wealth and the very low living standards of the indigenous population. The third is to make more fundamental reforms in the whole relationship between the centre and the regions which would, in practice, if not in name, take Indonesia further down the road of federalism than has ever been the case since 1949.

The first option has, I am sure, many powerful advocates in Jakarta, in both the military and civilian bureaucracies. After all, why change a system which has in many respects served Indonesia well over the past twenty-five years? On the one hand, continuing centralization of resource revenues can be justified on both equality and efficiency grounds; if the provincial governments of Aceh, Riau or East Kalimantan were allowed to keep all the revenues accruing from exploitation of oil and gas it is quite possible that much of it would be wasted on ill-advised projects with low rates of economic return, rather than on projects which enhanced the longer run growth prospects of the particular region. Surely it is more desirable that the revenues be used by the central government for the national development effort, which will benefit all citizens in the longer run?

On the other hand, it is likely that there is, within the public at large, considerable sympathy for the argument that some regions are so disadvantaged by their relative isolation and their legacy of colonial neglect that they do deserve special treatment, especially where they happen to be important producers of natural resources. Indonesian public opinion does appear to be sensitive to arguments couched in terms of equity, and I suspect many would agree that Irian Jaya, for example, has been unfairly treated by the centre over the New Order period. There may be dispute over what should be done, and what sort of policies are likely to be most beneficial to the indigenous population of the province, and there may be concern that too much pampering by the centre, especially in the form of better access to education, will produce the kinds of problems which have so tarnished Indonesia's international image in East Timor. But certainly there is a growing awareness in Indonesian government and academic circles, and in parts of the media, that the present development path will lead to a widening gap between the eastern and western parts of the country, and that in the medium term this will place serious strains on the fabric of the nation state.

Given this awareness, how many would support a more fundamental approach to reforming the whole nature of the relationship between centre and regions in Indonesia? There are those who think that any change, even in the relatively narrow sphere of financial relations between centre and regions, would open up a whole Pandora's box of demands for changes in the political status quo in Indonesia, leading inevitably to thorough-going constitutional change. They may well be right. If provinces are to be given greater control over the income produced within their boundaries, then should there not be a much greater measure of popular control over the selection of governors, bupatis and regional assemblies? And if such popular control is conceded, then what is to stop a region from demanding further autonomy, and even the power to secede altogether? In short, can the central government take any steps at all towards economic decentralization without irrevocably setting the country on the path to political disintegration?

This is obviously a risk that any reform programme in Indonesia would have to face. At the moment it seems clear that the government is only prepared to contemplate slow and piecemeal change, in the hope that the main defects of the present highly centralized system can be remedied without setting in train centrifugal forces that cannot be controlled. Although the government has been talking about a new law on central-regional financial relations for some years, progress has been glacially slow, and 'there is as yet no sign of the law being introduced into, let alone passed by, the parliament in the near future' (Pangestu and Azis, 1994, p. 44). In the meantime, many Indonesians would agree with the conclusions of Ranis and Stewart (1994, p. 71), that 'while Indonesia's system of delegation and constrained devolution has thus been associated with considerable achievements in human development and economic growth over the past twenty years, there is still great potential for real decentralisation'. In October 1994, the Minister of Internal Affairs announced that twenty-six districts would be given 'greater autonomy' from central government control as part of a new decentralization initiative, although it is not clear exactly what the greater autonomy will involve (see the report in *Kompas*, 13 October 1994). Apparently, poorer districts are being encouraged to fund more projects jointly with private business, although it remains to be seen whether the private sector would find, for

121

example, water supply projects in East Timor sufficiently profitable to undertake without a substantial subsidy.

Without doubt, there is a need to encourage the poorer provinces to tackle their poverty problems directly, using their own resources supplemented where necessary by funds from the centre. As the root causes of poverty differ by province, individual provinces could be given the primary responsibility for designing and implementing poverty alleviation strategies, and could also be given first call on all income accruing within their boundaries in order to fund such strategies. Where regional income is inadequate, as it certainly would be in the case of East Nusatenggara, West Kalimantan or East Timor, for example, the centre must be prepared to supplement local resources with subventions from the centre. However, such subventions should be more specifically targeted towards those provinces with the greatest development needs, rather than simply distributed on a lump sum basis or according to population as is now the case. In addition, there is a strong case for rewarding those poor provinces who do manage to achieve higher than average ratios of own-revenue to GDP with higher grants from the centre.

The most recent evidence from the early 1990s, which I reviewed above, does indicate that targeting of INPRES grants to poorer regions has become more pronounced. In addition, the new INPRES DESA TERTINGGAL is important both because it is more explicitly targeted to poorer villages, and because it gives more responsibility to local populations to decide on the kinds of projects that are most likely to raise incomes in their area. But if the targeting of central government grants to the regions on the basis of needs is to accelerate, then it follows that those provinces which are judged to be relatively well-off in terms of living standards will probably end up receiving less from the centre than they do at the moment. To compensate, they must be encouraged to raise more revenues themselves. This can only be done by giving them a greater share in those taxes and royalties which are currently the exclusive preserve of the centre. Now that non-oil taxes once again comprise well over seventy-five per cent of total central government revenues (excluding aid and borrowing), and are projected to increase to almost eighty-five per cent by the end of the century, there is in my view a strong case for turning over at least a proportion of the revenues from both the income and the value added taxes to the regional governments. Provinces should also be given the option of imposing surcharges on taxes such as the VAT in order to raise more revenues. Both urban and rural districts should be given more scope for increasing PBB (land and property tax) revenues by raising rates, without interference from the centre. In addition, as royalties from oil and gas become only a minor part of total central government revenues, there is a much stronger case to be made for turning over a proportion (perhaps half) to the producing regions.[10]

Measures such as those outlined above would be designed to give the regions more responsibility for planning development expenditures on the one hand, and more revenue raising (or revenue retention) powers on the other, and would go part of the way towards remedying the tensions created by an over-centralized fiscal system. If, for example, East Java needs more infrastructure in order to achieve medium and longer term development targets, then the provincial government would have the option to intensify collection of existing taxes or to levy new taxes. But it would, I think, be wrong to suggest that Indonesia's regional problems can be resolved through fiscal measures alone, important though they may be. There remains the crucial issue of devolution of political power. There seems to me to be little reason to expect that provinces and sub-provincial levels of government will use additional revenues responsibly unless control can be exercised over their behaviour through the ballot box. In the longer run, discussions of reform of the present system of inter-governmental financial relations in Indonesia cannot be divorced from the wider issues of political and constitutional reform.

Notes

1. According to Jones (1994), the term 'Indonesia' was not created by the German ethnographer Adolf Bastian in the late nineteenth century, as is commonly thought. Jones argues that the term was first coined by the English lawyer and writer, George Windsor Earl, in an article written in 1850, although he subsequently rejected it. Nevertheless, the term was taken up in an article written by another English lawyer working in Singapore, J. R. Logan. Bastian, in turn, took the term from Logan.

2. See de Wit (1973) for a discussion of the original INPRES *kabupaten* programme.

3. For more detailed discussions of economic development in the resource-rich provinces until the mid-1980s, see Hill (1989, chapters 3-6).

4. The central government initiated a process of tax reform in the mid-1980s, which involved the introduction of a value-added tax, and substantial reform of personal and corporate income tax. However, there was no attempt to reform the system of local government finance.

5. For a discussion of the INPRES DESA TERTINGGAL, see Pangestu and Azis (1994, pp. 32ff.).

6. Data on provincial and district own-revenue collections in 1991-92 are taken from the sources cited in Tables 5.3 and 5.4.

7. The dispersion of agricultural value added per farm household and per agricultural worker by province is not very great, and the data on value added per hectare and land per agricultural worker, when graphed, fall along a rectangular hyperbola. For more discussion of the implications of this, see Booth (1991).

8. As is clear from Table 5.6, the incidence of poverty in Kalimantan (excluding East Kalimantan) was actually much higher than in Sulawesi.

9. According to the Sixth Plan projections, by 1998-99 manufactured exports will be eighty-nine per cent of all non-oil exports, which in turn will be eighty-seven per cent of total export earnings.

10. Decentralizing tax and expenditure policies does not mean that the centre should abdicate its powers of supervision and audit. Indeed, the audit powers of government and parliament in Indonesia have traditionally been weak, and need to be strengthened, both at the centre and in the regions.

Table 5.1
Percentage breakdown of INPRES expenditures,
1989-90, 1993-94, 1994-95
(Rp.billion)

	1989-90	%	1993-94	%	1994-95	%
Grants to regions:						
Village	112	9.0	390	8.2	423	7.9
District	270	21.8	1025	21.7	2418	45.3
Province	324	26.1	783	16.5	1219	22.8
Sub-total	706	56.9	2198	46.4	4060	76.0
Sectoral grants:						
Primary schools	100	8.1	698	14.7	498	9.3
Markets	3	0.2	4	0.1	-	-
Health clinics	122	9.8	377	8.0	393	7.4
Re-afforestation	16	1.3	104	2.2	-	-
Roads	294	23.7	1352	28.6	-	-
Sub-total	535	43.1	2535	53.6	891	16.7
Backward villages	-	-	-	-	389	7.3
Total	1241	100.0	4733	100	5340	100.0

INPRES as a % of total Government expenditure:

	3.3		7.3		7.7

Real INPRES expenditures: *

	1288		3728		n.a.

* 1990 prices, deflated by the wholesale price index (excluding oil)

Source: *Indonesian Financial Statistics, Bank Indonesia,* Jakarta, various issues

Table 5.2
Estimating inequality aversion[a] parameter using CES function

Explanatory variable[b]	Dependant variable (as a ratio of consumption expenditures)		
	All INPRES[b]	Regional INPRES[b]	Road INPRES[b]
ln PCE			
(per capita conumption	-0.969	-0.82	-1.37
expenditure)	(7.216)	(5.758)	(7.905)
ln POPDEN	-0.138	-0.6	-0.293
(population density)	(5.197)	(2.135)	(8.558)
ln POP	-0.427	-0.387	-0.491
(population)	(10.602)	(9.066)	(9.435)
ln POV	0.279	0.312	0.176
(incidence of poverty)	(2,709)	(2.848)	(1.322)
Adjusted R^2	0.96	0.93	0.97
SEE	0.153	0.163	0.198
F statistic	155.06	87.52	185.06

a   A Constant Elasticity of Substitution (CES) function is fitted so that the inequality aversion perameter is 1 minus the coefficient on the PCE variable (see Ravallion, 1988, p. 59)

b   Data refer to 1993. There are 27 observations. Data on INPRES expenditures (natural log of the ratio of INPRES expenditures to consumption expenditures) refer to the calendar year 1993-94. Regional INPRES refers to the grants to provinces, *kabupaten* and villages.

Sources: INPRES data: *Lampiran Pidato Kenegaraan,* Department of Information, Jakarta, 1994, Tables XIV-1 to XIV-10; PCE estimates: *Expenditure on Consumption of Indonesia per Province 1993,* Central Bureau of Statistics, Jakarta, 1994; Poverty estimates: *Penduduk Miskin dan Desa Tertinggal 1993: Metodologi dan Analisis,* Central Bureau of Statistics, Jakarta, 1994, Table 3.3.

Table 5.3
Comparison of provincial and district own-revenue collections (PAD) with
INPRES grants, 1991-92 (Rp. billion)

Type of Revenue	Western Indonesia	Eastern Indonesia	All Indonesia
PAD (Province)	1441.9	162.1	1604.0
PAD (District)	574.6	130.7	705.3
INPRES (Province)	286.1	307.9	594.0
INPRES (District)	466.2	124.6	590.8
INPRES (Village)	174.6	75.3	249.9
ROAD INPRES			
Province	147.0	142.7	289.7
District	367.0	318.1	685.1

Sources: INPRES data: as for Table 5.2; Provincial and district own-revenue data; *Rencana Pembangunan Lima Tahun Keenam, 1994-95 to 1998-99,* 6th Five Year Development Plan, Bappenas Staff Cooperative, Jakarta, 1994, Vol. 2, Tables 16.4, 16.5 and 16.6.

Table 5.4
Estimates of revenue buoyancies with respect to GDP
and per capita expenditures[a]

	PAD 1[b]	PAD 2[c]	PAD[d]	PBB[e]
GDP	0.766	0.293	0.639	0.567
GDP (non-oil)	1.226	0.782	1.087	1.061
PCE	2.875	1.464	2.383	1.911

a   Buoyancies are calculated by regressing the log of revenues against GDP or PCE

b   PAD 1 — Provincial own-revenue per capita in 1991-92

c   PAD 2 — District own-revenue per capita in 1991-92

d   PAD — Provincial and district revenue in 1991-92

e   PBB — Land and Buildings Tax in 1992-93

Sources: Provincial and district own-revenue data: as for Table 5.3; Population data: *Statistical Year Book of Indonesia,* 1993, Central Bureau of Statistics, Jakarta, 1994, Table 3.1.4a; PCE data: as for Table 5.2; GDP data: *Gross Regional Domestic Product of Provinces in Indonesia by Industrial Origin, 1986-91,* Central Bureau of Statistics, Jakarta, 1993, pp. 250-1

Table 5.5
Provincial and district revenues as a percentage of provincial GDP

Province[*]	Own-revenues as a percentage of GDP:	
	1986-87	1991-92
Aceh	0.235	0.334
Riau	0.218	0.337
East Kalimantan	0.345	0.473
South Sumatra	0.476	0.594
Irian Jaya	0.496	0.646
Central Kalimantan	0.539	0.670
Maluku	0.663	0.694
West Kalimantan	0.652	0.695
Southeast Sulawesi	0.906	0.762
Lampung	1.128	0.823
South Kalimantan	0.838	0.831
Central Java	0.911	0.880
West Java	0.725	0.883
North Sumatra	0.976	0.916
Jambi	1.010	0.950
Bengkulu	1.224	0.956
East Java	0.824	0.956
South Sulawesi	1.110	1.058
West Sumatra	1.115	1.080
Central Sulawesi	0.988	1.179
West Nusatenggara	1.032	1.350
East Timor	1.722	1.423
Yogyakarta	1.400	1.507
East Nusatenggara	1.345	1.537
North Sulawesi	1.464	1.671
Bali	1.193	1.896
Jakarta	1.828	2.674

*   Provinces ranked in terms of ratio of revenues to GDP, 1991-92

Sources: As for Table 5.4

Table 5.6
Percentage breakdown of GDP, population and poverty incidence, 1993

Region	GDP[a]	Population	Poor Population	Poverty incidence[b]
Jakarta	12.0	4.7	1.9	5.6
Java/Bali	46.8	56.2	55.3	13.4
Mining 4[c]	17.1	6.0	6.4	14.5
Sumatra	14.2	16.9	16.0	13.0
Kalimantan	3.5	4.1	6.6	21.9
Sulawesi	4.1	7.0	5.1	9.9
Eastern Islands[d]	2.3	5.1	8.6	22.6
INDONESIA	100.0	100.0	100.0	13.6

a   GDP data refer to 1991

b   Percentage of population under the Central Bureau of Statistics 1993 poverty line

c   Aceh, Riau, East Kalimantan and Irian Jaya

d   Provinces of West and East Nusatenggara, Timor Timur and Maluku

Sources: *Statistical Yearbook of Indonesia 1993* and *Penduduk Miskin dan Desa Tertinggal 1993: Metodologi dan Analisis,* Central Bureau of Statistics, Jakarta, 1994

Table 5.7
Regional breakdown of GDP by sector, 1990

	Jakarta	Java/ Bali	Mining 4[*]	Sumatra/ Kalimantan	Eastern Indonesia	Whole Nation
Agriculture	0.6	54.5	8.1	24.7	12.1	100.0
Mining	0.0	15.9	73.2	9.2	1.7	100.0
Manufacturing	16.3	49.6	16.9	15.0	2.1	100.0
Utilities	37.9	41.7	3.9	12.6	3.8	100.0
Construction	19.6	54.0	5.4	14.7	6.3	100.0
Trade	13.2	52.9	7.9	20.3	5.7	100.0
Transport	20.9	40.4	8.3	21.4	9.0	100.0
Financial servs.	47.1	31.7	3.4	14.1	3.8	100.0
Govt./Defence	7.1	55.1	7.5	19.2	11.0	100.0
Other services	30.9	52.6	3.0	9.8	3.7	100.0

*   Aceh, Riau, East Kalimantan and Irian Jaya

Source: *Gross Regional Domestic Product of Provinces in Indonesia by Industrial Origin, 1986-91*, Central Bureau of Statistics, Jakarta, 1993, pp. 250-1

Table 5.8
Regional breakdown of the labour force by region and sector of employment, 1990

	Agriculture	Manufacturing	Trade	Public services	Total
Jakarta	0.1	7.8	7.9	10.1	4.1
Java/Bali	53.9	70.7	67.4	57.7	58.8
Mining 4*	6.0	2.8	3.3	4.8	5.1
Sumatra/ Kalimantan	25.4	10.9	14.0	16.8	20.4
Eastern Indonesia	14.6	7.7	7.4	10.6	11.7
INDONESIA	100.0	100.0	100.0	100.0	100.0

*   Aceh, Riau, East Kalirnantan and Irian Jaya

Source: *Labour Force Situation in Indonesia, 1990*, Central Bureau of Statistics, Jakarta, 1992

Table 5.9
Percentage breakdown of GDP, INPRES, PAD and PBB

Region	GDP 1991	INPRES 1993-94	Own-revenue, 1991-92: Province	District	PBB[a] 1992-93
Jakarta	12.0	2.3	43.7	0.0	24.4
Java/Bali	46.8	31.1	32.8	64.3	50.6
Mining 4[b]	17.1	14.5	6.5	6.5	4.4
Sumatra	14.2	20.1	9.7	14.8	11.4
Kalimantan	3.5	9.5	1.9	3.6	1.3
Sulawesi	4.1	11.5	3.5	6.9	5.5
Eastern Islands[c]	2.3	10.9	2.0	3.8	2.3
INDONESIA	100.0	100.0	100.0	100.0	100.0

a   Rural and urban revenues only
b   Aceh, Riau, East Kalimantan and Irian Jaya
c   Provinces of West and East Nusatenggara, Timor Timur and Maluku

Sources: *Statistical Yearbook of Indonesia, 1993*, Central Bureau of Statistics, Jakarta, 1994; INPRES and own-revenue data: as for Tables 2 and 4

Table 5.10
Growth in infrastructure, 1968 to 1992

Type of Infrastructure[a]	1968	1992	1992% in Western Indonesia
Asphalt Road (000 Km)	20.85	137.06	71.2
Other Roads (000 Km)	62.42	178.40	53.2
Total Roads (000 Km)	83.27	315.46	61.0
Electricity (000 MWh)	1780.46	41937.60	92.5
Cars (000)	201.12	1875.10	93.2
Trucks (000)	93.42	1126.26	88.0
Buses (000)	19.61	539.95	92.6
Motorcycle (000)	308.40	6941.00	87.2

a   Data on the length of roads refer to 1965 and 1991 respectively

Sources: Lampiran Pidato Kenegaraan 1994, Department of Information, Jakarta, Table IX-20; *Statistical Pocketbook of Indonesia 1968-69,* p. 270; *Statistical Yearbook of Indonesia 1993,* p. 416 and pp. 425-7

Table 5.11

**Twenty richest regions in Southeast Asia ranked by
per capita GDP (US$), 1985[a]**

Region	Per capita GDP	Per capita private consumption expenditure	Difference in ranks[b]
East Kalimantan	3319	293	-14
Riau	2659	295	-12
Sarawak	2427	558	-1
Sabah	2420	790	2
Greater Bangkok	2079	730	2
Peninsular Malaysia	1867	1102	5
Metro Manila	1345	517	1
Aceh	1300	282	-8
Jakarta	1220	530	4
Central Thailand	792	430	3
South Sumatra	737	268	-7
Southern Tagalog	703	303	0
Southern Midanao	631	251	-8
Irian Jaya	620	167	-31
Central Luzon	578	366	6
Southern Thailand	572	394	8
Northern Mndanao	556	231	-10
Central Visayas	527	190	-23
Central Kaliinantan	519	300	6
Bali	491	316	9

a   Excludes Singapore and Brunei. Data in local currencies converted to US dollars at the prevailing exchange rate

b   Shows differences between rankings according to per capita GDP and per capita consumption expenditures (pcce). A negative ranking indicates that the region was ranked lower in terms of pcce than in terms of per capita GDP

Sources: Indonesia: *Provincial Income in Indonesia by Expenditure,* Central Bureau of Statistics, Jakarta, 1989; Malaysia: *Siaran Perangkaan Tahunan, Sabah; Annual Statistical Bulletin, Sarawak; Yearbook of Statistics,* Department of Statistics, Kuala Lumpur, various years; Philippines: *1990 Philippine Statistical Yearbook,* National Statistical Coordination Board, Manila, 1990 and unpublished data from the *1985 Family Income and Expenditure Survey* supplied by the National Statistics Office, Manila; Thailand: *1989 Statistical Yearbook of Thailand,* National Statistical Office, Bangkok, 1989, and unpublished data from the National Economic and Social Development Board, Bangkok

Table 5.12
Poverty, per capita income and per capita GDP in Aceh, Peninsular Malaysia, Sabah and East Kalimantan, 1987

	Percentage below the Malaysian Poverty Line[a]	Per capita expenditure[b] (US$)	GDP per capita (US$)
Aceh	93.2 (74.5)	168	1021
Peninsular Malaysia	17.3	426	1914
East Kalimantan	94.2 (80.4)	224	2560
Sabah	35.3	443	2716

a Poverty line of M$68.09 per capita in Peninsular Malaysia and M$99.44 per capita in Sabah, as reported in *Mid Term Review of the Fifth Malaysia Plan*, p. 45. Figures in brackets refer to the % of the population in Aceh and East Kalimantan below the Malaysian poverty lines when these are adjusted to allow for differences in the purchasing power of the Malaysian and Indonesian currencies in 1985, as estimated by Summers and Heston in the *Review of Income and Wealth*, 1988

b In Malaysia, the data refer to average per capita household income as reported in the *Mid Term Review of the Fifth Malaysia Plan*, 1989, p. 45. In Indonesia, the data refer to average per capita household expenditure as reported in *Pengeluaran untuk Konsumsi Penduduk Indonesia per Propinsi 1987*, Central Bureau of Statistics, Jakarta

Sources: *Mid Term Review of the Fifth Malaysia Plan*, National Printing Department, Kuala Lumpur, 1989; *Pengeluaran untuk Konsumsi Penduduk Indonesia per Propinsi* 1987, Central Bureau of Statistics, Jakarta. GDP data: as for Table 5.4

References

Asher, M. and Booth, A. (1992), 'Fiscal Policy', in Booth, A. (ed.), *The Oil Boom and After: Indonesian Economic Policy and Performance in the Soeharto Era*, Oxford University Press, Singapore, pp. 41-76.

Behrman, J. R. and Sah, R. K. (1984), 'What Role Does Equity Play in the International Distribution of Development Aid?', in Syrquin, M., Taylor, L. and Westphal, L. E. (eds), *Economic Structure and Performance*, Academic Press, Orlando, pp. 295-315.

Booth, A. (1977), 'Inter-provincial Comparisons of Taxable Capacity, Tax Effort and Development Needs in Indonesia', *Malayan Economic Review*, Vol. XXII, No. 2, pp. 71-87.

Booth, A. (1989), 'Central Government Funding of Local Government Development Expenditures', in Devas, N. (ed.), *Financing Local Government in Indonesia*, Ohio University Monographs in International Studies— Southeast Asia Series No. 84, Ohio University Center for International Studies, Athens, pp. 191-212.

Booth, A. (1991), 'Regional Aspects of Indonesian Agricultural Growth', in Hardjono, J. (ed.), *Indonesia: Resources, Ecology and the Environment*, Oxford University Press, Singapore, pp. 36-60.

Booth, A. (1992), 'Income Distribution and Poverty', in Booth, A. (ed.), *The Oil Boom and After: Indonesian Economic Policy and Performance in the Soeharto Era*, Oxford University Press, Singapore, pp. 323-62.

Booth, A. (1994), 'Repelita VI and the Second Long-term Development Plan', *Bulletin of Indonesian Economic Studies*, Vol. 30, No. 3, pp. 3-40.

Central Bureau of Statistics (1994a), *Penduduk Miskin dan Desa Tertinggal 1993: Metodologi dan Analisis*, Central Bureau of Statistics, Jakarta.

Central Bureau of Statistics (1994b), *Gross Regional Domestic Product of Provinces in Indonesia by Expenditure, 1983-91*, Central Bureau of Statistics, Jakarta.

Devas, N. (ed.) (1989), 'Local Government Finance in Indonesia; An Overview', in Devas, N., et. al., *Financing Local Government in Indonesia*, Ohio University Monographs in International Studies—Southeast Asia Series No. 84, Ohio University Center for International Studies, Athens, pp. 1-51.

Feith, H. (1962), *The Decline of Constitutional Democracy in Indonesia*, Cornell University Press, Ithaca.

Glassburner, B. (ed.) (1971), *The Economy of Indonesia: Selected Readings*, Cornell University Press, Ithaca.

Hill, H. (ed.) (1989), *Unity in Diversity: Regional Economic Development in Indonesia since 1970*, Oxford University Press, Singapore.

Jones, R. (1994), 'George Windsor Earl and 'Indonesia'', *Indonesia Circle*, No. 64, November, pp. 279-90.

Kahin, G. M. (1952), *Nationalism and Revolution in Indonesia*, Cornell University Press, Ithaca.

Kelly, R. (1993), 'Property Tax Reform in Indonesia: Applying a Collection-Led Implementation Strategy', *Bulletin of Indonesian Economic Studies*, Vol. 29, No. 1, pp. 85-104.

Legge, J. D. (1961), *Central Authority and Regional Autonomy in Indonesia: A Study in Local Administration 1950-60*, Cornell University Press, Ithaca.

Legge, J. D. (1990), 'Review: Indonesia's Diversity Revisited', *Indonesia*, No. 49, pp. 127-31.

Leeuwen, R. van (1975), 'Central Government Subsidies for Regional Development', *Bulletin of Indonesian Economic Studies*, Vol. XI, No. 1, pp. 66-75.

Mackie, J. A. C. (1980), 'Integrating and Centrifugal Factors in Indonesian Politics since 1945', in Mackie, J. A. C. (ed.), *Indonesia: The Making of a Nation*, Research School of Pacific Studies, Australian National University, Canberra, pp. 669-684.

Mahadi, K., Schroeder, L. and Wang, H-H. (1993), 'Provincial Motor Vehicle Taxation in Indonesia', *Bulletin of Indonesian Economic Studies*, Vol. 29, No. 3, pp. 95-110.

Morris, E. (1985), 'Aceh: Social Revolution and the Islamic Vision', in Kahin, A. (ed.), *Regional Dynamics of the Indonesian Revolution*, University of Hawaii Press, Honolulu, pp. 83-91.

Niel, R. van (1979), 'From Netherlands East Indies to Republic of Indonesia: 1900-45', in Aveling, H. (ed.), *The Development of Indonesian Society*, University of Queensland Press, St. Lucia, pp. 106-65.

Paauw, D. S. (1960), *Financing Economic Development: The Indonesian Case*, Free Press, Glencoe.

Pangestu, M. and Azis, I. J. (1994), 'Survey of Recent Developments', *Bulletin of Indonesian Economic Studies*, Vol. 30, No. 2, pp. 1-47.

Ranis, G. and Stewart, F. (1994), 'Decentralisation in Indonesia,' *Bulletin of Indonesian Economic Studies*, Vol. 30, No. 3, pp. 41-72.

Ravallion, M. (1988), 'Inpres and Inequality: A Distributional Perspective on the Centre's Regional Disbursements', *Bulletin of Indonesian Economic Studies*, Vol. 24, No. 3, pp. 53-72.

Ricklefs, M. (1981), *A History of Modern Indonesia*, Macmillan, London.

Tabor, S. (1992), 'Agriculture in Transition', in Booth, A. (ed.), *The Oil Boom and After: Indonesian Economic Policy and Performance in the Soeharto Era*, Oxford University Press, Singapore, pp. 161-203.

Taylor, A. D. (1960), *Indonesian Independence and the United Nations*, Stephens and Sons, London.

Wit, Y. de (1973), 'The Kabupaten Programme', *Bulletin of Indonesian Economic Studies*, Vol. IX, No. 1, pp. 65-85.

6 Industrial development and the impetus to regional economic integration in Pacific Asia

Fu-Kuo Liu

Introduction

Where regional economic integration is concerned, the countries which put forward cooperation programmes have always taken into account any economic advantages which might accrue to them. Although political incentives have been crucial in advancing the progress towards regional integration, for the private sector, profits have remained the most fundamental motive for economic integration. This is what the theoretical approach to economic integration has suggested about the mutual benefits of the 'trade creation' effect. In particular, an integrated market allows economic factors, i.e. capital, goods, services, and personnel, to be able to move freely across national boundaries thereby making the best use of resources. Without the presence of mutual economic advantage, therefore, there is little hope for individual national economies to boost their prospects for regional integration and to maintain their commitment to existing regional groupings.

The purpose of this chapter is to explore, in general, economic development in the context of incremental Asia-Pacific economic cooperation and, in particular, the impact of industrial restructuring in the Asian Newly Industrialized Countries (hereafter ANICs[1] i.e. Hong Kong, Singapore, Taiwan, and South Korea) on the development of subregional economic groupings in the West Pacific Rim. It is an analysis of their attempts to resolve structural problems by developing economic interdependence with their neighbouring economies, which in turn has inched forward regional economic integration. Furthermore, through an examination of the division of labour in regional economies, the prospects for economic integration can be evaluated. The analysis focuses on the extent to which, although countries in Pacific Asia are pursuing a strategy of globalisation, their efforts have brought about the regionalisation of industrial development and the accelerated progress of economic integration in Pacific Asia. This exploration also tries to examine what the proposition of regional economic integration motivated by economic development implies for our understanding of regional integration in an interdependent world economy.

New momentum for Asia-Pacific economic integration

Since the late 1980s, a number of international trends have been shaping the context of Asia-Pacific regionalism.[2] Firstly, the collapse of communism in the Soviet Union and Eastern Europe has, more or less, soothed the Cold War in the Pacific area, and reminded China, one of the lone communist 'fortresses' in East Asia which has been implementing a more pragmatic policy towards the market economy, to keep up with the prosperous Asia-Pacific economy. Secondly, the relative decline of the United States has been reflected in its suffering a huge trade deficit with the East Asian export-led economies. An increasingly protectionist orientation has emerged in North America as a result. Therefore, East Asian export-led economies will have to increase the volume of intra-Asian trade to replace their traditional export market to the US, so that their economic growth will not be slowed. Thirdly, the effect of North America and the European Union (EU) becoming more protectionist has boosted the importance of Japan for the East Asian export-led economies. Japan has not only become an investor, banker, trader, and technology supplier for all East Asian export-led economies, but has also provided a large market for their exports. This Asia-Pacific economic cooperation may be leading to a new phase of economic integration. Furthermore, China has re-affirmed its reform and open door policy to the world which implies that it, like Japan, will continue to promote Asia-Pacific economic cooperation.

However, there are two sources of uncertainty which could decisively affect Asia-Pacific regionalism. Firstly, the global trading regime is likely to be feeble, 'as regional integration proceeds, as intra-firm trade continues to grow, and as trade among strategic alliance partners increase' (Drobnick, 1992, p. 15). Although the prolonged Uruguay Round negotiations of the General Agreement on Tariffs and Trade (GATT) has finally reached a compromise in December 1993, it does not mean that it has brought about immediate assurance for economies and regional blocs around the world over trade problems. Whether the new trade regime, the World Trade Organization, will eventually bring about increasing protectionism or deregulation remains to be seen. As many have believed that 'the end of the Uruguay Round will not be the end of trade talks — or trade battles' (Branegan, 1993, p.30), the future for freer trade could be more troubled, as *The Economist* (18 December 1993), for example, suggests.

Secondly, the trade friction between Japan and the US could jeopardize the world trade regime under the GATT, and also block trans-Pacific regional cooperation. While Japan has continued to benefit from a huge trade surplus with the US, Japan has kept its domestic markets relatively closed to foreigners. Since the US Omnibus Trade Act of 1988 was introduced, US administrations have made use of 'Super 301' legislation as a foreign policy instrument pressing Japan and others for bilateral trade negotiations.[3] Trade surpluses, protected domestic markets, and the US threat of imposing 'Super 301', characterize the current picture of the US-Japan's trade row.

In February 1994, a showdown over US access to Japanese markets brought about renewed tension. Subsequently, the US has threatened to cite Japan in a 'Super 301' action.[4] Many observers, at the time, feared that it might trigger a trade war.[5] Most recently, in May 1995, the US threatened to impose 100 per cent of import tariff on Japanese luxury cars unless Japan agreed measures to open its market to US cars and car parts. The sanction imposed by the US would cost Japanese car makers about US$5.9 billion (Hamilton and Williams, 1995). The US believes that because the Japanese economy is different from other industrialized countries, increased unilateral pressure is the only way to bring about change (Hamilton, 1995). In spite of a trade pact finally reached on 28 June, which dramatically eased the tension, it is still doubtful that the pact has resolved all differences between the US and Japan. Indeed, after this spat there have been a number of issues ready to be raised, such as US landing rights for air passengers and cargo, and Kodak's trade complaint against Fuji film (Borrus et al., 1995).[6] Predictably, this uncertainty will undoubtedly continue to undermine not only any plans for Asia-Pacific regional economic integration but also the critical US relationships with the Asia-Pacific exporting economies. The desire for a larger political framework to provide a mechanism of dialogue has, in part, contributed to the emergence of Asia Pacific Economic Cooperation (APEC).

Economies in Pacific Asia have been sharing very similar patterns of economic development, i.e. considerable levels of dependence upon US and Japanese technologies and industrial techniques, and US markets. Japan, the ANICs, the Association of South East Asian Nations (ASEAN) and China together, have constituted a dependent and interdependent pattern at different levels of skill, wage rate, and economic development. 'The flow of investments from the upper to lower tier of countries acts as a transmission belt in transmitting growth momentum from one tier to the next' (Low, 1991, p.378). Since the mid-1980s, the ANICs have been commonly suffering from the 'NICs disease' — namely rapidly appreciating currencies, soaring property prices, and shortages of labour, thereby losing their comparative advantages in labour-intensive industries. As a consequence, international competition has driven industrialists in the ANICs to relocate their industries in Southeast Asia and China, as part of their strategy of restructuring industries to regain competitiveness (Kim, 1993).

Regional economic development has increased the momentum of economic integration in the region. The economic framework of an international division of labour in production (resulting from the ANICs-based foreign investment flows, their upgrading of technology, and industrial cooperation in the region) has raised the possibility of further economic integration. However, economic integration will be meaningful only if regional economies have been actively participating in an international division of labour (Panic, 1988). It is quite clear that the ANICs' industrial restructuring has contributed to exports of capital, technology, and industrial experience to other East Asian developing economies. Furthermore, cross border investment and inter-industry cooperation has not only created comprehensive economic ties between regional economies, but also generated certain common business interests such as a commitment to keep the world trade system free and open.

The growing trend of economic tie-ups, occurring amongst a group of neighbouring economies in Pacific Asia, is parallel to the general development of Asia-Pacific economic cooperation. The impact of the ANICs' policy for industrial restructuring has been to change both the pace of structural adjustment and the political circumstances in the rest of the Asia-Pacific area as a whole, resulting in the rise of economic groupings. The clearest example can be seen in the case of the emergence of 'subregional economic groupings' in the Asia-Pacific area[7], such as the Growth Triangle amongst Singapore, Malaysia, and Indonesia; and the Southern China Economic Area amongst Taiwan, Hong Kong, and the Fujian and Guangdong provinces in China. Nevertheless, East Asian subregional groupings today have made their own way towards economic integration by relying upon industrial cooperation in which the full endorsement of governments has followed rather than led such developments, especially in the case of the emergence of the Chinese Economic Area, the Bohai Sea Economic Circle, and the Yellow Sea Economic Circle.[8]

The emergence of subregional groupings in the context of Asia-Pacific economic cooperation

For decades, a number of pan-Pacific economic cooperation initiatives have been presented in various forms by academics, businessmen and government officials, e.g. the Pacific Trade and Development Conference, the Pacific Basin Economic Council (PBEC) and the Pacific Economic Cooperation Conference (PECC). Details of the development of such initiatives can be found in Drysdale (1988), Palmer (1991) and Woods (1991), while Hadi Soesatro (1983) provides a review of Pacific economic cooperation. Since the mid-1980s, economic development in the Asia-Pacific area has been going through a transitional phase following the ANICs' industrial restructuring process. Although there have been different situations in each ANIC depending on its own political and economic environment, some general factors have contributed to this change: the appreciation of the Japanese Yen and the currencies of the ANICs against the US dollar; democratization, rising wage rates and stricter environmental protection regulations in the ANICs; the 1989 elimination of the Generalized System of Preference (GSP) status of the ANICs by the US; and China's open market (Drobnick, 1992).

Due to demands for self-adjustment of industrial structures in order to regain competitiveness, the ANICs have allowed some of their low-level skilled

140

industries to relocate in Southeast Asian countries and China. At the same time, they have pressed ahead with the upgrading of their domestic technology. This restructuring process in the ANICs has not only reinforced the existing regional trade structure, but also built up much more comprehensive economic ties, based on this industrial division of labour, with Japan and regional developing countries. A new economic East Asian map has appeared based around subregional groupings. According to geographical charactersistics, subregional groupings generally can be divided into three groups: the Japan Sea Zone, including the Yellow Sea Zone and the Tumen Delta; the Southern China Zone; and the ASEAN Free Trade Area plan, including the Growth Triangle, the Northern Triangle and the Baht Economic Zone[9] (There are also four 'mini strategic triangles': the 'manufacturing triangle' of Japan, Thailand and Indonesia; the 'Chinese triangle' of China, Taiwan and Hong Kong; the 'growth triangle' of Singapore, Malaysia and Indonesia; and the 'trade triangle' of South Korea, North Korea and China's Shandong Peninsula (Kanmao Wang, 1992)). The rush to triangulate in the Asia-Pacific area has been largely driven by the efforts of industrialists to cope with 'the world economic recession and the perceived threat of protectionism from emerging trade blocs in Europe and North America' (Burton, 1994, p.24).

Although the ANICs have not been the only contributors to the impetus bringing forward regional economic cooperation in general, they do offer the possibility of subregional economic groupings which contribute to a larger framework of pan-Pacific cooperation. Without fully involving the tedious formality of governmental scrutiny, the ascendence of subregional groupings, to some extent, driven by the private sector, results from the anxiety of regional economies concerning the prospects for the wavering world trade regime and for yet far from successful regional economic integration. It may be more accurate to state that the emergence of subregional groupings is partly a pragmatic response of regional economies to regional autarky, and partly a natural result of East Asian traditional business links through personal contact rather than bureaucratic practices (Burton, 1994).

Economic development and Asia-Pacific economic cooperation

Stuart Harris once said that 'the interest in regional economic cooperation in the Asia-Pacific region has not always been motivated by a logical understanding of the need. It was often a response to what appeared to be happening elsewhere' (Harris, 1991, p.308). Indeed, for decades, the dynamics of the economic cooperation movement in this region have resulted partly from some sort of 'defensive stand' against the emergence of regional integration in Europe and North America (Funabashi, 1993; Gibney, 1993; Low, 1991). Since the early 1960s, partly in response to the progress of European integration programmes (Wijkman and Lindstrom, 1989), a series of initiatives have brought forward economic cooperation and continued shaping up the progress of economic integration in Pacific Asia. Table 6.1 provides further details of the many proposals over the last three decades.

Table 6.1
Initiatives for Pacific economic cooperation: a chronology

1960	A Pan-Pacific organization[a] (M. Kajima)
1963	In a report for the JERC[b] calling for annual meetings of five developed Pacific nations (S. Okita)
1965	Pacific Free Trade Area (K. Kojima)
1967	Pacific Basin Economic Council (Japanese and Australian Business groups)
1967	Association of Southeast Asian Nations (A. Malik & T. Khoman)
1968	Asian Pacific Bloc Establishment Plan (T. Miki)
1968	Pacific Trade and Development Conference (K. Kojima & T. Miki)
1969	A System of Collective Security in Asia & the Pacific Community (L. Brezhnev)
1977	Fukuda Doctrine (Fukuda)
1977	Organization of Pacific Trade and Development (P. Drysdale & H. Patrick)
1978	Pacific Basin Cooperation Study Group (M. Ohira)
1980	Pacific Economists Community (K. Kojima)
	Pacific Basin Cooperation Concept (PBC Study Group)
	Pacific Economic Cooperation Conference
1981	ASEAN-Pacific Forum (K. Kojima)
1989	Asia-Pacific Economic Cooperation (R. Hawke)
1990	East Asian Economic Caucus (D. Mahathir)
1992	ASEAN Free Trade Area
1993	ASEAN Regional Forum

a   It became 'Union of Asian Countries' in 1973.
b   Japan Economic Research Centre

Sources: Based mainly on Hadi Soesastro (1983), 'Institutional aspects of Pacific Economic Cooperation', in Hadi Soesatro and Sung-Joo Han, (eds.), *Pacific Economic Cooperation: the New Phase*, Centre for Strategic and International Studies, Jakarta, pp. 1-52.

None of these programmes has yet developed a consensus amongst all economies in the region in terms of European patterns of regional integration. Some have argued that, in general, Pacific Asia lacks the favourable conditions for regional integration present in Europe (Wijkman and Lindstrom, 1989), not only because the wide differences in levels of industrial development, and in cultural, political and economic preferences, have made a desire to form 'a common and equitable mandate' less likely (Linder, 1986, p.114), but also because the East Asian export-led economies have not relied so much on regional markets per se. Although intra-regional trade has in recent years steadily increased, regional economies still remain heavily dependent upon the rest of the world markets. In 1980, for example, the exports of the West Pacific accounted for 37.3 per cent of its intra-regional trade; by 1989 this had risen to 46.6 per cent (Kwan, 1991). While in Europe strong political pressure promoted the emergence of economic integration, the Asia-Pacific area appears to have little similar political motives.

The Japanese Professor Kiyoshi Kojima, observed in the early 1970s, that: 'the enlarged Eurobloc will continue and strengthen its inward-looking policies, intensifying intra-regional development and raising the degree of its self-sufficiency...these Pacific basin countries (Japan, Australia, New Zealand, the US, and Canada) should join efforts in obtaining a bargaining power equal to the Community'(Kiyoshi Kojima, 1972, pp. 586-7). While in the second half of the 1980s the relaunching of European integration put forward a target for the completion of the European Single Market in 1992 and the US-Mexico-Canada North American Free Trade negotiation started off, the effect of the promotion of these forms of regional economic integration was to encourage the APEC concept, with the background to its emergence being trade tension between East Asian economies and Western countries (Elek, 1991). These external factors spurred on regional economic cooperation to a 'G7 summit alike influential intergovernmental mechanism' (Hughes, 1991, p.125).

In the past few decades, with limited governmental commitment (Hiroshi Kitamura, 1983), the general efforts for economic integration in the Asia-Pacific region have focused principally on the construction of transnational networks on a non-governmental basis. Although those institutions, characterized by non-governmental features, have yet to claim complete success for their efforts to lead regional economic integration, they have generated a prevalent interest in the goal of Pacific cooperation. From the onset of the Asia-Pacific economic cooperation movement, this has largely stemmed from a tripartite network of academics, business people, and governmental officials, which has meant that economic cooperation has been based more on bargaining between different individual interests than on the definition of common interest. Nevertheless, these efforts for Asia-Pacific economic cooperation have never been so important as to water down those official regional organizations which have been continuously devoted for decades to regional economic integration.

The PECC's network for cooperation has been advancing considerably towards its political objective, in which negotiation between states, and between societal sectors, is facilitated. This function has credited the PECC with a means of enhancing official relationships in the discussion of common problems and policies through informal elements.[10] The PECC's successful presentation of a Pacific perspective on the Uruguay Round of multinational trade negotiations has shown its capacity for expressing a common regional interest to a transnational forum (Woods, 1991). Moreover, increasing governmental commitment to regional cooperation programmes may well have created the context for the emergence of the APEC as an influential institution.

The APEC concept was originally conceived as 'an informal forum of officials from Asia-Pacific countries in response to the rise in economic regionalism — notably the European Community (EC) and the North American Free Trade Area (NAFTA) (Susumu Awanohara and Nayan Chanda, 1993, p.16). In 1991, the third APEC annual ministerial meeting in Seoul sought to gather the members' commitment to an 'open regionalism' of free trade and economic collaboration. A 'Seoul APEC Declaration' which recognized their need to establish a secretariat has further progressed the institutional development of APEC (*Korea Newsreview,* 1991). Moreover, the Clinton administration of the US has sought to transform the forum from 'a 'talking shop' to an achievement-based group' especially at the Seattle APEC summit meeting in November 1993 (Susumu Awanohara and Nayan Chanda, 1993, p.17). Whether the APEC will gradually evolve into a mechanism for regional economic integration remains to be seen. Its main objective has, nevertheless, been to co-ordinate and congregate regional interests for improving the global multilateral trading framework. Furthermore, the APEC provides an excellent vehicle for achieving regional trade liberalization that will enhance more ambitious Asia-Pacific integration (Clark, 1992).

Asia-Pacific regional economies see themselves as global rather than 'regional traders' (Harland, 1993, p.16). Since their outward-looking strategy has made them very vulnerable to external factors, particularly developed countries' trade policy, protectionism, and exchange rate fluctuation, the economies in Pacific Asia have sought to defend themselves against such external challenges by forming their own regional groupings. The hopes for establishing a regional grouping to reduce regional economies' vulnerability to international competition and protectionism have enabled APEC to play a leading role. Their outward-looking perspective has been a major reason why Japan and the ANICs have yet to show 'much sense of community, or much interest in regional cooperation' in spite of their increasing economic interdependence (Harland, 1993, p.16). This may also explain why Asia-Pacific economic cooperation has been more successful thus far in non-governmental rather than in inter-governmental forms. The relationships between these are summarized in Figure 6.1.

The rise of subregional groupings

Against the background of general efforts for Asia-Pacific economic cooperation, growing economic development has brought about an economic interdependence which 'has begun to forge a sense of cohesion across the Pacific'(Clark, 1992, p.386). If the momentum for pan-Pacific economic cooperation resulted from a passive reaction to the threat of regional economic integration elsewhere, the dynamics of economic integration in the region appear to be driven by rapid

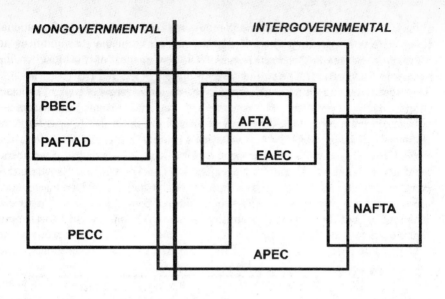

PBEC

PAFTAD

AFTA

EAEC

NAFTA

PECC

APEC

Figure 6.1   Asia - Pacific Economic Cooperation

regional economic development. To some extent, external factors have served as a trigger to push forward economic cooperation initiatives.

More and more practical indices suggest that the increasing economic interdependence amongst Asia-Pacific countries has been brought into being by intra-regional trade, investment, inter-industry cooperation, and division of labour. According to APEC's definition, intra-Asia-Pacific trade in terms of total trade shares has risen from 57 per cent in 1970 to 66 per cent in 1988.[11] However, the most impressive development amongst East Asian economies in the last decade has been rising intra-investment from not only those previously developed countries, such as Japan, the US, and European countries, but also from the ANICs, which shows 'a phenomenon reflecting growing economic cooperation and integration in this region' (Chen, 1991, p.32). Such new patterns of investment reveal that the transformation of East Asian economic development is under way by 'an extensive industrial restructuring and a sophisticated subregional division of labour'(Chen, 1991, p.33). The emergence of the division of labour across all East Asian economies has, to some extent, deflected them from any possible political rows caused by trade disputes over competition for export markets. It will be the progress of economic development that activates the initiatives for regional economic integration.

Before the Uruguay Round was finally concluded, Asia-Pacific economies had already made a few efforts via the private and public sectors to form trading groupings in order to safeguard their market competitiveness and strengthen negotiating leverage in case of a collapse in the GATT negotiations. The concept

145

of the 'Chinese Economic Area' and the 'Growth Triangle' searching for 'natural allies' reflects in particular Hong Kong, Taiwan, and Singapore's aspirations to maintain their market competitiveness. The emergence of the East Asian Economic Caucus (EAEC) and the ASEAN Free Trade Area (AFTA), implies even more so the search for a consensus in the region in terms of trade. The keen efforts made have been the outcome of regional economies' industrial restructuring process and the development of regionalism in the EC and NAFTA (*Asiaweek*, 13 January 1993, p.42). Malaysia's Prime Minister, Dr. Mahathir, has warned that economic blocs in Europe and North America are forcing East Asian countries to follow suit (*Time*, 22 November 1993, p.57). Graham Hayward, the executive director of the Singapore International Chamber of Commerce, has stressed that the formation of AFTA or a similar body, has become 'a useful insurance policy' for regional economies (*Asiaweek*, 13 January 1993, p.42) (see Figure 6.2).

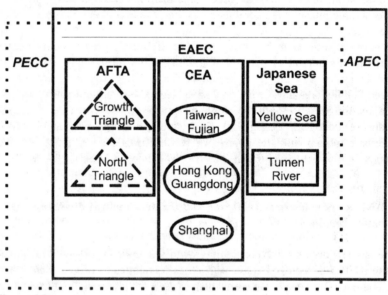

Figure 6.2   Asia - Pacific Subregional Groupings

In general, regional trade groupings are making common stands to cope with other trade blocs by establishing common regulations for their own internal markets and a consensus in international negotiations. The interest of individual countries will supposedly be protected by projecting a common stand against external challenges. Such a decisive move is entirely dependent on governmental commitment and policy cooperation. However, the development of a subregional economic grouping in Pacific Asia does not comply with Western conventional knowledge of inward-looking trade blocs, partly because there is yet to exist a comprehensive economic grouping to generate a common interest, and partly because increasing economic ties between regional economies have not been based on political motivations, but rather on economic development.

During the period of the ANICs' industrial restructuring, a political motivation behind economic cooperation has appeared to consolidate security arrangements in the post- Cold War era. Singapore, through the development of the Growth Triangle which ties in Malaysia and Indonesia, has seen advantages for its city state's security. Hong Kong has been especially keen to develop economic interdependence with China, which could be the only way for Hong Kong to remain economically active after 1997. In accelerating economic transactions across the Taiwan Strait, possibly resulting in the creation of the Chinese Economic Area, the political tension between Taiwan and China has, at least until recent tensions in summer 1995, largely abated. Although China remains a potential political and military threat to Taiwan, their all round relationship has improved at an unprecedented speed. This has clearly suggested that the more their economic interests are combined together, the less likely will it be for China to use force.

In terms of security in Northeast Asia, while North Korea remains a potential threat, China's pursuit of peace and stability as its most important goal in the region is rather convincing to South Korea.[12] The increasing economic ties between South Korea and China may have blended economic interests with South Korea's willingness to sooth the continual tension in the Korea Peninsula. South Korean President Kim Young Sam, for example, hoped to persuade his Chinese counterpart to step into the quarrel of North Korea's development of nuclear weapons, in his visit to Beijing in March 1994 (*Time*, 28 March 1994, p.28).

The ANICs' industrial restructuring and the development of subregional economic groupings

In the last few decades fast economic growth and their export-led strategies have led the ANICs to focus on trade with other economies to propel their economic development. The comparative advantage based on low cost production had led the ANICs to compete successfully with their trade counterparts in developed economies in certain sectors, such as textiles, electronics, automobiles, steel, shipbuilding and electrical equipment.

However, since the 1980s, the ANICs have suffered from a loss of comparative advantage because of the mounting pressure to their exports from low cost products from other developing countries, such as Indonesia, Malaysia, Thailand, the Philippines, and above all China (OECD, 1988, p.8). These countries are equipped with abundant low cost production factors, notably cheap land, labour and natural resources, and are eroding the ANICs' share of the world markets, mainly in the labour-intensive industrial products, e.g. textile, footwear, toys, and electrical products for domestic consumption. As soon as these regional low cost developing countries started the catching-up to ANICs process by adopting export-led strategies for economic development in the early 1980s, the ANICs' trading position as a group of low cost manufacturing exporters was at stake.

Table 6.2
Thomson's survey of labour costs

Countries:	labour cost per hour (Fr.)
Germany	120
France	100
UK	60
Taiwan	25
Hong Kong	22
Singapore	20
Thailand	6
Malaysia	5
China	2.5

Source: *The Times*, (7 October, 1992), p. 28.

In addition, the ANICs' position as an attractive low cost production base has also been weakened, above all in labour-intensive industries. For example, as Thomson Consumer Electronics, French electronics giant, is chasing lowest-cost labour to keep its products competitive, the company has been operating in East Asia since 1975 because of cheap labour cost. (See Table 6.2) In response to the increase of labour cost in the ANICs, as with the relocation of ANICs' indigenous industry, Thomson has cut production in Taiwan and Hong Kong and opened plants in South China and Indonesia (Tiernan, 1992, p.28).

Moreover, at the other end of the economic development spectrum, developed countries, facing intensifying competition from their trading counterparts, have quietly imposed protectionist measures, notably by setting up import restrictions, including tariff and above all non-tariff barriers, against exports from other economies; vide the EC's import quotas, export restraints, and unfair trade measures, despite the free trade spirit always being claimed. In particular, during the worldwide economic recession, the ANICs have steadily expanded their shares in the world markets, with an increase in trade surplus against most of their trade partners, and this has incurred new protectionism in the EU and the US. According to an Organization for Economic Cooperation and Development (OECD) study, discriminatory trade restrictions by OECD countries have risen in recent years and mainly focused on Japan and the ANICs (OECD, 1988, p.73). Focusing on the EC's trade policy to the ANICs in the 1980s, one study suggests that the EC import barriers not only increasingly target developing countries in general and the ANICs in particular, but also their new export items, e.g. colour TVs, and computers that provide fierce competition with EC products (Sun-Taik Han, 1992, p.27). The other study points out that the ANICs, for example, have often become the targets of the EC anti-dumping charges, due to their substantial trade surplus against the EC and their lack of bargaining power (Chien-Nan Wang and Jui-ling Hsu, 1992) (see Table 6.3).

Table 6.3
EC anti-dumping cases against its trade partners

Exporting countries:	1981-1984	1985-1988
Developed countries	60	31
Developing countries	45	79
ANICs	3	27
Taiwan	3	6
South Korea	1	14
Non-Market countries	98	31

Source: Chien-nan Wang, and Jui-ling Hsu (1992), 'The impacts of the European integration on Taiwan and Taiwan's responses', paper presented to the Sino-European Conference on *'Economic Development: Impacts of the European Integration and Responses of Non-EC Countries'*, Chung-Hua Institution for Economic Research, Taipei, Taiwan, 6-7 May.

To fortify their international competitiveness, the ANICs have, since the mid-1980s, launched a process of industrial restructuring, seeking to upgrade their industrial structure, on the one hand, by increasing investment in quality improvement of their products and upgrading technology, and on the other hand, allowing more inefficient sun-set industries to die or relocate in lower cost countries, instead of merely sticking to their previous strategy of cutting production costs. These processes of restructuring have been derived, to a large extent, from external competition for markets and advantage. As a result, the ANICs' efforts at industrial restructuring have reinforced the existing regional industrial division of labour that has been exploited by the Japanese for years.

A large part of the ANICs' outflow of investment and industrial relocation into Southeast Asian countries and China that happened in the last few years has dramatically changed East Asian economic structure. This new trend of investment from the ANICs has been more substantial than investment from the transnational corporations (TNCs) because the ANICs' investment in those neighbouring countries has involved many more companies, which is crucial to economic integration. For example, according to the Taiwanese official figure in 1993, there were about 2,600 companies investing about US$900 million in

Mainland China.[13] South Korea has also increased its investment in China sharply from US$42.4 million in 69 projects in 1991 to US$597 million in 616 projects in 1993 (Shim Jae Hoon, 1995, p.37). Subregional economic groupings have emerged as a result of the ANICs' pursuit of industrial adjustment together with their efforts to globalize their enterprises and markets (for the ANICs investment in ASEAN countries see Table 6.4).

Table 6.4
The Asian NICs investment in regional developing countries (US$ million)

HK:	China	Indonesia	Thailand	Malaysia	Philippines
1987	1,947	135	125	11	28
1988	3,466	240	451	50	27
1989	3,160	407	561	42	133
1990	na	993	na	na	34

Taiwan:	China	Indonesia	Thailand	Malaysia	Philippines
1989	552	158	892	815	148
1990	1,011	618	782	2,383	140
1991	1,737	1,056	583	1,314	12
1992	6,430	563	290	602	9

Sing:	China	Indonesia	Thailand	Malaysia	Philippines
1986-88	111	116	157	112	1
1989	124	166	411	338	24

S Korea:	China	Indonesia	Thailand	Malaysia	Philippines
1986-88	na	78	171	7	1
1989	na	466	41	70	17
1990	22	722	na	32	10

					ASEAN-4*
1991	42				1,141
1992	205				1,424

*   ASEAN-4 comprises Indonesia, Thailand, Malaysia, and Philippines

Sources: Chen (1993); Hoon (1993); Kim (1993); Paisley (1992), and the Majestic Trading Co. Ltd., (1993), *Annual Report*, London;.

Since the mid-1980s, the US has investigated the ANICs' advantages in trade with the US and has tried to deal with East Asian economies individually rather than in 'a monolithic whole'.[14] In the late 1980s, while the US has continuously conferred the GSP to most Southeast Asian countries and China, allowing their products easy access to the US market, the ANICs' GSP status has been eliminated.[15] These factors are further weakening the competitive advantage of the ANICs. Moreover, the increasing pressure on the appreciation of the ANICs' currencies has sharpened the threat to the competitive advantage of their exports.

The ANICs' capital- and technological-intensive industries which were linked with the developed markets were hit by the worldwide recession and savage competition in the late 1980s, especially shipbuilding, auto, and machinery industries, as well as the computer industry. The fast growing South Korean and Taiwanese computer makers were among the list of victims of world recession and the computer price war in 1991 launched by the big three, International Business Machines Co. (IBM), Apple, and Compaq Computer Co. (*Far Eastern Economic Review*, 17 October 1991, p.105). Taiwan's Acer Inc., the leading computer maker, suffered a loss of revenue.[16] In South Korea, while Samsung Electronics was expected to post a loss of US$40 million on exporting personal computers, Koryo Systems, the country's 1990 Silver Tower Trophy holder of export performance award and the fifth largest computer maker, actually went bust in October 1991 (*Far Eastern Economic Review*, 17 October 1991, p.105).

The structural problems of the ANICs are clearly shaped by two-way pressures: the low production costs of other regional developing countries facing their downstream industries; and the technological constraints on the upgrading of their higher value-added industries. In fact, for the ANICs these are not solely problems of industrial restructuring itself, but also a political challenge ahead with regards to the re-organization of regional economic cooperation (see Figure 6.3). In the process of industrial restructuring, which projects global business strategy, the ANICs have invested domestic capital in Southeast Asia and China to strengthen their competitiveness. These flows have transferred technology and management practices, and have increased local employment, which has created a regional framework for the division of labour (Drobnick, 1992, p.25). A momentum for further regional economic integration will only be generated by regional economies successfully pursuing continual economic development.

The international division of labour and regional economic integration

In East Asia, a 'vertical development' which links neighbouring economies in the context of an industrial division of labour has been going on substantially and spontaneously, through mainly business and other economic pursuits.[17] To some extent, this trend has demonstrated a strong impetus to endorse the likely regional economic grouping, notwithstanding that political cooperation within the region has been less likely to take the lead in the efforts for regional economic integration. In this favourable economic context, with the ANICs projecting their innovative economic capacity into the region, a number of subregional economic groupings have emerged. Regional economies have already benefited from their complementarity to each other through certain industrial divisions of labour.

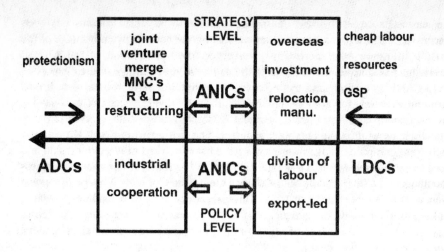

Figure 6.3   The ANICs trade structure

The Hong Kong-Guangdong-Shenzhen Triangle

The most outstanding example of a subregional economic grouping is Hong Kong's efforts to participate in and benefit from China's economic development. The growing triangular economic zone of Hong Kong, Guangdong, and the Shenzhen Special Economic Zone is to be the next growing star in prosperous East Asia. The Province of Guangdong itself has become the fastest growing area in the world, and will within two decades become the 'fifth tiger' following the current four tigers of Hong Kong, Singapore, Taiwan and South Korea.[18] Whilst Southern China has a huge potential due to its cheap labour, especially when coupled to the government's special preference for export-orientation, Hong Kong is pouring large amounts of capital, technology, marketing expertise, business and financial services, and skills and management into economic cooperation. Japanese and US investment has been playing the same role in Taiwanese and Korean economic development, as has Hong Kong investment in China. Hong Kong enjoys the low cost of production in China, but is nonetheless prepared to share its advanced market and manufacturing experience. The industrial structure of this combined economy has been focused on manufacturing due to its cheap labour and easy access to raw materials and markets.

In the long run, China's heavy industrial experience may well be a critical driving force for the absorption of Hong Kong's commodity economy. As most of Hong Kong textile and electrical industries are limited in their access to most of the OECD's markets by various non-tariff barriers, especially anti-dumping regulations and Voluntary Export Restraint, it offers in cooperation with China

152

the easiest access to these markets for manufacturers. This is a way of circumventing trade restrictions protecting developed markets. In turn, Hong Kong's informed business and development experience has benefited China's development. In addition, notwithstanding the fact that Hong Kong is about to be handed over to China in 1997, the British colonial linkage gives it a pivotal position to cement the relations between this triangle and the EU. With respect to the exchange of information, marketing experience, and market resources, this triangular development is critical to China and to those who are concerned with the China market. If Hong Kong keeps its free trade orientation after 1997, it will need to expand its access to markets to further strengthen its competitiveness. The spontaneous linkage of the triangle tells us that the ANICs with narrow domestic markets and poor resources are expecting to amplify their own economic scope by linking up with other economies.

The Singapore-Johor-Riau Growth Triangle

Another triangular economy, which is to be an innovative example of joint marketing at the national level, is comprised of Singapore, the Malaysian state of Johor and the Indonesian Riau Islands (Batam and Bintan). Following a series of Singapore-Indonesia and Singapore-Malaysia ministerial meetings from 1988 to 1991, the Growth Triangle has officially come into being. The initiatives for this subregional economic grouping were derived partly from Singapore's desire to strengthen its international competitiveness, and partly from Singapore's new thinking on ASEAN which has rallied fruitlessly to economic cooperation (Vatikiotis, 1990, p.15). This again is another complementary economic complex. Speaking at an investors forum in Jakarta in 1990, Lee Hsien Loong, Singapore's then Trade and Industry Minister, said:

> Singapore is short of land and labour, but has more developed infrastructure and a higher concentration of manufacturing and service industries. Indonesia (as well as Malaysia) has abundant labour and natural resources, and potential for tremendous growth once these are organized and developed (quoted in Vatikiotis, 1990, p.15).

As the Singaporean industrial structure is heavily dependent upon foreign investors, which consist of many transnational corporations (TNCs), the triangle is intended to develop higher technology by offering an enormous investment opportunity and environment to those investors who come from the developed countries with their high technology. In order to globalize its economy to cope with future competitive challenges, Singapore which has learned from the experience of the TNCs, has been trying to extend its hinterland to its neighbouring economies as a way of expanding its economy. Allowing neighbouring economies to share its successful economic performance, Singapore has been trying to portray itself as an economic powerhouse in the triangle, as the

153

broker for introducing more updated advanced high technology from the TNCs, on the one hand, and as the manager for economic development, on the other. Tun Daim Zainuddin, a former Malaysian Finance Minister, realizes that 'Prosperity is our goal, and that prosperity should be shared' (quoted in Burton, 1994, p.24). It is this which has brought the triangle economic complex into effect.

The concept of the triangle has stemmed from the global competitive strategy of the TNCs which have diversified their production processes in different countries. The purpose of the diversification of production has been the search for competitive advantage. The Japanese electrical giant Sony, for example, has been producing some electronics components in Taiwan, assembling in Malaysia, but retaining its marketing and management operations in Japan. Indeed, with Batam and Johor's ready labour and land availability at competitive rates, coupled with Singapore's efficient infrastructure and technical expertise, the triangle is making itself more attractive to foreign investment and competitive in world markets. This is what Singapore's former Prime Minister, Lee Kuan Yew, has envisioned: Singapore as a hub 'can serve not only their home market, but also the regional and world markets. Furthermore, they can tap the region's bigger and cheaper labour pool. Labour-intensive parts of a product can be done in neighbouring countries and exported to Singapore for more capital- or skill-intensive operations'(Salem, 1988, p. 77).

If a single subregional grouping is thought of as a process of Asia-Pacific regional economic integration in a limited area, the drive will certainly come from a common interest in economic development. The Growth Triangle was initiated by the governments of Singapore, Malaysia, and Indonesia, but their movement has lagged far behind the businessmen's pace of development' (Aoki and Ohashi, 1992, p. 27). Although some sceptics in Malaysia and Indonesia see this project as having specific Singaporean objectives, by 1991 there were twenty-eight multinational corporations, including the region's biggest business group Liem Sioe Liong's Salim Group and companies controlled by Suharto's family, planning to invest in Batam Island in response to Singapore's proposal for the development of the Triangle (Vatikiotis, 1991, p.35). It is also said that the close relationship of the Indonesian tycoon Liem Sioe Liong with the Singapore government has facilitated the development of the triangle concept (*Central Daily News*, Taipei, 13 March 1994).

Taiwan's economic sphere of influence

Taiwan's economic activities for competitive advantage stretch both to the developed economies for higher technology and the developing economies for low cost production factors. Many have already noticed that Taiwan as Asia's newest banker is challenging the Japanese role 'as the paymaster of regional industrial integration' (*Time*, 13 January 1992, p. 15; Moore, 1990, pp. 82-87). It is outstandingly cash-rich, according to a recent report. Its foreign exchange reserves have reached the highest in the world at over US$90 billion (in 1992), and has become an attractive investor in the region (See Table 6.5). Taiwan has been going through a process of industrial restructuring and structural adjustment during the last decade. Many small and middle enterprises, especially those inefficient and labour-intensive industries on which the Taiwan miracle was based, have barely survived international competition because of rising labour cost and land prices, currency appreciation, and tighter pollution controls at home. The adjustment itself through outflow investment and manufacturing relocation has facilitated a hope for regional economic integration.

Table 6.5
The top four foreign exchange reserves holders (US$ million)

	Taiwan	Japan	Germany	USA
1992	90.1	71.6	91.0	60.3
1993	84.2	98.5	77.9	62.4

Source: *The Economist*, 12 March 1994, pp. 153-154.

To break through its diplomatic isolation and to maintain its competitive advantage, the Taiwanese government is actively promoting overseas investment. Overseas investment as an instrument of foreign policy tightly links investors and the host countries. These international economic linkages are expected to tie the interests of countries more closely together. Such diplomatic concerns are especially meaningful for Taiwan since direct investment can be an effective approach to both markets and friendship. Perhaps its investment capital is the only trump card in Taiwan's hand (*Far Eastern Economic Review*, 18 March 1993; *The Economist*, 19 February 1994). Companies seeking low-cost bases for manufacturing products destined for the US and the EC markets started the latest investment wave in 1987. Most are labour-intensive industries making shoes, garments, toys, handbags and consumer electronics in South East Asia (Moore, 1990, p.86). Apart from the low-cost manufacturers of Southeast Asian countries, the overseas Chinese communities which have been easily tied to Taiwanese business and offered powerful local marketing allies for Taiwanese entrepreneurs, have been another attractive incentive for investment by Taiwanese companies. The similarity of social and cultural background is also an important factor for investors.

Since the investment wave started, Taiwanese investment has rapidly increased in Southeast Asian countries. Investment to the region which accounted for over US$500 million in 1987 and for US$2.5 billion in 1989 including China, was recognized as 'the key to a second spring for Taiwan industry' (Moore, 19 April 1990, p. 86) even before the further expansion of the early 1990s, with outflow investment to the region reaching US$12 billion in 1993, accounting for almost half of Taiwan's total outflow investment of US$25 billion (*Far Eastern*

Economic Review, 18 March 1993). Indeed, this is especially important for labour-intensive and low-technology industries, such as Hua Loong Textile Co., the nation-run China Steel Co. in Malaysia, and the Yuen Foong Yu Paper Manufacturing Co. in Indonesia. Moreover, Taiwanese investment in this region has become ubiquitous not only to ASEAN members but also to Vietnam. A new figure shows that Taiwan and Hong Kong are the biggest foreign investors in Vietnam. Up to early 1994, together they have proposed more than US$2.7 billion (total $6.8 billion) in 269 projects (of a total 787), and far outpaced the regional number one investor — Japan (*Financial Times*, 24 February 1994, p. 7).

Today, the Taiwan-China complementary trade is becoming much more significant, as both sides have gradually eased the decades-long political constraint on communication between their people. Although for political reasons trade is still indirect, most of it via Hong Kong, and the rest via Japan and Singapore, the competitive advantage for investors is attractive. Recently, Taiwan entrepreneurs have been focusing their investment to China in the Southeast coastal province of Fujian — Xiamen, due to kinship, the same dialect and geographical proximity (Xu Xinpeng, pp. 142-153; Tung, pp. 154-168; both in Klintworth, 1994). Indeed, Taiwanese businessmen recognize that kinship and the same dialect as Fujian residents are sometimes even more important than the short-term winning of a business contract given the longer term importance of establishing *guanxi* (personal relationships) in Chinese society, and of introducing management knowledge.

Nevertheless, Taiwanese investment is dependent upon market conditions, which means that investment is following Chinese economic indicators. Because the Beijing regime may change its policy after the communist old guards leave the scene, the uncertain political situation has cast some doubt on long-term investment. In addition, bureaucratic red tape, management problems and a shortage of raw materials has frustrated not only hundreds of manufacturers already operating there but also a great number of investors (Baum, 1990, p. 68). But in spite of some scepticism about the future, economic and even political contacts between Taiwan and China are still increasing steadily. According to a recent survey by the Chinese National Federation of Industries (Taipei), most of the sample of 300 Taiwanese companies operating in China expressed an optimistic view of further investment in the mainland (*Kun Sung Shi Pao* (Commercial Times), 29 September 1995, p. 13). Apart from increasing trade and investment figures, and the regular basis of the quasi-official talks between the Strait Exchange Foundation and the Association for Relations Across the Taiwan Straits, recently, the Taiwanese government has proposed a joint venture with Singapore to explore oil, natural gas, and tourism on China's Hainan Island (Dawson, 1994, p. 24).

In terms of economic development, what Taiwan is really short of is the high technology to upgrade its industrial high value-added products. With respect to technology, Taiwanese investment in the region is almost nothing to do with the procurement of technology. Rather, regional economic integration is much more concerned with production and market cooperation. In the sense of regional integration, Taiwanese economic development has been tied firmly to the regional countries through the export of direct investment, low- and middle-level technologies and manufacturing experience, and the import of raw materials and labour forces. One might expect the 'spillover' effect of regional integration to come in the scope of industrial cooperation and of policies concerned with this. In other words, their mutual interest will converge in international trade negotiations for the products concerned. For example, in early 1992, when the US Congress was seeking to link the annual renewal of China's Most Favoured Nation (MFN) trading status to fulfilment of US demands on human rights, missile proliferation, and trade practices as a way of disciplining China, Hong Kong and Taiwan feared that they might suffer a great loss. Therefore, both Taiwan and Hong Kong took action to urge 'the United States to maintain China's MFN status' (Harding, 1992, p. 22).

The Northeast China-Korea-Japan Triangle

Since South Korea's development is focused on large and heavy industry, this direction has resulted in its industry being characterized by rapidly changing comparative advantage, highly concentrated export markets prone to protectionist pressures, a high degree of industrial concentration, and a strong technological dependence on Japan (Leipziger, 1988, p. 126). South Korean industries have been through structural adjustment for a decade or so, and comparative advantage has shifted from traditional and labour-intensive industries (such as textile yarn and thread, cotton fabrics, wood manufactures, printed matter, sound recorders, and office supplies) to capital-intensive industries (such as ships, electrical equipment, metal products and iron and steel). Although this adjustment did enable some industries to survive international competition, South Korea like other ANICs is encountering a technological threshold which may not be easy to break through by national R & D spending.

South Korea's recent main industrial strategy has concentrated on moving it up the technology ladder (OECD, 1988, p. 37). In spite of having the highest spending in R & D among the ANICs and trying to reduce technology imports from Japan, South Korea is still heavily dependent upon Japanese technology (See Table 6.6). For instance, Samsung, the then biggest conglomerate in Korea and probably the biggest single non-Japanese electrical producer in Asia (*Business Week*, 27 January 1992), has suffered from the shortcoming of its core technologies i.e. sophisticated computer IT and semi-conductors. In addition, as South Korean industrial restructuring has changed the focus of its industrial activities to capital-intensive sectors, traditional overseas markets have been replaced by the developed markets of the EU and North America. To compete with these developed economies and other Asia-Pacific subregional economic groupings, South Korea's need to develop its technology ladder has increased its close relationship with Japan (*Korea Newsreview*, 19 February 1994).

157

Table 6.6

South Korea technology imports from Japan (US$ million)

	Amount	No.	Amount (%)	No. (%)
1962-80	168.3	1017	36.8	58.8
1985	35.4	108	25.2	50.2
1990	341.4	333	31.4	45.1
1991	372.5	277	31.5	46.8
1992	266.3	232	31.3	43.5

Source: From Korea Institute for International Economic Policy, *Korea Newsreview*, 19 February 1994, p. 16.

Whilst in recent years South Korean producers of light industrial goods have rushed to take advantage of China's cheap labour costs in order to extend industrial capacity and to survive international competition, big firms in the heavy and chemical industries have also been targeting China's huge domestic market by setting up sales bases (*Business Korea*, May 1993, p. 18). Part of South Korean industrial restructuring strategy has been to move home-based manufacturing sectors away from labour-intensive products, and enterprises have been steadily increasing investment in North East China (Shim Jae Hoon, 1993, p. 44). A common business interest has been brought about as a result.

Korea, like Japan, has also entered into China's domestic market, albeit less rapidly than Hong Kong and Taiwan but since the normalization of the Beijing-Seoul relationship in August 1992, the two-way trade has been increasing. The figures show that while its imports from China have steadily grown from US$3.4 billion to $3.9 billion, South Korea's exports to China have doubled in the same period from US$2.37 billion to $5 billion (Kun-Ha Yu, 1994, p. 26). In the degree of economic development, South Korea is playing the middleman role to Japan and China. The industrial focus of Japan (advanced technology), Korea (skilled and marketing experience) and China (low-cost production and manufacturing base) represent, respectively, three different development levels of a complementary economy which is conducive to their further economic cooperation.

It is clear that Seoul's rush towards China is not purely for business (*Business Week*, 11 April 1994, p. 19). Politically, South Korea's desire to strengthen its position against North Korea has served as a drive to develop relations with China. Seoul's political intention is in accordance with Beijing's policy which centres on maintaining peace and stability in the peninsula in order to assure a peaceful environment for China's development. A 'dual track' approach, which ties simultaneously to Pyongyang and Seoul, has become China's recent Korean policy. As far as economics is concerned, China's huge domestic market is attractive to Korean entrepreneurs. The rapidly growing Chinese economy helps

158

support the restructuring of the South Korean economy. China is now the most preferred country and has been the number one for investment by South Korean enterprises (Kun-Ha Yu, 1994, p. 36; *Beijing Review*, 2-8 January 1995, p. 37). With geographical proximity, ethnic connection, and historic links to Korea and Japan, Shandong and Liaodong Peninsulas as well as the area along the Yellow Sea, have become the main economic zones targeted by Korean and Japanese investment.

Therefore, South Korea has been increasing investment in, and cooperation with, China, as this cooperation will not only allow Korean industries access to the market and therefore improve their international competitiveness, but will also win Chinese assurance in regional security, by diminishing tension from any potential threat from North Korea. Targeting the China market potential, Hyundai Group has boosted its car sale from shipment to 714 units in 1992 worth US$9.5 million up to the first quarter of 1993 14,700 units worth US$148 million (Shim Jae Hoon, 1993, p. 46). Already, because South Korean heavy industrial companies have made investments in China (such as Daewood's cement factory in Shandong, Samsung Electronics' Video-Cassette Recorders (VCRs) assembly in Tianjin, and Goldstar's industrial water pipe plant), more small- and medium-sized firms are following suit (Paisley, 1992, p. 12). Further, although Japan's investment in China is behind Hong Kong, Taiwan, and the US due to its concerns about the high risk of investing in China, recently, some Japanese big firms (Toshiba, Sanyo, Canon, Sanyo-Nissho Iwai, Matsushita), perhaps reassured by Korean involvement, have poured in capital and technology to Dalian, a port for Liaodong Peninsula (*Business Week*, 14 March 1994, p. 22).

Through existing economic links, a new subregional grouping in Northeast Asia has emerged. The concept of Northeast Asian Economic Cooperation has included two economic development areas: the Yellow Sea Economic Zone combining South Korea, Japan, and the Chinese provinces of Liaoning and Shandong; and the Tumen River programme with China, two Koreas, Japan, Russia, and Mongolia (Guo Zhen Yuan, 1993; Manguno 1993). The Yellow Sea Economic Zone, as yet an academic sketch, has been characterized by complementary economic links between China-South Korea-Japan.

The Tumen River programme now envisioned under the United Nations Development Program (UNDP) has become attractive because it is also a complementary economic complex which will combine China, Russia, and North Korea's abundant natural resources and manpowers with South Korean and Japanese capital. Moreover, its enormous potential regional market 'could encompass nearly 300 million population, have a collective GNP of almost US$3 trillion, and account for nearly one-third of world trade' (Manguno, 1993, p. 7). Again, like other subregional economic groupings in East Asia, these two concepts to make up a Northeast Asian trade bloc as a whole, are driven mainly by academics and businessmen, and less by any governmental commitment (Guo Zhen Yuan, 1993, p. 172). However, most recently, South Korean President Kim has brought his vision of the Yellow Sea Economic Zone to China's leaders. As a result, both China and South Korea have agreed to cooperate in four key industries: autos, aerospace, telecommunication, and electronics (*Business Week*, 11 April 1994, p. 18).

Conclusion: the prospects for regional economic integration in the Asia-Pacific region

In terms of economic development, the growing economies of the ANICs, as a whole, are threatened by both low-cost producers in other developing countries and also developed countries' protectionism and pressure to open the ANICs domestic markets. Kim provides a detailed analysis of the restructuring of the ANICs (Kim, 1993). The challenges the ANICs have faced can therefore be generalized as 'exogenous industrial structural problems'. The export-led economies of the ANICs are very much vulnerable and sensitive to external challenges. In the context of the development of regional groupings for reinforcing competitiveness, the ANICs' efforts towards industrial restructuring have generated a momentum of regionalization upon which the formation of the Asia-Pacific subregional groupings has been based. Instead of being driven by political motivations, the emergence of Asia-Pacific subregional groupings has been driven by pressure from private sector interests. By contrast, the development of the Pan-Pacific or Asia-Pacific economic cooperation movement, has been characterized by more talking and theorizing than action. Regional groupings with high political profile have not, as yet, been fully accepted by countries of the region. Whilst President Clinton wished to move APEC towards becoming some sort of 'free trade vehicle' at the Seattle summit in November 1993, some Asian leaders remained suspicious of his motives (Walsh, 1993, p. 53).

The ANICs' structural problems, including the erosion of the comparative advantage of their products, and their shortcomings in advanced technology, have served as a drive to boost the possibility of forming subregional economic groupings. Projecting their economic strength in the region, the ANICs have taken practical action by way of increasing foreign direct investment in the region itself. The ANICs, since the mid-1980s, have undertaken an industrial restructuring process, and not only have regional economic structures been changed, but also more sophisticated subregional divisions of labour have been developed, as a result. Consequent to this industrial restructuring, subregional economic groupings have become the most effective way to further the economic development of each of the ANICs. This trend is very likely to continue, as regional economies have been intensifying their links with each other, and as regionalism elsewhere remains a head-on trade issue.

The Asia-Pacific subregional grouping does imply for the ANICs a need both to improve their competitiveness, and also the prospect of mutual benefits. The biggest part of the ANICs structural problems has been the shortage of labour and falling profit margins resulting from their rising production costs at home.

160

Subregional groupings have provided an extensive economic space to allow the ANICs to regain their competitive advantage by exchanging their economic development expertise. To a large extent, Asia-Pacific economic integration at the subregional level offers an effective means of overcoming labour shortages and of balancing differences in regional economic development.

Notes

1. In defining the NICs, the OECD's use is adapted here. The OECD (1979) categorized ten countries as NICs: Hong Kong, Singapore, South Korea, Taiwan (Asia), Mexico, and Brazil (America), Greece, Spain, Portugal, and Yugoslavia (Europe). Hereafter, 'the NICs' refers to only three Asian countries and one economy.

2. Richard Drobnick (1992, p. 15). The project was under the direction of Charles Oman and produced as part of the research programme on Globalization and Regionalization.

3. For detail see US Senate, 'Super 301: Effectiveness in Opening Foreign Markets', hearing before the subcommittee on international trade of the Committee of Finance, 101th Congress, second session, April 27, 1990.

4. 'Super 301', the centre of the Omnibus Trade Act of 1988, provides 'a mechanism through which U. S. trade negotiators can threaten the eventual imposition of special surcharges on a country's imports if that country does not agree to modify its 'unfair' trade practices (as unilaterally defined by the US), but gives the President great flexibility in determining whether or how far to apply the sanctions.' See Lawrence and Schultze (eds) (1990, p. 5).

5. For example, Shintaro Ishihara, a maverick Liberal Democratic Party member, said that 'Now it is time for us to say no sometimes and then make counter-proposals.' Ibid.

6. For details of recent trade rows between the US and Japan see reports 'Tough talk', *Business Week* (28 February, 1994, pp. 14-16); for Japanese response to the showdown see 'The Japanese are hardly heading for the bunkers', *Business Week* (28 February, 1994, pp. 17-19); and the reasons Japanese took tough stand towards the US see 'Saying no', *The Economist* (19 February, 1994, pp. 74, 77). See also Bollus et.al. (1995).

7. There have been various terms used, such as 'economic circle', 'economic zone', and 'triangle', but 'subregional grouping' is used here as a general term to be distinguished from Asia-Pacific regional economic cooperation.

8. In his contribution to China's economic cooperation network in Asian-Pacific region, Jin identified three basic economic circles based on China's coastal area. In stead of the CEA, he described the area covering Taiwan, Hong Kong, Fujien, and Guangdong provinces, as the Taiwan Straits Economic Circle (Huongfan Jin, 1990).

9. Although recently there have been different arguments about subregional groupings in East Asia, the category here is based on a Japanese work (Aoki and Ohashi, 1992).

10. In January 1980, the then Australian Prime Minister, Malcolm Fraser, and Japanese Prime Minister, M. Ohira, agreed to hold a non-governmental seminar to further explore the Pacific economic cooperation, which brought about the 'unofficial' PECC in Canberra seminar later that year. See Kitamura (1983, p. 160) and Soesatro, 'Institutional aspects of Pacific Economic Cooperation' (p. 24).

11. This intra-regional trade figure including cross-Pacific trade is more eminent than the figure for the intra-West Pacific trade. Compare the discussion in Low, 'East Asia Economic Grouping' (p. 379); and C. H. Kwan, 'The emerging pattern of trade and interdependence in the Pacific region' (pp. 139-41).

12. As China is currently undertaking great reform for its economic development, a peaceful and stable Korea Peninsula remains in China's best interest. For China and North Korea relations see Bridges (1986, pp. 68-72).

13. The official figure was calculated by the registration in the Ministry of Economic Affairs. Although the actual figure remains unclear, the Ministry suggested figure put it around 4,000 companies in US$3 billion. See K. L. Kao (1992), *Kuo ton kan ling yu lian an kuen si* (National Guidelines for Unification and the Relationships between two Sides of the Taiwan Strait), Mainland Affairs Council, Executive Yuan, Taipei.

14. The differentiated US policy towards East Asian economies was identified in a report 'US trade relations with Asia' of a staff study mission to Korea, Taiwan, Hong Kong, China, Thailand, Singapore, and Indonesia, to the Committee on Foreign Affairs, US House of Representatives, (November 30 to December 27, 1986).

15. The GSP is based on duty-free treatment on most manufacturing products from developing countries with the exception of textiles and some leather products. The continuing GSP treatment has been linked to the actual trade performance of each developing country, by products. When exports to the US exceed an absolute threshold related to US GNP (around US$57 million in 1989) or account for more than 50 per cent of all exports from developing countries of that product, the US will call off the GSP treatment in the following year. See Cooper (1989, p. 303).

16. Although Acer's rapid expansion in the late 1980s was responsible for draining out its profit margin, worldwide recession faltered its pace. See Goldstein (1990), p. 62. Returned from stagnation since early 1993, Acer's ambition to be one of the world's top five PC maker remains alive. See special interview to Acer's Chairman Shih, I. L. Yany, 'Hong Gi Ru Her Fan Bai Wei Shern' (How did Acer stage a comeback?), *Tien Shia* (Commonwealth), (1 August, 1993, pp. 104-109).

17. Each of the ANICs is building its own 'market sphere of influence' with geographical proximity linking their neighbouring economies together. In terms of economic development timing, the term 'vertical development' hence implies the economic relationship between each ANIC and their neighbours.

18. Li Hau, Chinese Communist Party secretary for the city of Shenzhen, proposed in November 1991 that to develop the city in current economic growth rate, in twenty years Shenzhen will be able to keep pace with Hong Kong and Singapore. See *Sing Tao Daily News* (23 November, 1992) and 'The fifth tiger is on China's coast', *Business Week* (6 April, 1992, pp. 22-24).

References

Aoki, and Ohasi (1992), 'Asia: Integration of the World's Most Dynamic Economies', *Tokyo Business Today*, June, pp. 26-29.

Asiaweek (1993), 'Year of the Blocs?', 13 January, pp. 41-45.

Awanohara, S. and Chanda, N. (1993), 'Uncommon Bonds?', *Far Eastern Economic Review*, 18 November, pp. 16-17.

Beijing Review (1995), 2-8 January, p. 37.

Baum, J. (1990), 'Second Thoughts', *Far Eastern Economic Review*, 1 November, pp. 68-70.

Bollus, A., Templeman, J.,Naughton, K. and Updike, E. (1995), 'Good deal? Yes. Great Deal? No.', *Business Week*, 10 July, pp. 32-34.

Branegan, J. (1993), 'And That's a Wrap', *Time*, 27 December, p. 30.

Bridges, B. (1986), *Korea and the West*, Routledge & Kegan Paul for the Royal Institute of International Affairs, London.

Burton, S. (1994), 'Growing By Leaps-and-Triangles', *Time*, 17 January, p. 24.

Business Korea (1993), 'A West-bound Gold Rush?', Vol. 10, No. 11, May, p. 18.

Business Week (1992), 'Samsung: Korea's Hope for High Tech', 27 January, pp. 22-24.

Business Week (1994a), 'A Golden Gate on the Yellow Sea', 14 March, p. 22.

Business Week (1994b),'South Korea Plays the China Card', 11 April, pp. 18-19.

Central Daily News, International Edition, Taipei (1994), 'Special Report', 13 March, p. 3.

Chen, E. K. Y. (1991), 'Foreign Direct Investment in East Asia', *Asian Development Review*, Vol. 11, No. 1, pp. 24-59.

Clark, W., Jr. (1993), 'The Asia-Pacific Area Needs a Stronger Sense of Community', Address to the Mid-America Committeee, Chicago, 4/12/1992, *ASEAN Economic Bulletin*, Vol. 9, No. 3, pp. 381-386.

Cooper, R. (1989), 'Trade policy as foreign policy', in Robert M. Stern, (ed.), *US Trade Policies in a Changing World Economy*, (Cambridge, Massachusetts: The MIT Press.

Dawson, M. (1994), 'The Taiwan Strait Never Seemed So Narrow', *Business Week*, 24 January, p. 24.

Drobnick, R. (1992), '*Economic Integration in the Pacific Region*', Technical Papers, No. 65, OECD Development Centre, Paris.

Drysdale, P. (1988), *International Economic Pluralism: Economic Policy in East Asia and the Pacific*, Columbia University Press, New York.

Elek, A. (1991), 'Asia-Pacific Economic Co-operation (APEC)', *South East Asia Affairs*, pp. 33-48.

Far Eastern Economic Review (1991), 'Computer Crash', 17 October, pp. 105-107.

Far Eastern Economic Review (1993), 'Taipei's Offshore Empire', 18 March, pp. 44-50.

Financial Times (1994), 'Asian Investors Lead the Way in Vietnam'', 24 February, p. 7.

Funabashi, T. (1993), 'The Asianization of Asia', *Foreign Affairs*, Vol. 72, No. 5, November/December, pp. 75-85.

Gibney, F.B. (1993), 'Creating a Pacific Community: A Time to Bolster Economic Institutions', *Foreign Affairs*, Vol. 72, No. 5, November/December, pp. 20-25.

Goldstein, C. (1990), 'Acer in the hole', *Far Eastern Economic Review*, 13 December, pp. 62-63.

Guo Zhen Yuan (1993), 'The Related Factors and Prospects for the Development of Northeast Asian Economic Cooperation', *The Korean Journal of International Studies*, Vol. 24, No. 2, Summer, pp. 171-183.

Hamilton, D. (1995), 'US Revisionists on Japan are Heard', *Asian Wall Street Journal*, 9-10 June, p. 1.

Hamilton, D. and Williams, M. (1995), 'Japanese Car Makers Pit Stamina Against Threatened US Tariffs', *Asian Wall Street Journal*, 12 June, p. 1.

Han, Sun-Taik (1992), *European Integration: The Impact on Asian Newly Industrializing Economies*, OECD, Paris.

Harding, H. (1992), 'The US and Greater China', *The China Business Review*, May-June, pp. 18-22.

Harland, B. (1993), 'Whither East Asia?', *The Pacific Review*, Vol. 6, No. 1.

Harris, S. (1991), 'Varieties of Pacific Economic Cooperation', *The Pacific Review*, Vol.4, No. 4, pp. .

Hoon, S.J. (1993), 'China Market Roars', *Far Eastern Economic Review*, 27 May, p. 44.

Hughes, H. (ed.)(1988), *Achieving Industrialisation in East Asia*, Cambridge University Press, New York.

Hughes, H. (1991)'Does APEC Make Sense?', *ASEAN Economic Bulletin*, Vol. 8, No. 2, pp. 125-136.

Jenkins, R. (1991), 'The Political Economy of Industrializing Countries: a Comparison of Latin American and East Asian Newly Industrializing Countries', *Development and Change*, No. 22, pp. 197-231.

Jia, Hao and Zhuang, Qubing (1992), 'China's Policy Toward the Korean Peninsula', *Asian Survey*, Vol. 32, No. 12, pp. 1137-1156.

Jin, Huongfan (1991), 'China's Open Door Policy and Asian-Pacific Economic Cooperation', *The Korean Journal of International Studies*, Vol. 22, No.1, Spring, pp. 125-147.

Kim, W. B. (1993), 'Industrial Restructuring and Regional Adjustment in Asian NIEs', *Environment and Planning A*, No. 25, pp. 27-46.

Kitamura, H. (1983), 'Asian-Pacific Economic Cooperation: the Role of Governments', in Soesatro, H. and Han, S-J (eds), *Pacific Economic Cooperation: the New Phase*, Centre for Strategic and International Studies, Jakarta.

Klintworth, G. (ed.) (1994), *Taiwan in the Asia-Pacific in the 1990s*, Allen & Unwin, Canberra.

Kojima, K. (1972), 'A Pacific Free Trade Area Proposed', *Pacific Community*, Vol. 3, No. 4, July, pp. 585-596.

Korea Newsreview (1991), 'APEC Announces Seoul Declaration', 23 November, pp. 4-5.

Korea Newsreview (1994), 'Technology Imports From Japan Dwindling', 19 February, pp. 16-17.

Kwan, C.H. (1991), 'The Emerging Pattern of Trade and Interdependence in the Pacific Region', *Tokyo Club Papers*, Vol. 4, No. 2, pp.139-141.

Lawrence, R. Z. and Schultze, C. L. (eds.), (1990), *An American Trade Strategy Options for the 1990s*, The Brookings Institute, Washington D. C.

Leipziger, D. M. (1988), 'Industrial Restructuring in Korea', *World Development*, Vol. 16, No. 1, pp. 121-135.

Linder, S. B. (1986), *The Pacific Century: Economic and Political Consequences of Asian-Pacific Dynamism*, Stanford University Press, Stanford, California.

Low, L. (1991), 'East Asia Economic grouping', *The Pacific Review*, Vol. 4, No. 4, pp. 375-382.

Manguno, J. P. (1993), 'A New Regional Trade Bloc in Northeast Asia?', *The China Business Review*, March-April, pp. 6-8.

OECD (1979), *The Impact of the Newly Industrializing Countries on Production and Trade in Manufactures*, OECD, Paris.

OECD (1988), *The Newly Industrializing Countries: Challenge and Opportunity for OECD Countries*, OECD, Paris.

Paisley, E. (1992), 'The Harvest to Come', *Far Eastern Economic Review*, 3 September, p. 12.

Palmer, N. D. (1992), *The New Regionalism in Asia and the Pacific*, Lexington Books, Lexington, Massachusetts.

Panic, M. (1988), *National Management of the International Economy*, Macmillan, London.

Salem, E. (1988), 'Twinned Hinterlands', *Far Eastern Economic Review*, 18 August, p. 77.

Soesatro, H. and Han, S-J (eds) (1983), *Pacific Economic Cooperation: the New Phase*, Centre for Strategic and International Studies, Jakarta.

Stern, R. (ed.) (1989), *US Trade Policies in a Changing World Economy*, The MIT Press, Cambridge, Massachusetts.

The Economist (1993), 18 December, pp. 13-14.

The Economist (1994), 'China. Taiwan and Hurt Feelings', 19 February, pp. 73-74.

Tiernan, R. (1992), 'Broadening Horizons of Asia Pacific Extend Opportunities for the West', *The Times*, 7 October, p. 28.

Time (1992), 13 January, p. 15.

Time (1993), 'The Stubborn Holdout', 22 November, p. 57.

Time (1994), 'Interview: South Korea's Kim Young Sam - Making a Plea for Patience', 28 March, p. 28.

US Senate (1990), '*Super 301: Effectiveness in Opening Foreign Markets*', hearing before the subcommittee on international trade of the Committee of Finance, 101st Congress, second session, 27 April.

Vatikiotis, M. (1990), 'Triangular Vision', *Far Eastern Economic Review*, 26 July, p. 15.

Vatikiotis, M. (1991), 'Search for a Hinterland', *Far Eastern Economic Review*, 3 January, p. 35.

Wang, Chien-nan and Hsu, Jui-ling (1992), 'The Impacts of European Integration on Taiwan and Taiwan's Responses', *Sino-European Conference on Economic Development: Impacts of the European integration and Responses of Non-EC Countries*, Chung-Hua Institution for Economic Research, Taipei, Taiwan, 6-7 May.

Wang, Kanmao (1992), 'The Pacific and the Global Economy', *The Pacific Review*, Vol. 5, No. 2, pp. .

Wijkman, P.M. and Lindstrom, E.S. (1989), 'Pacific Basin Integration: a Step Towards Freer Trade', in Nieuwenhuysen, J. (ed.), *Towards Freer Trade Between Nations*, Oxford University Press, Melbourne, Australia.

Walsh, J. (1993), 'Toward the Pacific Age', *Time*, 22 November, p. 53.

Woods, L. T. (1991), 'Non-governmental Organisations and Pacific Cooperation: Back to the Future?', *The Pacific Review*, Vol. 4, No. 4, pp. 312-321.

Yu, K-H. (1994), 'Korea-China Economic Ties Rise to New Peak', *Korea Newsreview*, 26 February, p. 26.

7 Pacific Asia as a region: A view from business

Cho-Oon Khong

Introduction: the liberalization revolution[1]

The extraordinary growth rates in the Gross Domestic Products (GDPs) of certain Asian nations catalyzed a dramatic shift in business interest and investment funds from the developed West to the developing East. The message for business companies was that their future, if not indeed their very survival, lay in the booming economies of the Pacific Rim, rather than the stagnating, or at best minimally expanding, markets of Western Europe. This message of the rising economic power of the Pacific Asia region has proved to be one of the most compelling themes of the present time, driving business strategies, shaping business policies, and challenging old ways of thinking about where business believes its fundamental interests lie.

While this furore over Asian growth has led many business companies to follow the herd in 'looking East', there is also a growing concern to understand the context of Asian growth, and to try to evaluate its substance over the excited hyperbole-ridden advocacy. The growth in Pacific Asia exists as part (albeit a critical part) of a world poised on the threshold of major revolutionary change. This *Weltanschauung* is premised on the belief that the collapse of the Soviet Union in the late 1980s was a defining moment, sending shockwaves right through the international system. But this collapse was only part of a much larger revolution of political and economic liberalization, which has since swept across the world. The message of this revolution was summarized by Fukuyama as 'the end of history' (Fukuyama, 1992). Authoritarian systems do not work. There is a democratic tide — Huntington's 'Third Wave' — unsettling Third World regimes, which we see in events such as the collapse of apartheid, and also moves towards privatization and free markets (Huntington, 1991).

However, continuing liberalization is not inevitable. This is a tremendously turbulent time. People may seize the opportunities; and if they succeed in initiating growth, they raise expectations in the wider society for more change, and thus for more liberalization. A positive feedback loop is set up. This archetypal future world may be characterized as one of expanding horizons and new frontiers, in which vast new, highly competitive markets open up. Change is rapid, but unsettling. The business environment is both exciting and unnerving. There is, however, another possible response. Liberalization threatens entrenched social interests, who may then seek to resist change. People reinforce the barriers between themselves, setting up a negative feedback loop. Development becomes inward-oriented in this archetypal future world, characterized by a 'barricades' mentality. Nevertheless, there would still be opportunities for business, provided it can home in on the market imperfections created by these barriers, tariffs and other protective devices.

Global liberalization therefore sparks off two quite separate possible reactions — one of expanding horizons, the other of contracting horizons — each of which feeds on and reinforces itself.[2] The problem for business lies in trying to see how this seemingly mutually exclusive dichotomy applies to perceptions of the Asian region. Of course, the real world cannot be expected to replicate exactly either one or the other archetypal response. Nevertheless, it seems reasonable to presume that a high growth region such as Pacific Asia will more closely approximate an expanding frontiers, new horizons world; while the closed mentality of a barricaded world would be equated with low growth regions in the Third World, resisting change and liberalization. In any case, the term 'barricades' begs the question: who is within the protective barrier, and who is kept outside?

Such seemingly straightforward thinking does not, however, generate a useful strategic debate on possible futures for business when applied to Pacific Asia. To begin with, people in the region are clearly imbued with an expanding frontiers motivation, a 'can do' philosophy which believes that anything is possible, so long as one tries. Yet Pacific Asia, despite being a hot growth stock, is riven — as a region, and also in so many individual countries — by a barricades mentality, in which business is conducted within an environment characterized by closed, communitarian, patriarchal societies, that is difficult for outside forces to penetrate. Even the labels themselves become confusing. 'New Frontiers' would presumably connote expanding horizons, open to innovation and new ideas — an Asian future driven by an explosion of political and economic liberalization, sweeping all before it. For example, the Japanese, in their current political realignments, appear to show an understanding of the label that is both much more complex and much less obvious. The recently formed New Frontiers Party purported to represent a clean break with the past. But it was set up by an old-fashioned power broker, Ichiro Ozawa, and led by a former Liberal Democratic Party politician of the old school, Toshiki Kaifu. The 'newness' had all to do with image, not substance. The lesson for observers of the Pacific Asia region is to avoid stereotyping. They are left with the uneasy surmise that openness to change does not provide a clear-cut yardstick to evaluate different societies, and that what

168

is presented as reform may in substance be its opposite. This uncertainty is symptomatic of a number of deep concerns which business has in trying to assess the significance of the phenomenon of growth in Pacific Asia.

The East Asian growth model

There is no consensus on what constitutes the Asian region, and no clearly understood concept of Asian growth. Our distinctive model of Asian growth was set by a handful of countries: Japan and the four Newly Industrializing Countries (NICs) of Singapore, Hong Kong, Taiwan and South Korea. Together, they encompass a population of just under 200 million, responsible for a Gross Domestic Product (Purchasing Power Parity adjusted) of well over US$3,900 billion. But what we call Asia is now much more. Indonesia, Malaysia and Thailand today claim to be valid growth models, treading the path laid down by the NICs. There is a massive transformation of scale as the big players come on board, with China and India both opening up to trade and investment. A host of other countries — notably Vietnam, Myanmar and the Philippines — together with areas such as the Russian Far East, have signalled their intention to follow suit, and the first sparks of economic growth have been registered. This is an Asian region of some 2,800 million people, with a Gross Domestic Product (Purchasing Power Parity adjusted) of almost US$9,000 billion. The potential for growth in Asia is enormous — and so, given the vast disparities in wealth across this huge region, are the corresponding uncertainties. There is a major question of whether the old growth model defined by Japan and the NICs can apply on this much expanded scale.

There is also no real understanding of how this old model actually worked in the first place. What were the ingredients responsible for growth? The recent World Bank study on the 'East Asian Miracle' observed: 'In some countries, in some instances, particular government interventions appear to have resulted in higher and more equal growth than otherwise would have occurred' (World Bank, 1993, p. 6). Similar policies, it concluded, if pursued elsewhere, could possibly be beneficial, though this was by no means certain. The World Bank study uncovered no single East Asian model. While some governments, such as South Korea, have been heavily interventionist, others, like Hong Kong, have tended to prefer a laissez faire approach. What caught the Bank's attention was the strong performance of East Asian countries in savings and investment, which it characterized as the economic fundamentals. But each country used a different mix of market incentives and state intervention to achieve its own particular results. Indeed, the mix even varies for each country across time, with a country like South Korea, for instance, only now beginning to see the merits of more liberal policies.

So, even in those countries whose practice defined the East Asian model, the ground is now shifting. Whichever way the old model worked in the past, it may well be becoming increasingly irrelevant in mapping out these countries' future experiences. In particular, the idea of state-directed capitalism may be part of the baggage that must be off-loaded. But to shed this baggage requires a radical redefinition of the role of the state. Japan may serve as an example. The conventional understanding of Japan's governing structure is based on the so-called 'Iron Triangle' between government bureaucrats, politicians and big business, with each group ingratiating itself with the others. Companies fund political factions; bureacrats practise *amakudari*, 'descending from heaven' into advisory positions in business. In Japan, Korea and Taiwan, this has become the distinctive East Asian model of state-directed capitalism (Amsden, 1989; Johnson, 1995; Wade, 1990). But this model has come under increasingly intolerable stress. Companies are under increasing pressure to widen pay differentials between employees and senior management. Consumers are increasingly less willing to subsidize inefficiencies in the old system. In Korea, Kim Young Sam has launched a globalization drive because Korean companies (in particular, the large *chaebols*) find that the competitive pressure of opening up global markets requires them to have the sort of international mind-set fostered by open liberal domestic markets. A signal of the new government attitude came in February 1995, when it allowed the Duksan Group, one of the smaller *chaebols*, to fall into bankruptcy. The *chaebols*, never particularly popular with the general public in Korea, are now very much on the defensive.

The East Asian growth model of Japan and the NICs is today poised on the verge of major change. But the question remains how these countries will forge a new path to growth. Will they manage to build change on the traditional strengths which have so effectively brought about growth in the past, or will their businesses become increasingly governed by the same criteria as their Western counterparts? For example, the Japanese 'Iron Triangle' may well succeed in reforming itself, and a new effective governing structure may emerge, which is rid of the inefficiencies and cartels of the past — or in the effort to reform itself, it may fail, rather in the manner of Karel van Wolferen's 'leaderless society' (Van Wolferen, 1990). For without effective direction, the ruling system may drift and the economy stagnate; and Japan may become to Pacific Asia what Argentina once was to Latin America. Or else, the Iron Triangle may succeed in resisting change seemingly imposed from the outside, and present interests may entrench themselves in the governing structure. The point is, we simply cannot tell how distinctive the Japanese model will remain in the future, given the present, enormous pressure for change.

East Asian values

Some East Asian leaders — led most notably by the Singaporean patriarch Lee Kuan Yew — claim to be evolving a Confucian model which is distinctively Asian, epitomized to the outside world by the Michael Fay case, where an American teenager convicted of vandalism by a Singaporean court was sentenced to corporal punishment: 'spare the rod and spoil the child'.

We have here a cultural definition of Asia-Pacific regionalism, to be understood as part of a process of region-building, just as nations invent national myths when building up their national identities. East Asian peoples (so it is argued) are somehow uniquely different to everyone else; they are better fitted to cope with the challenges of growth because they are not individualistic, they cling to groups, and they prefer to reach a consensus by avoiding open disagreement. Confucianism, thus interpreted, is now the fashionable defining characteristic of East Asian regionalism.

Of course the cultural context must have a fundamental impact, but this should not be taken as an invitation to make a crude dichotomy between exaggerated and mutually exclusive notions of conformist 'Asian' as opposed to individualistic 'Western' values. The Confucian political tradition is far too broad and rich to be so neatly characterized. Confucian teaching, for instance, does require a role for the criticism of authority. For example, the story is told of the irascible scholar Hai Rui, who took the precaution of buying his own coffin before criticizing the Emperor (fortunately he lived on for another twenty odd years). The moral of the story is that one is duty-bound to criticize the ruler, whatever the consequences. But this criticism is not a democratic right; it is an elitist prerogative incumbent on those people who uphold the government and whose criticisms are aimed at maintaining it. (Today, these people would be the bureaucrats rather than scholars) Thus, an action which fits readily into democratic liberal practice, as understood in the West, is seen in a qualitatively different light in Confucian culture.

How Confucian mores shape the day-to-day choices of ordinary people is even more relevant to determining their economic behaviour. This popular Confucianism is no more than an amalgam of residual, ethical beliefs and a bias towards particular practices, not necessarily amenable to rational analysis. Nevertheless, certain attitudes are prompted: the family is the focus of attention and close affections; education is respected; and public service honoured — although government is viewed with suspicion. There is a concern to keep some distance between one's family and the state, whose intentions cannot be fully trusted, and which has in the past been predatory. These are not attitudes which are instinctively authoritarian; they lend themselves to populism as well as participation.

In any event, the tremendous economic growth in the coastal provinces of Southern China has been achieved by people turning their backs on supposed traditional values and 'plunging into the sea of commerce' (the current Chinese buzz-phrase). East Asian values today are undergoing tremendous change, within a tightly compressed time frame. An equally striking phenomenon is the rise of religion. The activist, Christian sects burgeoning through Singapore, Hong Kong and Korea, together with the growth of new religions in Japan and the construction of new temples throughout the region, are signs of rapid change. As economic development forces East Asian societies to ineluctably leave their past behind, their peoples have become increasingly concerned to retain some point of reference to guide them into a challenging, hopefully rewarding, but nevertheless unknown and therefore uneasy future.

The advocacy of Confucianism by East Asian governments to define their regional identity becomes, in this environment, one among a host of competing anchor points for peoples' loyalties. The interpretation of Confucianism that is on offer is selective, and defined to justify certain forms of government rule, which are believed to be necessary to maintain order and stability against both internal and external pressures for change. The process of regional definition is similar to Benedict Anderson's view of nations as 'imagined communities' (Anderson, 1991). Certain people with particular interests decide that some relationships are important for their interests, and these relationships then become relevant to defining the regional community.

Not all East Asian governments, however, agree on the appropriate cultural model that can be regarded as genuinely Asian. The political discourse has pitted Lee Kuan Yew against Fidel Ramos of the Philippines, and Goh Chok Tong (the current Singaporean Prime Minister) against aspects of Taiwanese democracy — although Goh is not the most prominent critic of the current Taiwanese form of rule. Similarly, China has become increasingly concerned that democracy in Taiwan has enabled a resurgent populism to articulate expressions of Taiwanese self-identity and separation from China. In any event, the sweeping political changes in countries like Taiwan and South Korea have not given rise to a simple replication of Western democratic models. Change reflects the influence of Western practices, but the political traditions taking root, while democratic, are firmly based on indigenous modes of behaviour and traditional populist cultures. The question must remain open whether or not East Asian values are distinctive in the kind of authoritarian way that some of the region's governments claim them to be.

The sustainability of growth

Another issue of deep concern to Western business is the sustainability of East Asian development, particularly in the light of arguments over total factor productivity in Asia. Business planning should be premised on the belief that it is unwise to make simple straight-line extrapolations from existing trends. However, most current growth projections for East Asia are derived from extending the present high growth rates into the future. Paul Krugman has argued that such projections are infeasible. East Asian growth, in Krugman's view, has been achieved by throwing more and more inputs of labour and capital into the production process, not by squeezing more output from a given level of input (Krugman, 1994). The parallel Krugman draws is with the Soviet Union in the 1950s in which this pattern of growth led to diminishing returns over the long run, when there were no more surplus inputs to be drawn into the production process. East Asian growth will inevitably lose steam, since there is a limit to how many more resources can be squeezed out of the populations of a small economy, like that of Singapore. Likewise, Japan is a mature economy, with an increasingly elderly and dependent population, and China may well continue to grow respectably, but not spectacularly.

Krugman bases his arguments on research by Alwyn Young (1994) who carried out a cross-country comparison of factor productivity.[3] Young's data shows an outstandingly high level of growth of output per person (a measure of productivity growth per capita) in the populations of Japan and the four East Asian NICs, compared to the populations of Western developed countries. However, when growth of output is measured per worker in the active labour force (a measure of gains in labour productivity), the relative performance of the four East Asian NICs begins to slip, and is no different from a number of other developing countries elsewhere in the developing world (such as Egypt or Greece).[4] This difference between producing growth per capita and per worker would imply that output growth has been fuelled, in part, by engaging a higher proportion of the country's population in the wage economy — no more than a natural consequence of the early stages of economic development. And when growth in total factor productivity is compared (a measure of efficiency of production and technological change, which takes into account increasing inputs of capital as well as labour in the production process), the performance of the four East Asian NICs from 1966 to 1990 is distinctly poor when set against the performance of the established developed countries of Germany, Japan, the United States, the United Kingdom in their own periods of highest growth.[5] Indeed, Singapore registers a negative rate of growth in total factor productivity (-4.4 per cent), implying that overinvestment has brought about a contraction in output per unit of additional input.

Young's figures, in measuring such broad aggregates, are presumably not incontrovertible. Singapore continues to register high rates of economic growth, despite its negative change in total factor productivity. And Lester Thurow (1994) has argued that successful expanding economies must over-invest by conventional economic criteria, because the returns on investment accrue not immediately but over the long-term.[6] Indeed, we may note that increasing capital inputs in the production process requires a high level of domestic savings (a characteristic of all the East Asian NICs), in order to accumulate the capital for investment; and high saving and investment rates are conventionally regarded as important for economic growth. Also, generous depreciation allowances could lead to an overweighting of production inputs, with the payoff in terms of output coming later.

One other argument which suggests that the East Asian NICs may buck the trend decreed by Krugman is the intensification of Asia-Pacific regionalism, as intra-regional trade grows and production processes spread themselves across the different Asian countries. This synergy in Asia-Pacific regionalism may allow growth in the East Asian NICs to feed off the growth of other Asian countries further down the development ladder, as the latter open up. China and India have large quantities of spare resources which can be deployed, Krugman fashion, in the production process. Provided intra-regional barriers to trade and investment are lowered, then the growth of these large economies could help fuel growth in the wider Asian region.

Nevertheless, the argument over total factor productivity points clearly to the limitations of the East Asian growth model. As population sizes decline and labour participation rates peak, and as the limits to capital accumulation and investment are reached; and indeed may be pulled downwards, as Asians tend to consume more of what they produce; future economic growth in Asia will have to come from a more efficient organization of production, and especially from incorporating higher levels of technology into the production process — in other words, from total factor productivity. Promoting low value-added investment to gain international market share, and engaging in dirigiste interventionist policies to subsidize and to target investment, as a country like South Korea has done, will no longer be viable strategies for successful Asian governments to pursue.

Overseas Chinese networks

Another area of interest — indeed a major focus for Western business in looking at the Asian market — is how overseas Chinese business works. But why is this a concern in assessing Asia-Pacific regionalism? Our starting point is a recognition that there is indeed a growing regional identity in Pacific Asia. However, the 'glue' holding this regional identity together is not provided by institutional arrangements such as the Asia Pacific Economic Cooperation (APEC) or the Association of South East Asian Nations (ASEAN). These institutions do at the moment provide useful fora for discussions between the political leaders of different countries in the Pacific Asia region. But while they hold the promise of further growth to perhaps eventually match the formal structures, regulatory and policy-making powers of regional counterparts elsewhere, such as the European Union (EU), they do not as yet provide much more than an encouragement to the informal ties holding the region together.

Pacific Asia, as a region, is also riven by a very strong 'barriers' mentality. Thus China claims as its 'historic waters' (a different category of claim from

174

'territorial waters'), a large swathe of the South China Sea, almost up to the coastlines of Vietnam, Brunei, Malaysia and the Philippines. As these other littoral states stake out their interests, competing jurisdictional claims have led to tension and, on occasion, to hostilities. National boundaries, presumably, hinder rather than allow (never mind promote) regional integration. The key enabling characteristic of regionalism in Pacific Asia is neither institutional nor nation-state bound; it comes from a highly distinctive form of spontaneous integration by business, whose efforts are aimed at getting around the barriers imposed by the region's politics, and which pulls the reluctant politicians along in its wake. Asia-Pacific regional integration is market-led, not policy-led, and the catalyst in this process is the network of overseas Chinese communities, emanating from one small part of coastal Southern China, and linking the region together in a web of informal ties based on personal contacts. It is overseas Chinese business that is the primary source of the capital and foreign direct investment driving the economic growth in the region.

The Pacific Asia region is therefore defined as an economic network. The issue, however, is the direction of the causal relationship. In Europe, it is the politicians who are driving the integration process; but in Asia, it is the business. For example, the government of Taiwan is now having to address its banning of the *San Tong*, or 'Three Flows', with China: no direct transport, trade or postal links. And this reappraisal comes about because business is blatantly circumventing the ban. So, a transshipment centre is set up in Kaohsiung for goods from third countries going into China. The action bringing the region together is taking place elsewhere from its politics, and East Asian politicians are having to devise policies which respond to, rather than set the direction for, regional economic integration. However, these business linkages do not constitute the transnational network of Kenichi Ohmae's 'borderless world' (Ohmae, 1990). Networking is done not through the Internet, but rather through closely guarded, and intensely private, personal connections based on *shinyung* (trustworthiness). In this network of verbal agreements, foreigners are largely shut out. It is a 'barricades' response to a barricades environment. When business cannot rely on the legal and regulatory frameworks of the countries it operates in to govern its operations in a non-discriminatory manner, and to adjudicate impartially in contractual disputes, then business people have to rely on personal friends and their own family relationships. However, this barricade-determined activity appears to those outside the networks as a world of open liberalization because of its transnational characteristics.

Again, this is another defining characteristic of regionalism in Pacific Asia in the throes of major change. Overseas Chinese business today is carried out on a vastly expanded scale and now ties in, rather than excludes, the region's political elites, bringing in state-owned capital with political patronage to invest in conjunction with private overseas Chinese funds. There is intense pressure on overseas Chinese businesses to modernize and to open up, so that they can compete in global markets; and they also need to acquire high technology and to diffuse it within their organizational structures. Hence, increasing possibilities of linking in with the interests of Western firms may emerge, provided that these firms can bring in modern professional skills and technological knowledge, and provide access to Western developed country markets. This change can be mapped in the actions of individuals. When the Hong Kong entrepreneur Gordon Wu switches his investments in power plants from China to India, he is purely seeking a better return on his capital and a desire to diversify his investments, thereby avoiding over-exposure in any one market. His behaviour is one that outsiders can readily understand, as it conforms to conventional economic criteria. It appears more normal and open than the traditional overseas Chinese business stereotype, which might well prefer a less profitable business transaction within the network of personal contacts, to a more profitable one elsewhere (of course, balancing the higher cost against the greater feeling of security in dealing with a personally known contact).

Moreover, in defining the Pacific Asia region in terms of the network of economic relationships linking the countries along the Asia-Pacific Rim, we also imply that regional governments are not necessarily in charge of the regional integration efforts. A GDP growth rate of thirteen per cent in 1994 was too much of a good thing for the Chinese economy; but when Vice-Premier Zhu Rongji squeezed the deflationary brakes, the high growth regions in the coastal provinces of Southern China blithely carried on, shaking off the fiscal austerity measures emanating from the political centre. They could do so because the bulk of their investment funds comes not from Beijing, but from the secretive connections which they have established with overseas Chinese interests based across the border with Hong Kong. A bargain of convenience has been struck in China between the provinces, who have been given their head in terms of economic growth, and Beijing, that maintains a control which is at least in part nominal. This is a situation with many precedents in Chinese history.

Measuring Pacific Asia in terms of economic relationships also leads to a loss of focus. Pacific Asia does not form a closed economic bloc; its regionalism is open and outward-oriented. Businesses do not see their operations as region-bound. The overseas Chinese networks now stretch, as a matter of course, to California, Seattle and Vancouver, and even, in many instances, further afield. This Asian economic game is played on a global stage. Within Pacific Asia, there is a marked trend towards intra-regional trade, but the North American market still remains critically important for Asian export-manufacturing; and exports to North America continue to increase in absolute terms. Also, much of the intra-regional trade is of intermediate products, whose eventual destination, in their final form, is again North America. Indeed, for China, the region's fastest growing exporter, dependence on the US market is increasing at a dramatic rate: trade flows, which more or less kept in balance over the 1980s, have opened up a trade deficit in the bilateral relationship for China of US$6.4 billion in 1989, rapidly escalating to US$23.3 billion in 1993.[7]

Strategic considerations

Such economic links, as have been discussed, carry strategic implications. The United States is the lingering spectre haunting this Asian banquet. It is not a spectre about to be banished from the feast; indeed, all the diners would prefer it to remain. Yet, it is also the spectre of a hegemon in decline, impelled by growing isolationism at home and a feeling of being rebuffed abroad. There are a number of difficult political transitions to be worked through in East Asia. Kim Jong Il has yet to establish his rule in North Korea, the contenders for power are establishing their rival positions in Beijing, and the question remains as to how long Suharto intends to linger in Jakarta. Each of these transitions has the potential for destabilizing change, not just in the countries concerned, but throughout the region. Policy-makers in Pacific Asia are increasingly having to grapple with the difficult questions posed by change. They realize that the United States cannot be fully relied on to keep the peace in Asia after the Cold War, no matter what its public pronouncements may be to the opposite effect, and they do not fully trust any of the other candidates for hegemonic office from within the region. Pacific Asia is defined in economic terms within the region and without. Every player in this game has an increasing economic stake in Asian stability, but the political commitment to Asian regionalism is as yet fragile: either absent, wavering or suspicious. It is this political lacuna which makes the long-term future of regionalism in Pacific Asia so unclear.

Suspicion over political motives leads to concern over a potential arms race in the region. Here the conventional view is that defence spending has increased in Asia, though not dramatically (it has declined in Vietnam). However, the value of East Asian arms imports has actually fallen off in recent years.[8] The figures for defence spending and arms transfers may be suspect. Russia, for instance, is coming to prominence as a major supplier of value-for-money arms from its former Soviet arsenal. Nevertheless, taking the figures at face value, if spending is up but arms imports are down, these trends suggest the establishment of indigenous arms industries in many Asian countries. These arms industries may not yet have reached the technological sophistication of Japan (which has recently unveiled its latest FSX fighter aircraft, based on the United States F16), but the higher the proportion of weapons that can be locally sourced, the more uncertain will the regional politics become.

We need to be concerned about whether or not an Asian military build-up can be contained, or at least controlled, given the growing independence of domestic arms sourcing. Questions are also raised over the development of countries like Taiwan and South Korea, as they face an increasingly uncertain international

177

environment, with increasingly rickety support from their United States patron. Will they feel impelled to pump even more funds into their arms industries, thus diverting resources away from economic growth?

On strategic issues, the only possible approach to take in assessing future Asian growth is to temper optimism with caution. Economics cannot be separated from political or strategic considerations. Pacific Asia, like the rest of the world, is in a period of transition; it is still groping towards a new, post-Cold War order. The old assumption of a stable pattern of bipolar allegiances no longer holds, but has not been replaced. In this complex strategic environment, each country decides its own policies on a calculation of costs and benefits to itself. The desire for economic growth that Asian countries share in common may prove inadequate to preserve the peace. Indeed, the Mischief Reef incident, in which China built four structures on a reef within the Philippines' 200 nautical mile exclusive economic zone in the South China Sea, makes the point (Walker, 1995). An economically resurgent China open to the outside world and driving economic growth in the wider Asia region will also be a China increasingly confident and assertive in pressing its sovereign claims to the full and demanding due deference from the rest of Asia. A stable, prosperous China domestically is not incompatible with a nationally assertive, potentially destabilizing Chinese posture abroad.

A pattern of Asia-Pacific regionalism

The concerns of business that we have identified are no more than straws in the wind when thinking about the future of Pacific Asia. On the one hand, globalization is not the same thing as liberalization. Much of state industrial policy in the NICs is globally focused, but not liberal. On the other hand, the efforts of the United States to push Japan and China to liberalize, by opening up their markets, is characterized by a bilateral, and hence anti-globalizing, approach. We need to find some way to combine the idea of globalization with the idea of a strong nation-state. Indeed, the boundaries of the international system are increasingly blurred. Singapore, for example, has a strong government committed to modernization. A subnational player like Guangdong or Fujian province can interact with multilateral agencies and other non-government organizations in ways which undermine the effectiveness of central government power. Such a system has no locus of final authority, and its structure is highly complex and difficult to delineate.

Another argument to consider, in mapping the pattern of regionalism in Pacific Asia, is that the choice between liberalization leading to expanding horizons, as against resistance to change, poses a false dichotomy, especially when looking at alternative futures for Asia. Rather than attempt to draw alternative archetypes for how the regional picture might eventually turn out, we need to ask what is the nature of change, and what is the growth dynamic in Pacific Asia? Is the choice between opening up or resisting change a useful characterization, not of alternative end points, but of alternative processes of change? Perhaps then, instead of dichotomy, we have a mutual dependence, rather in the nature of Yin and Yang. The Pacific Asia region may have a liberal open structure, but it is driven internally by closed, barricades-type processes. Alternatively, we could characterize regional change in Pacific Asia as a defensive structure, which is motivated by a liberal dynamism. Opposites need not necessarily be antagonistic; they can co-exist with each other. Both expanding horizons and an exclusive identity, feeding off each other, may be the critical drivers of Asia-Pacific regionalism.

Notes

1. The author of this chapter is writing in his personal capacity, and expressing his own personal views.
2. This is the characterization given in Shell (1992).
3. The subsequent figures were calculated from the Alwyn Young data.
4. The average growth of output per worker per annum over the period 1960 to 1985 was 5.5 per cent for Taiwan, 5.0 per cent for South Korea, 4.3 per cent for Singapore, 5.3 per cent for Egypt and 4.7 per cent for Greece.
5. Over the relevant periods indicated for each country, total factor productivity contributed 11.1 per cent of South Korean growth, 20 per cent of Taiwanese growth, 30 per cent of growth in Hong Kong, 44.9 per cent of West German growth and 28.9 per cent of growth in Japan.
6. Lester Thurow, 'The Plate Tectonics of Capitalism', three public lectures given at the London School of Economics and Political Science, 31 January, and 1 and 2 February, 1995. Directing resources towards investment is also a major theme of Thurow (1994).
7. Source: United States Department of Commerce.
8. Source: *Strategic Survey* published annually by the International Institute for Strategic Studies, London.

References

Amsden, A. (1989), *Asia's Next Giant: South Korea and Late Industrialization*, Oxford University Press, New York.

Anderson, B. (1991), *Imagined Communities*, Verso, London.

Fukuyama, F. (1992), *The End of History and the Last Man*, Hamish Hamilton, London.

Huntington, S.P. (1991), *The Third Wave: Democratization in the Late Twentieth Century*, University of Oklahoma Press, Norman.

Johnson, C. (1995), *Japan: Who Governs? The Rise of the Developmental State*, W.W. Norton, New York.

Krugman, P. (1994), 'The Myth of Asia's Miracle', *Foreign Affairs*, vol. 73, no. 6, November-December, pp. 62-78.

Ohmae, K. (1990), *The Borderless World: Power and Strategy in the Interlinked Economy*, Collins, London.

Shell (1992), *Global Scenarios 1992-2020*, Shell International Petroleum Company, London.

Thurow, L. (1994), *Head to Head: The Coming Economic Battle Among Japan, Europe and America*, Nicholas Brealey, London.

Van Wolferen, K. (1990), *The Enigma of Japanese Power*, Vintage Books, New York.

Wade, R. (1990), *Governing the Market: Economic Theory and the Role of Government in East Asian Industrialization*, Princeton University Press, Princeton, NJ.

Walker, T. (1995), 'The Waters Beyond Mischief Reef', *Financial Times*, 15 March, p. 23.

World Bank (1993), *The East Asian Miracle: Economic Growth and Public Policy*, Oxford University Press, Oxford.

Young, A. (1994), 'Lessons from the East Asian NICs: A Contrarian View', *European Economic Review*, vol. 38, pp. 964-73.

8 Burma: Prospects for regional integration

John Bray

Burma[1] exemplifies both of the main themes in this book: the fear of political fragmentation at the national level, combined with increasing pressure for greater economic and political integration at the regional level.

The first theme, the search for national unity, has been a constant leitmotif of Burmese politics since independence in 1948. The search is complicated by the country's wide ethnic diversity. The Karen insurgency began within a year of independence and has continued ever since. Similarly, Kachin, Shan and an array of other minority groups have been at war with the central government for much of the period since the 1960s. In recent years fifteen groups have signed ceasefire agreements with the central government, but there has as yet been no sustained attempt to resolve the political problems which led to ethnic insurrection in the first place.

The second theme, the trend towards regional integration, is a more recent development. Burma has long had a tradition of isolationism, and Gen Ne Win built on it when he established his 'Burmese Path to Socialism' between 1962 and 1988. During this period Burma minimised external economic contacts and eschewed regional groupings. However, since 1988 the ruling State Law and Order Restoration Council (SLORC) has introduced a policy of economic liberalization, including the legalization of cross-border trade with the country's neighbours and the promotion of foreign investment. SLORC is currently trying to build up its external political relationships, especially with China and the Asociation of South East Asian Nations (ASEAN) countries.

There is therefore no doubt that Burma's integration — or re-integration — with East and Southeast Asia is already taking place. The outstanding questions concern the pace and beneficiaries of this integration. Will Burma's increased exposure to the outside world act as a force for renewal, or will it lead to further national fragmentation?

This chapter has two main sections. The first discusses the three main factors which influence Burma's search for national unity: the constitutional debate, the role of the ethnic minorities, and the economic environment. The second section examines the implications for Burma's developing relationship with its neighbours and the wider international community. The chapter concludes with an assessment of the prospects for both national unity and regional integration.

The search for national unity

The constitutional debate

The central issue in the Burmese national debate is a dispute over the army's political role. SLORC claims to be leading a transitional government, but insists that the army must continue to play a decisive role in any future administration, even if the country's official leaders are civilians. By contrast the opposition, led by Nobel Peace Prize laureate Aung San Suu Kyi, insists on the unqualified primacy of democratically elected civilian leaders. Burma will not be able to achieve either unity or stability until the dispute is resolved.

SLORC is entirely made up of military officers. It defines its three aims as the non-disintegration of the Union, the non-disintegration of national solidarity, and the consolidation of national sovereignty. The army claims that it is specially qualified to achieve these aims because of its part in the independence struggle, and in the preservation of national unity since then.

The army's founder was Aung San (the father of Aung San Suu Kyi): he led a group of 'Thirty Comrades' who went to Japan for military training in 1941. After the Japanese conquest of Burma the following year, Aung San served as Defence Minister in the Japanese-backed 'independent' government in Rangoon. Aung San turned against Tokyo when the new government's independence proved to be no more than nominal. He lent his support to the British campaign to expel the Japanese and subsequently led independence negotiations with London. However, he was assassinated in July 1947, six months before the British finally left. His place was taken by U Nu, who became the first Prime Minister of independent Burma.

The newly independent government soon found itself fighting a desperate campaign against both Karen and communist insurgents. At one point the Karen came close to taking Rangoon. In the 1950s Burma achieved a fragile equilibrium, although stability was undermined by political factionalism in Rangoon, and by continuing insurgencies in the border areas. However, in 1962 Gen Ne Win deposed U Nu's civilian administration — ostensibly to prevent him introducing policies which might have split the country — and the army has dominated Burmese politics ever since.

182

The next major turning point in Burmese politics came in 1988. In July, Ne Win formally resigned from his last official position as chairman of the ruling Burma Socialist Programme Party (BSPP), although he continued to influence the administration behind the scenes. In August and September, thousands of people took to the streets in Rangoon and other towns to demand comprehensive democratic reforms. The army responded brutally: at least 5,000 people were killed in a series of massacres across the country (see Lintner, 1989). Ordinary soldiers were told that the demonstrators were communists bent on destroying the country. In September 1988 SLORC seized power.

SLORC represented continuity in that all its members had held senior positions in the previous regime and were personally loyal to Ne Win. However, it espoused a different political strategy. It abolished the BSPP and legalized opposition groups, pending national elections. SLORC insisted that it would in due course hand over power to a new civilian administration, but it has never given a firm timetable for the transfer of power.

In May 1990 the government held national parliamentary elections. SLORC may have hoped that the opposition would be divided and that the National Unity Party (NUP), the successor to the BSPP, would gain sufficient seats to lead a compliant civilian government. In the event, Aung San Suu Kyi's National League for Democracy (NLD) won 392 out of the 485 seats, even though she herself was under house arrest. By contrast, the NUP won only ten seats. SLORC nonetheless continued in office, in effect treating the elections as a referendum whose results it was free to ignore.

In early 1993 SLORC launched a different strategy by inaugurating a National Convention to draw up the guiding principles of a new constitution. The Convention's 702 members include 156 elected MPs, but they are outnumbered by selected representatives of professional and ethnic minority groups — all of whom had been appointed by SLORC (Diller, 1994). The Convention's deliberations have continued intermittently ever since, but the debate has been carefully controlled. For example, the participants are not permitted to hold separate meetings outside formal sessions of the Convention.

Among other resolutions, the Convention has recommended that a quarter of the seats in the 440-seat lower chamber of parliament and the 224-seat upper house should be reserved for serving members of the armed forces. Similarly, the army would expect to control the defence, security/home affairs and border affairs portfolios, while the President should have had some form of military experience. These proposals may have been inspired by Indonesia, where the armed forces are allocated a quarter of the seats in the People's Consultative Assembly (which elects the President every five years), and serving officers sit in the House of Representatives as of right. Whatever the source of its ideas, the National Convention has little credibility either within Burma or abroad because its debates are so tightly controlled.

The Burmese political leader with the greatest claim to popular legitimacy is Aung San Suu Kyi. As noted above, she is the daughter of Burma's main independence leader, but has spent much of her career abroad and is married to an English academic, Michael Aris. In 1988, she returned to Burma to look after her sick mother, and — partly out of a sense of family duty — became caught up in that year's pro-democracy demonstrations.

Aung San Suu Kyi points out that her father founded the army and claims to have a special affection for it, but insists on the primacy of elected civilian leaders (Aung San Suu Kyi, 1991, 1994). Perhaps partly because of her long residence abroad, she has proved much more outspoken than other political leaders. This quality helped build up her support, but her criticisms of Ne Win reinforced the regime's hostility. In July 1989, she was placed under house arrest, and remained there for six years despite her party's victory in the 1990 elections.

According to SLORC's own calculations, the legal justification for Aung San Suu Kyi's detention was due to expire in July 1995 and — somewhat to the surprise of most international observers — she was released on 10 July. International pressures almost certainly played a role in persuading SLORC to make this move. Japan had been following a policy of 'quiet diplomacy', involving a partial resumption of aid with the promise of more to come if she were released. In the US, Republican Senator Mitch McConnell was planning to introduce a bill calling for economic sanctions against Burma unless it introduced political reforms. A further factor may have been the ASEAN Minister's Meeting which was due to take place in Brunei in late July. Foreign Minister Ohn Gyaw intended to attend the meeting as a guest of the host government, with a view to strengthening Burma's links with ASEAN. SLORC no doubt hoped that Aung San Suu Kyi's release would improve its international standing both in Asia and in the West.

However, internal political considerations would have been paramount in SLORC's calculations. It evidently judged that it was sufficiently well-entrenched to weather any resurgence of opposition activity following Aung San Suu Kyi's release. It may also have hoped that economic growth and new opportunities for personal enrichment would have diverted the energies of ordinary Burmese away from politics. Aung San Suu Kyi herself expressed cautious optimism. She re-iterated her affection for the armed forces and said that she was prepared to work with them, but again emphasized the need for genuine political dialogue. Her own release was no more than the first step.

Prospects for future dialogue In the month following her release, SLORC gave no indication that it intended to take up the possibilities for dialogue. It emphasized that Aung San Suu Kyi had the rights of an 'ordinary citizen', but implied that it did not recognize her claim to represent any particular political constituency. On 8 July, shortly before her release, the official *New Light of Myanmar* newspaper ran a lengthy article hinting that her marriage to a foreign citizen implied some sort of conspiracy against Burma's national interests. The official line is that her foreign connections disqualify her from playing a political role in Burma. It is doubtful whether this assertion carries any credibility among ordinary Burmese. It is well known that SLORC offered to release Aung San Suu Kyi if she would leave the country. Her refusal to accept this offer demonstrated her commitment to Burma.

The failure to resolve the dispute over Burma's constitutional future will make it more difficult to address other critical questions such as the relationship between the centre and regions dominated by ethnic minorities.

Ethnic minorities

The minorities between them make up some thirty-five per cent of Burma's total population of some forty-five million (this is a rough estimate: there has been no plausible census since 1931). Whereas the majority Burman population is concentrated in the lowland central regions, most of the minorities are scattered in the highland frontier areas. Burma's political frontiers do not coincide with ethnic boundaries. For example, there are Karen and Mon in Thailand; Kachin in China; and Nagas and Chin/Mizo in India. Political controversies surrounding the minorities therefore impinge both on Burma's national politics and on its relations with its neighbours.

As noted above, the Karen rebellion began in 1948 (see Bray, 1992a; Lintner 1994a; Smith 1991). Other insurgencies followed and by the 1970s there were active guerrilla groups among the Karen, the Mon, the Kachin, the Shan, the Karenni, the Pao, the Palaung, the Rohingya and the Naga peoples. In 1976, the Karen National Union (KNU) and the Kachin Independence Organisation (KIO) helped form the National Democratic Front (NDF) to act as an umbrella group loosely uniting the main factions. Rebel groups outside the NDF included Khun Sa's Shan United Army (SUA, now known as the Mong Tai Army — MTA), the Communist Party of Burma (CPB) and some small Rohingya Muslim groups in Arakan state. In November 1988. the NDF joined with Burman opposition groups, notably the All Burmese Students' Democratic Front (ABSDF), to form the Democratic Alliance of Burma (DAB).

Until 1989, the government's military campaigns seemed to fall into a regular pattern of dry season offensives followed by retreats during the rains. However, in that year the CPB collapsed. With 15,000 guerrillas under arms, the CPB was once the most powerful guerrilla group, but it had been weakened by a severe cut-back in Chinese support and some elements within it had resorted to drug running as a source of finance (see Lintner, 1990). The final blow came from within its own ranks. The majority of the CPB's leaders were ethnic Burmans, but most of the rank and file belonged to ethnic minorities, notably the Wa. They came to feel that they were being used as cannon-fodder in someone else's war and therefore mutinied. The result was the emergence of a set of new groups, notably the United Wa State Party (UWSP) and the Myanmar National Democratic Alliance Army (MNDAA), which has a support base among the Kokang Chinese (the Kokang Chinese are indigenous to north-eastern Burma). SLORC succeeded in negotiating ceasefire agreements with these groups.

Under the terms of the ceasefires the UWSP and the MNDAA were allowed to keep their weapons and maintain a high degree of local autonomy in return for promises not to attack government forces. The privileges of local autonomy have included the continued production of opium for the international narcotics trade. From SLORC's point of view, the main benefit was that it was able to concentrate its military resources elsewhere, notably in the Karen region in the east.

The ceasefires with the former CPB factions set the pattern for similar negotiations with other insurgent groups, and by mid-1995 the government had agreed to ceasefires with a total of fifteen organisations.[2] The most important of these was the Kachin Independence Organisation (KIO) whose armed wing had some 5-6,000 guerrillas in northern Burma. The factors which encouraged the KIO to seek a ceasefire included: war-weariness among ordinary Kachin; the judgement that there was little hope of external assistance for the minorities; and the hope that the Kachin would be able to share in new economic opportunities arising from the growing border trade with China.

However, several groups remained at war with Rangoon in mid-1995, notably the Karen National Union (KNU) on the country's eastern border with Thailand. The KNU is the longest-lasting guerrilla group, but since late 1994 it has suffered a series of major setbacks. Many of its senior leaders are Christians, and in December a faction of Buddhist Karen broke away to form their own group, the Democratic Kayin Buddhist Organisation (DKBO). In January 1995, government troops acting with DKBO assistance captured the KNU headquarters at Manerplaw, and the last remaining major Karen base at Kawmoora fell a month later. Some 30,000 refugees fled into Thailand adding to the 100,000 already in the country. These setbacks forced the KNU to consider a change of strategy. Some sections of KNU opinion are believed to favour negotiations with Rangoon, but by August 1995 there had been no sign of progress in this direction.

Other groups still at war include the ABSDF, a handful of smaller Rohingya groups and Khun Sa's MTA, which has acquired international notoriety because of its role in the international drugs trade. In 1994 and the first half of 1995, the government launched a series of offensives against Khun Sa. One of its motives may have been the hope that it would win Western plaudits for attacking the drugs trade. If so, it was unsuccessful: Khun Sa remains one of the most wanted men of the US Drug Enforcement Agency (DEA), but most of Burma's opium crop is produced to the north of his territory. He continues to deal in narcotics but new export routes have emerged via China and India, and Khun Sa is no longer as pivotal in the drugs trade as he may once have been. His army lost ground as a result of the government offensive but remains well-entrenched.

Meanwhile, there has been a fresh outbreak of fighting in Kayah state. The Karenni National Progressive Party (KNPP) signed a ceasefire agreement in March 1995, but fighting broke out again in late June. It appears that one of the underlying causes of the fighting may have been a struggle for the control of the local logging trade. Whatever the cause, the breakdown of the KNPP ceasefire underlines the potential fragility of other ceasefire agreements.

Ethnic minorities and the future The most critical question for the future is whether the ceasefires can lead to a permanent political settlement. In this respect, progress has been limited. The Kachin hoped that their ceasefire would lead to substantive negotiations which ultimately would involve all the minorities, but so far there is little sign of this happening. The National Convention has made proposals for limited devolution, but the Convention lacks credibility and none of its proposals will stand without military backing. In December 1994, the Wa and the Kachin formed an alliance known as the People's Democratic Front (PDF) to press for swifter progress towards a political settlement. When discussing this issue, Kachin spokesmen take a long view. They are prepared to move slowly provided that they are at least moving forward, but their underlying tone is one of frustration.

The ceasefires have benefitted thousands of ordinary people previously caught up in fighting. They have been able to begin reconstructing their local economies, and take advantage of the new opportunities from the expansion of trade with neighbouring countries. Much of this is happening independently of Rangoon. If present trends continue, the most likely scenario is the consolidation of semi-autonomous regional power centres. The minorities are unlikely to revive their demands for outright independence, and Burma will avoid outright political fragmentation. However, the central government's influence over the border areas will become increasingly tenuous as they enter the economic orbit of neighbouring countries.

Economic pressures

The economic changes which have taken place in Burma since 1988 are in many respects more far-reaching than the political ones. Overall, Burma lags far behind its ASEAN neighbours but economic liberalization has opened up new opportunities for the future. At the same time, recent developments are widening social disparities to a degree unprecedented in the country's previous history. Current economic developments impinge both on the question of national unity and on Burma's re-integration with its neighbours.

Burma's inheritance Burma is rich in natural resources and, as many commentators point out, has the potential to be one of the richest countries in Southeast Asia. Until the Second World War its economic achievements surpassed those of Thailand, a neighbouring country of comparable size. However, in the last thirty years it has sunk to the status of an economic backwater. This is the legacy of Ne Win's Burmese Path to Socialism.

The first aspect of this legacy is sheer neglect. The country's transport and communications infrastructure is in disarray. Hospitals are short of basic facilities, often including medicines, and the educational system has declined. Among the reasons for this neglect was the high level of defence expenditure: no reliable figures are available, but it almost certainly amounted to at least fifty per cent of the government budget.

State Economic Enterprises (SEEs) absorbed two thirds of public investment as well as some sixty-two per cent of foreign aid between 1978 and 1988 (Tin Maung Maung Than, 1994), but their performance was similar to their equivalents in Eastern Europe. Factories typically were poorly managed, operated at levels far below their capacity, and produced second- or third-rate goods. In the countryside, farmers were forced to sell a large proportion of their crop to the state at fixed prices, and this removed the incentive to increase production.

SLORC's economic reforms   Since 1988, the government has introduced a series of reforms, as much out of necessity as conviction. It has lifted restrictions on private business; legalised cross-border trade with neighbouring countries; and introduced a foreign investment law which — on paper — compares favourably with many other countries. However, the process remains incomplete. The most important deficiency — at least from an international point of view — is the government's failure to rationalize exchange rates. The official exchange rate is some six kyat to the US dollar: the unofficial rate, which reflects the currency's market value, is 100-120 kyat to the dollar. At the same time, high levels of military spending continue to distort the economy, and the banking system remains rudimentary.

If Burma is to resolve its economic problems, it will require external sources of finance. Most countries suspended aid in 1988 and have yet to resume it. SLORC has therefore turned to the private sector as a source of foreign exchange.

The legalization of the cross-border trade with neighbouring countries has brought immediate benefits. For example, Burma's trade with China is now estimated to be worth US$800 million or even US$1 billion a year. Trade with Thailand and, to a lesser extent, India and Bangladesh has also expanded. However, the artificial exchange rate means that importers often have difficulty getting paid unless they are prepared to arrange payment in Burmese goods such as rice, pulses or timber.

At the same time there has been growing interest in foreign investment. The most promising prospect has been offshore gas. Unocal (US) and Total (France) are jointly developing the Yadana offshore gas-field. Gas reserves in the field are estimated at some 5.8 trillion cubic feet, and total investment is expected to reach some US$1 billion (Buckman, 1995). In February 1995, the consortium signed a formal agreement to export gas to the Petroleum Authority of Thailand (PTT), which requires it for a 2,100 MW power station at Ratchaburi on the Gulf of Thailand. The gas will be exported by pipeline. A second consortium, consisting of Premier (UK), Texaco (US) and Nippon Oil (Japan), is developing the neighbouring Yetagun field.

Hotels and tourism make up the second main area of foreign investment interest. The government has designated 1996 as 'Visit Myanmar Year'. It hopes to attract 500,000 tourists in that year, compared with 21,600 in 1993-94. Singaporean companies have invested in eight hotel projects; Thailand in five; and Hong Kong and the United Kingdom have two each. The other key foreign investment sectors are forestry and fishing (where Thai companies have been particularly prominent) and light manufacturing (an area of particular interest to East Asian companies). The country's mineral potential means that there is great interest in mining, although the lack of political stability has so far discouraged major long-term investments.

Economic outlook   The benefits of economic reform are most apparent in the cities — particularly Rangoon, Mandalay and, to a lesser extent, provincial centres such as Taunggyi. New buildings are being constructed; roads have been widened; imported electronic goods are widely available; and exotic fashions such as *karaoke* bars are gaining popularity among the new rich.

This prosperity would appear to be confirmed by growth figures. After a period of contraction, the economy reportedly grew by 10.9 per cent in 1992-93, and by 5.8 per cent in 1993-94. As with all Burmese statistics, these figures must be treated with some caution. Even if they are valid, the economy is only now returning to the levels of the mid-1980s. Inflation rates remain high and aid officials report that social indicators — of literacy, child mortality and so on — are disquieting.

In the next two to three years the Burmese economy will continue to grow, but from a low base. Widening inequalities are a particular source of concern, and Burma will continue to lag far behind its ASEAN neighbours.

Burma's Asian neighbours

Burma has faced fierce criticism from the West, particularly the US, on account of its record of human rights abuses (see, inter alia, Bray, 1992b, 1995; *Human Rights Watch/Asia* 1995). Washington welcomed the release of Aung San Suu Kyi in July 1995, but on 31 July Senator Mitch McConnell, a Republican from Kentucky, introduced a bill calling for unilateral economic sanctions against Burma. The proposed 1995 'Free Burma Act' called for a ban on US trade, investment and tourist traffic to Burma, unless the President could certify that the government of Burma had released all political prisoners, fully implemented the results of the 1990 elections and implemented an effective narcotics eradication and control regime. The US administration called for further reforms in Rangoon but opposes sanctions, arguing that they would be ineffective without the participation of China and ASEAN. In September 1995 McConnell withdrew his bill.

By contrast, Burma's Asian neighbours have tended to be more pragmatic in their relations with Rangoon. There have been two main reasons for this. The first is economic: as noted above, Burma has a justified reputation as a country rich in economic resources whose potential has scarcely been tapped. The second is strategic: by culture and geography Burma belongs most naturally to Southeast Asia, but it also borders on both China and India. China, the ASEAN countries and — to a lesser extent — India all compete for influence there.

China

Since 1988 China has proved to be Burma's most reliable ally. No Burmese government can afford to neglect China, and a sense of shared experience may have contributed to the sense of affinity between the two administrations. China suffered from international opprobrium after the Tiananmen Square massacre in 1989, just as Burma had done a year earlier. SLORC may hope that it will be able to emulate China by facing down Western pressure. China has expressed its support by expanding economic links and by exchanging a series of senior ministerial delegations. In December 1994, Chinese Prime Minister Li Peng visited Rangoon, and he was followed in July 1995, by Defence Minister Chi Haotian.

China's economic interests in Burma revolve around the southern province of Yunnan, which traditionally has been one of the poorer, wilder and more remote regions of the country (d'Hooghe, 1994). This is beginning to change. Yunnan has a population of thirty-eight million, and is beginning to develop its own light industry. Burma offers a market for its goods. China has declared the Ruili district on the border with Burma's Shan state a 'special economic development zone' (see Lintner, 1994b). The road network between the two countries has been improved and since 1988 cross-border trade has grown to some US$800 million to US$1 billion a year. China has exported mainly factory goods, and receives in return commodities, such as timber and jade — as well as goods from further afield, such as East Asian cars.

China's economic expansion into northern Burma has alarmed many Burmese. For example, it has become a common complaint that Mandalay is increasingly dominated by Chinese businessmen, many of whom are recent immigrants who have purchased Burmese papers illegally (Mya Maung, 1994; Bridges, 1994). Economic development is contributing to racial tensions.

Yunnan also has had its share of social problems. Burma's principal exports to China have included narcotics and according to official figures, which may be an

190

underestimate, Yunnan has some 100,000 heroin addicts. It also has the highest rate of HIV infection in China. The Chinese authorities have taken stern measures against drugs smugglers: in 1994 they executed 466 criminals associated with the narcotics trade (Reuters, 1995). The United Nations Drugs Control Programme (UNDCP) supplied US$5 million for anti-narcotics operations in Southwest China between 1987 and 1992, and in May 1995 agreed on a new grant of US$2.9 million to finance equipment and training (Reuters, 1995), but such measures have so far made little impact.

In addition to its more conventional commercial activities, China sold Burma US$1.2 billion worth of military equipment between 1990 and 1993 (Lintner, 1993). In late 1994 Rangoon signed a second contract for some US$400 million worth of military goods. At the same time, Chinese technicians have been helping upgrade existing naval facilities in Sittwe, Bassein, Monkey Point (near Rangoon) and Mergui, as well as constructing new ones in Hainggyi (near Bassein) and the Coco Islands. China reportedly has been seeking access to two other islands for signals intelligence: Ramree island, south of Sittwe; and Zadetkyi island, off the Tenasserim coast. China naturally denies that it has any military ambitions in Burma, and the prime motive for its arms sales may have been commercial rather than strategic. Nevertheless, Beijing is certainly alert to the long-term benefits of strengthening its political and military influence in a country which could give it access to the Indian Ocean.

However, there are limits to the extent of Chinese willingness to assist SLORC. For example, China has made no attempt to protect Burma from criticism in the United Nations General Assembly. From Beijing's point of view, Burmese affairs are of minor importance, and it might well be prepared to sacrifice its friendship with SLORC if it could thereby gain a major advantage in some other international affairs arena.

ASEAN

Since 1989, the ASEAN approach to Burma has been one of 'constructive engagement', a term first used by those who opposed sanctions against South Africa in the 1980s. ASEAN leaders accept that political reform is desirable in Burma, but argue that it is inappropriate for non-Burmese to interfere in its internal affairs. If the outside world tries to isolate Burma by imposing sanctions, SLORC will become more inward-looking and repressive. Instead, the international community should increase diplomatic and economic contact with Rangoon. In due course such contacts will encourage SLORC to introduce reforms into Burma of its own accord.

One of the main underlying motives of this policy is commercial self-interest. Thai companies were among the first to enter Burma after SLORC lifted restrictions on foreign investment and trade in the late 1980s. More recently, companies from Singapore, Malaysia and Indonesia have signed a series of

191

lucrative contracts. Strategic interests also are important: the ASEAN states are concerned at China's increased influence in Burma, and wish to balance this by hastening Burma's integration with Southeast Asia. A third factor may be a sense of shared resentment against criticisms from Western human rights activists.

Opinions are divided on the success of constructive engagement. On the one hand, in early August 1995, Indonesian Foreign Minister Ali Alatas suggested that Aung San Suu Kyi's release showed that Burma is capable of solving its own problems, and that it 'deserves all the encouragement it can get' (Cooper, 1995). On the other hand, Thai academics and the Thai English-language press have repeatedly criticized constructive engagement (see below). Aung San Suu Kyi herself points out that the question is: for whom has the policy been constructive (*The Nation*, 1995)? Was it constructive for the forces of democracy, for the Burmese people in general, for a limited business community — or for SLORC? She implies the latter, but adds that it will be necessary to wait for a few years to evaluate how effective the policy was in inner government circles.

Notwithstanding such doubts, ASEAN has taken a series of steps to build up links with SLORC. In 1994, Thailand hosted the annual ASEAN Ministers' Meeting, and invited Burmese Foreign Minister Ohn Gyaw as an official guest. Brunei repeated the invitation the following year, and on 27 July, Ohn Gyaw formally signed the Treaty of Amity and Co-operation on his country's behalf. In December 1995, Thailand will invite Burma to a regional security summit: the other participants will be the seven ASEAN states plus Cambodia and Laos.

Accession to the Treaty of Amity and Co-operation is the first step towards ASEAN membership. The next step is for Burma to become an official observer at the ASEAN Ministers' Meetings, and this could take place in 1996 or 1997. The accession of Vietnam to ASEAN has set a precedent for the three remaining Southeast Asian states (Burma, Cambodia, Laos) and it is widely believed that Burma will become a full member before the turn of the century. However, this will not happen without consensus among the existing members of ASEAN. The organization has an opportunity to encourage Rangoon to introduce further reforms as a condition of membership. Whether it will do so will depend on the attitudes of individual member states.

Thailand   Thailand is the only ASEAN state bordering directly on to Burma, and has naturally taken the lead in formulating ASEAN's policy. Since late 1988, Thailand has been consistent in its advocacy of constructive engagement. However, Thai/Burmese relations have been more troubled than might have been expected.

In part, these troubles stem from the historical legacy. The two countries are similar in size, and they share a common allegiance to Theravada Buddhism, but their past history has been one of rivalry more often than friendship. While maintaining formal relations with Rangoon, successive Thai governments have tolerated the activities of Burma's ethnic minority guerrilla groups on their western border because these provided a useful buffer between Thai territory and the Burmese army.

Thai policy changed in December 1988, when then Thai armed forces commander Gen Chaovalit Yongchaiyut became the first senior foreign leader to visit Rangoon after the SLORC coup. Chaovalit appears to have established a personal rapport with SLORC chairman Gen Saw Maung. Soon afterwards, Thai timber companies — many of which were linked to families of senior Thai army officers — arranged for a series of lucrative logging contracts inside Burma (Kramer, 1994). Similarly, Thai companies have benefited from the opening of the border to expand their trading links throughout Burma.

At the same time, Thai officers became more accommodating to their Burmese counterparts. Many of the most important Karen and Mon bases lay directly on the Thai/Burmese border. Between 1989 and 1991, the Burmese army entered Thai territory several times to attack these positions from the rear, and this resulted in the fall of a string of guerrilla bases. Thai border forces made no attempt to stop these incursions.

Notwithstanding the apparent friendship between the two countries, a dispute over the demarcation of their common boundary led to new frictions in late 1991. Both countries claimed a certain 'Hill 492' on the southern border, and by early 1992, it seemed that the dispute might lead to outright conflict similar to the three-month war between Thailand and Laos in 1987. King Bhumibhol Adulyadej of Thailand used his influence to persuade the Thai authorities to adopt a more conciliatory attitude, and by mid-1992 relations appeared once more to be on a more even keel.

However, a new set of problems flared up in late 1994 and early 1995. As noted above, the split in the Karen National Union (KNU) and the emergence of the Democratic Kayin Buddhist Organisation (DKBO) led to the fall of the KNU headquarters at Manerplaw in January 1995. Thousands of Karen refugees, many of whom were directly linked to the KNU, fled across the border into Thailand, and DKBO guerrillas launched a series of raids on refugee camps in Thai territory. On several occasions Thai security personnel were killed in clashes with the DKBO.

The Burmese authorities in Rangoon claimed that Thailand had brought these problems on itself. For example, on 11 May, Col Kyaw Win, the deputy director of the Directorate of Defence Services Intelligence (DDSI), stated that, 'The problems along the Thai-Myanmar border have arisen because for various reasons, Thailand has admitted terrorist organisations opposed to Myanmar' (Kyaw Win, 1995). SLORC claims — implausibly — that it has no influence over the DKBO: 'The Myanmar authorities cannot take responsibility for the activities of the armed groups who have not yet officially returned to the legal fold' (Burmese Radio, 1995). However, in June Rangoon signalled its displeasure with the Thais by suspending work on the 'Friendship Bridge' across the Moei river at Myawaddy. The Burmese claimed that the Thais were trying to expand Thai by dumping earth into the Moei. In the same period, posters appeared in Myawaddy calling for a boycott of Thai goods.

The Thai reaction has been confused. The Thai English-language press pointed to these events as further evidence of the failure of 'constructive engagement'. The House Foreign Affairs Sub-committee called for a review of policy towards Burma (*Bangkok Post,* 4 May 1995) and Prof. Vitit Muntarborn of Chulalongkorn University suggested that constructive engagement was a 'slap-in-the-face policy' for Thailand (*The Nation*, 26 June 1995).

Nevertheless, official Thai policy remained unchanged. Thai Prime Minister Chuan Leekpai stated in early May that 'the border battles are specific incidents. We should not let them undermine the main policy' (*The Nation,* 7 May 1995*).* Similarly, M.R. Kasem Samosorn Kasemri, who was appointed Foreign Minister after the Chart Thai party's victory in the July 1995 national elections, has re-affirmed the country's commitment to constructive engagement. Chaovalit Yongchaiyut, who is Deputy Prime Minister and holds the defence portfolio in the new government, announced his intention of visiting Rangoon with a view to smoothing over frictions between the two countries.

In late July, Bangkok's Thammasat University renewed an invitation issued to Aung San Suu Kyi in 1991 to receive an honorary doctorate. The English-language press approved of the invitation; army leaders opposed it, on the ground that it might antagonize SLORC and thus damage Thai interests in Burma; the Thai government tried to remain neutral. This episode symbolized the contradictions in the Thai establishment's approach to Burma.

Other ASEAN countries   While Burma's relations with Thailand have been in the doldrums, its links with other ASEAN countries appear to be blossoming. Singapore is one of the main beneficiaries. In March 1994, Singaporean Prime Minister Goh Chok-tong became the second foreign head of government to visit Rangoon (the first was the President of Laos in 1992), and the two countries have exchanged a series of ministerial delegations since then. In June 1995, SLORC Chairman Senior Gen Than Shwe made an official visit to Singapore and Indonesia, and signed agreements to boost economic ties with both countries.

Singapore has now emerged as one of the largest foreign investors in Burma. By June 1995 Singaporean companies had already invested a total of US$135 million in twenty-five projects, mainly hotels. During Than Shwe's visit, the Singapore Technologies Industrial Corporation signed a memorandum of understanding for a S$500 million (US$359.7 million) project to build a new international airport in Mandalay (*Asian Wall Street Journal,* 7 June 1995). Indonesia and Malaysia are not far behind. For example, on 27 July 1995 the Malaysian company Idris Hydraulic signed a contract to invest US$157 million in two hotels in Rangoon (*Reuters,* 27 July 1995).

In recent years there has been increasing interest in the prospects for cooperation among the four northernmost countries along the river Mekong: Thailand, Laos, Burma and the Yunnan province of China. This has given rise to the phrase 'golden quadrilateral', an optimistic realignment of the region's political geometry which represents a change of emphasis from the 'golden triangle' of Northeastern Burma, Thailand and Laos (See Edwards 1995; Grant 1995; Robertson 1995). The 'triangle' specialized in narcotics production, whilst the 'quadrilateral' represents a new and more harmonious era of legitimate trade and investment.

The Asian Development Bank (ADB) has acted as a catalyst (Asian Development Bank 1993a, 1993b). It has organized a series of conferences in Manila (1992 and 1993), Hanoi (1994) and Rangoon (April 1995) to discuss the prospects for regional cooperation. In April 1995, Thailand, Laos, Cambodia and Vietnam set up a Mekong River Commission to increase regional coordination, and Burma and China will be invited to join. The ADB has been keen to particularly promote cooperation in Transport and Energy. Proposals include the construction of a 'ring road' joining Chiang Rai in Northern Thailand, with Kunming the capital of Yunnan, via Northern Burma. A second road would join Chiang Rai with Kunming via Northern Laos. Other projects under discussion include joint projects to improve regional energy supplies and promote tourism.

Such regional cooperation initiatives are undoubtedly an improvement on the past, but the new era will take time to emerge. The ADB can act as a coordinating body, but the US has used its influence to prevent ADB loans or aid grants to Burma. Moreover, the proposed transport links between Northern Thailand and Yunnan pass through parts of Shan state which are still unstable. More generally, the potential for political instability in Burma continues to deter would-be investors, while Thailand and the other Southeast Asian countries are nervous about China's increased strategic influence in the region, and this may temper their enthusiasm for joint economic initiatives.

The wider international community

Closer relations between Burma and its Asian neighbours have not saved it from condemnation among the wider international community. As noted above, the US has tended to take the lead in calling for increased international pressure to persuade SLORC to end human rights abuses. The European Union (EU) has adopted a similar line, although in late 1994, EU leaders suggested that the emphasis should be on 'critical dialogue' rather than isolation. Australia agrees with ASEAN in supporting dialogue and engagement with SLORC, but emphasizes the need for SLORC to reach certain 'benchmarks' before it can be re-integrated into the international community. Aung San Suu Kyi's release was one of those benchmarks. The others include a serious dialogue with the opposition, a clear timetable for the constitutional process, significant progress in the proposed dialogue between SLORC and the UN, and the cessation of forced labour and porterage.

Since 1991, the United Nations General Assembly in New York has passed four consensus resolutions condemning SLORC's human rights record. Boutros Boutros-Ghali, the UN Secretary General, has offered to use his 'good offices in assisting the Government of Myanmar to respond to the concerns of other Member States'. However, his representatives have so far made little progress in their discussions with SLORC.

International condemnation of SLORC has a practical impact in that it holds up multilateral as well as bilateral aid. The US has used its influence to prevent the IMF and the World Bank from expanding their Burma country programmes. Assistance from these bodies could help Rangoon tackle the problems of its unrealistic exchange rate as well as its international debt burden of some US$5.3 billion.

Conclusion: prospects for national unity and regional integration

Nearly 40 years ago, J.S. Furnivall, the doyen of Burma scholars in his day, pointed out that Burma could not lead a healthy national life in isolation from the outside world (Furnivall 1957, p. g.). He added that 'it is a law of political as of natural evolution that organisms which keep themselves to themselves survive if at all only as freaks, museum pieces, until, on exposure to the stress and pressure of the outside world, they break down and disintegrate'. His words were written five years before Ne Win introduced the isolationist Burmese Path to Socialism: they serve as a warning of the dangers which confront Burma as it tries to catch up with its neighbours in the 1990s.

Superficially, the prospects for national unity are better than they have been at any time since independence. SLORC's military power is overwhelming, and this limits the ability of any opposition movement — either in Rangoon or in the regions — to present a credible challenge to its authority. Moreover, the majority of the ethnic insurgent groups have now signed ceasefires with the central government, and even those who are still at war call for a 'genuine federation' rather than secession.

And yet the apparent strength of the regime masks deep divisions in Burmese society. The most obvious divide is between the army and the democratic opposition. In the 1990 national elections Aung San Suu Kyi's National League for Democracy showed that it had overwhelming popular support: the opposition campaign had united the country — at least temporarily — more convincingly than the army has ever done. The history of Burma since 1962 demonstrates the staying power of a well-entrenched military regime, but the world of the 1990s is more complicated than the 1960s. It is doubtful whether the Burmese army has the technical capacity — let alone the constitutional authority — to steer the country through the complicated political and economic choices which it will face in the next decade. If the country is to negotiate these choices, it will require political institutions which have more than a facade of popular legitimacy.

The regime's apologists point out that it is at least bringing economic development, and they suggest that this will divert the energies of ordinary Burmese away from politics. This argument may be true of a minority of entrepreneurs in Rangoon, Mandalay and Taunggyi, but the memories of 1988 and 1990 are too fresh — and the fruits of development are too unevenly distributed — for it to apply convincingly to the country as a whole. Even so, the impact of current economic developments should not be underestimated. One consequence, as noted above, is that the economies of border areas such as Eastern Shan state have increasingly come into the orbit of neighbouring countries rather than Rangoon. Burma's political boundaries may be relatively secure, but the pattern of its economy is becoming much more complex.

Improved communications at every level and the acknowledged failure of Burma's socialist experiment, mean that regional economic integration is gathering pace. In line with these changes, ASEAN leaders hope to welcome Burma as a member before the turn of the century. SLORC will try to minimize external contacts which might limit its freedom of political manoeuvre at home, but it will not be able to isolate the country from new ideas. If Burma can establish the political institutions needed to facilitate a genuine dialogue between its citizens it may eventually be able to achieve a new stability. Otherwise, regional integration and national fragmentation may prove to be two sides of the same coin.

Notes

1. In 1989 the government changed the country's official name to 'The Union of Myanmar'. This change remains controversial, and in this chapter I have chosen to stick to the traditional English usage except in quotations.

2. These are, in chronological order of ceasefire (men under arms):

   Myanmar National Democracy Alliance (2,000), 31 March 1989;
   Myanmar National Solidarity Party (Wa — 15,000), 8 May 1989;
   National Democracy Alliance Army (2,000), 30 June 1989;
   Shan State Army (2,000), 24 September 1989;
   New Democratic Army (400), 15 December 1989;
   Kachin Defence Army (900), 11 January 1991;
   Pao National Organization (500), 18 February 1991;

Palaung State Liberation Army (800), 21 April 1991;
Kayan National Guards (200), 27 February 1992;
Kachin Independence Organization (5,000), 1 October 1993;
Karenni National People's Liberation Front (300), 9 May 1994;
Kayan Pyithit Party (200), 26 July 1994;
Shan State Nationalities People's Liberation Organization (700),
    9 October 1994;
Karenni National Progressive Party (800), 21 March 1995;
New Mon State Party (1,500), 29 June 1995.

References

Asian Development Bank (1993a), *Subregional Economic Cooperation. Initial Possibilities for Cambodia, Lao PDR, Myanmar, Thailand, Viet Nam and Yunnan Province of the People's Republic of China*, Manila .

Asian Development Bank (1993b), *Economic Cooperation in the Greater Mekong Subregion*, Manila.

Aung San Suu Kyi (1991), *Freedom From Fear and Other Writings*, Penguin books, London.

Aung San Suu Kyi (1994), *'Empowerment for a Culture of Peace and Development'*, Address to a meeting of the World Commission on Culture and Development, Manila, 21 November.

Bray, J. (1992a), 'Ethnic Minorities and the Future of Burma', *The World Today*, Vol. 48, Nos 8-9, pp. 144-7.

Bray, J. (1992b), 'Burma: Resisting the International Community', *Pacific Review*, Vol.5, No. 3, pp. 291-6.

Bray, J. (1995), *Burma. The Politics of Constructive Engagement*, Royal Institute of International Affairs, London.

Bridges, B. (1994), 'Chinese Conundrums on the Road to Mandalay', *Eastern Express*, 24 August.

Buckman, D. (1995), 'New Lease of Life for Myanmar', *Petroleum Review*, Vol. 49, No. 582, pp. 316-18.

Burmese Radio (1995), 'Burma Rejects Thai Protest on Border Incident', BBC *Summary of World Broadcasts (SWB)*, FE/2273/ B/1, 8 April.

Cooper, M. (1995), "Diplomatic' Burma Keeps Low Profile at ASEANMeet', *Agence France Presse*, 31 July.

Diller, J. M. (1994), 'The National Convention: Lessons from the Past and Steps to the Future', *Burma Debate*, Vol.1, No.2, pp. 4-10.

Edwards, B. (1995), 'A river runs through it', *Euromoney*, February, pp. 66-9.

Furnivall, J.S. (1957), *An Introduction to the Political Economy of Burma*, Third Edition, People's Literature Committee and House, Rangoon.

Grant, R. (1995), 'Go with the flow', *World Link*, July/August.

d'Hooghe, I. (1995), 'Regional integration in Yunnan', in Goodman, D.S.G. and Segal, G. (eds.) *China Deconstructs: Politics, Trade and Regionalism*, Routledge, London.

Human Rights Watch/Asia (1995), 'Burma,. Entrenchment or Reform?', Vol. 7, No. 10.

Kramer, T. (1994), *Thai Foreign Policy Towards Burma 1987-1993,* Doctoral dissertation, Instituut voor Moderne Aziatische Geschiednis, Universiteit van Amsterdam.

Kyaw Win (1995), 'Defence Ministry News Conference on Thai Border Situation', *BBC Summary of World Broadcasts (SWB)*, FE/2300 B/1, 11 May.

Lintner, B. (1989), *Outrage. Burma's Struggle for Democracy*, Review Publishing House, Hong Kong.

Lintner, B. (1990), *The Rise and Fall of the Communist Party of Burma*, Cornell University Southeast Asia Program, Ithaca, New York.

Lintner, B. (1993), 'Arms for Eyes', *Far Eastern Economic Review*, 16 December, p. 26.

Lintner, B. (1994a), *Burma in Revolt: Opium and Insurgency*, Westview Press, Boulder.

Lintner, B. (1994b), 'Enter the Dragon', *Far Eastern Economic Review*, 22 December, pp. 22-7.

Mya Maung (1994), 'On the Road to Mandalay. A Case Study of the Sinonisation of Upper Burma'. *Asian Survey*, Vol. 34, No. 5, pp. 447-59.

Reuters News Agency (1995), 'UN Gives China Province $3 million to Fight Drugs', 22 May.

Robertson, D. E. (1995), 'The 'Golden Quadrangle': an accessible dream?', *The World Today*, Vol. 51, No. 5, pp. 82-4.

Smith, M. (1991), *Burma. Insurgency and the Politics of Ethnicity*, Zed Books, London.

Smith, M. (1994), *Ethnic Groups in Burma. Development, Democracy and Human Rights*, Anti-Slavery International, London.

The Nation (1995), 'People are More Important,' Interview with Aung San Suu Kyi by *Nation* Editor-in-Chief Suthichai Yoon, 1 August.

Tin Maung Maung Than (1994), 'Reforming Myanmar's State Economic Enterprises', *Business Times*, 27-28 August. Cited in *Foreign Broadcast Information Service (FBIS)* EAS-94-170 (1 September 1994), p. 158.

9 The rise of regionalism and the future of China

Ian Cook and Rex Li

Introduction

Observers of China have long been fascinated by its huge size and marvelled at its coherence through millennia; more recently, however, people have wondered whether the People's Republic of China (PRC) can continue to exist as a state, particularly in the light of the demise of the Soviet Union, but also because of the speed of transformation within China itself, and the internal and external pressures to which this transformation has given rise. Some suggest that the PRC will not follow the Soviet path of disintegration (Ferdinand, 1992), while others argue that the break-up of China is a distinct possibility (Cannon, 1993). In this chapter, we identify and analyze the key factors determining the national unity or division of China, and then consider the most likely scenarios for the future. Obviously, it is impossible for us (and indeed anyone) to predict the exact course of development in China, given the complexity of the political and economic situation in the country. What we wish to do is to raise some relevant issues for discussion and hopefully stimulate further research into this important topic. What happens in China in the coming decade will have very serious implications for the world, and for Pacific Asia in particular.

Economic development, centralization and decentralization

Modern China's economic development is based on such legacies as: the industrial development of the treaty ports of the nineteenth century; the Japanese-led industrialization of Manchuria; and the Communist-led drive for reconstruction, which originally utilized Soviet, and then Maoist, models of development; and, recently, Dengist development strategies. Indeed, the economic reforms introduced by the Chinese leadership under Deng Xiaoping have had a profound effect on every single aspect of Chinese society (Wen, 1984; Zhong, 1990), the most significant of which is arguably the rise of regionalism (*difang zhuyi*), as the reforms have a differential spatial impact.

It is useful to briefly consider these legacies of the past in terms of their expression of the tensions between centralization and decentralization. Firstly, the opening up of China in the nineteenth century was very much forced upon a weak China by militarily strong foreign powers, especially by Britain but also by France, the United States, Germany, Russia and later Japan. These imperial powers ensured decentralization of control to their own spheres of influence, mainly in coastal cities where the principle of extraterritoriality was enforced, or along the Yangzi river and, later, in Manchuria, where the Japanese established the puppet state of *Manzhouguo*. 'The extraterritorial concessions ensured the imperial powers *de facto* control of trade and industry in the coastal provinces. Inland trade was controlled through the railway concessions and the inland river treaty ports' (Chossudovsky, 1986, p. 136). China's modern economic development began, therefore, with a considerable loss of power and authority by the central Chinese government to outside powers and institutions.

After the establishment of the PRC in 1949, the Chinese not surprisingly responded to this legacy via the establishment of a rigid, Centrally Planned Economy, on Soviet lines. Five year plans were established in the early 1950s (Howe, 1978), and 'centralization was further intensified to serve the needs of large-scale economic construction' (Liu et al., 1987, p. 441). In parallel with the gradual collectivization of agriculture (designed not only to feed the people but also to extract surpluses from the peasantry for investment in industry), heavy industry became the cornerstone of the economy. The emphasis was very much on production rather than consumption. To some extent, development was concentrated in the pre-World War Two centres such as Shanghai or Manchuria, but large-scale inland sites were also developed for resource extraction, energy production and resource processing.

China was not the Soviet Union, however, and Mao was the most influential person to recognize that China was at a far different level of development in the 1950s compared to the Soviet Union in the 1920s. He envisaged that the role for China's vast peasantry had to be different from that in the Soviet Union. The emphasis shifted to extremely rapid agricultural collectivization, and the breathtaking Great Leap Forward (GLF) of 1958 witnessed the establishment of communes, throughout the country. Much has been written about the successes and failures of this extraordinary experiment in social engineering, but we note here that one key feature of the GLF was the decentralization of control of production to the local level, whether to the commune or to the state enterprise. In part, this reflects the Maoist emphasis on self-reliance, nurtured in the revolutionary 'base areas' under Communist control. 'One unit-ism' was the result, with the aim of locating the entire production process, from the manufacture of parts to final assembly, at one site (Yabuki, 1995, p. 35).

The Maoist model had many critics within the Chinese Communist Party (CCP), especially after the famine years following the GLF, and the alternative 'Four Modernizations' programme was outlined by Zhou Enlai in 1964 (Howe, 1978). This programme proposed the modernization of agriculture, industry, defence, plus science and technology (taken together), in part via the opening up of China to the outside world. The unleashing of the Cultural Revolution in 1966 postponed such a path until the late 1970s, however, by which time the majority of Chinese leaders were convinced that the Maoist model of development was inefficient and unpopular among the people, and had to be abandoned. In order to attract necessary Western investment, technology, management skills, and to earn foreign exchange, the Chinese government decided in the late 1970s to pursue an 'Open Door' policy, which markedly expanded its foreign trade and economic relations (Bucknall, 1989; Howell, 1993). This, however, has resulted in a different type of decentralization in China. Yabuki argues that 'one unit-ism ultimately has served as a shackle on modernization' (Yabuki, p. 36) due to the 'battlefield mentality' which requires the enterprise to provide for the workers' social and welfare requirements, plus the intrusive presence of the party cadres within the enterprise.

Now that this situation is being 'freed up', with local governments and the managers of enterprises being given more autonomy to make decisions and to deal with foreign companies, the centre is finding it more and more difficult to control them. In part, this reflects the opportunity for foreign capital to have multiple points of contact in 'Open Cities', 'Special Economic Zones' and other spatial entities. It also reflects the growing sophistication and complexity of interaction with the global economy. Once again, the Chinese economy is subject to the pull of outside forces, which threaten to undermine central authority.

It has been argued that central government has in effect lost control over the accumulation, storage and allocation of capital, and that regional authorities have become increasingly assertive in promoting and protecting their interests. They are often critical of decisions made by the centre and reluctant to pay tax to it. In short, much of China's foreign trade and economic activity is now in the hands of regional and local authorities (Breslin, 1995b; Chang, 1992, pp. 213-8; Segal, 1994, pp. 12-19).

The current decentralist tendencies, however, should be considered in historical perspective. The centre in China has never been able to exert complete control over the provinces. Historically, this was due largely to spatial factors, with distance and slow communications being barriers to the exertion of central control. Perceptions were also important, best described by an old Chinese saying: 'The mountains are high; the emperor is far away'. The Emperor tended to exert strong control at the beginning of a dynasty but his power waxed and waned over time and space until the dynastic cycle eventually moved on via his overthrow and the passing on of the 'Mandate of Heaven' (the right to govern). Some provinces were habitually associated with revolt; one such was Sichuan, as Zhou Enlai noted: 'An old saying has it that Szechuan [sic] always was the scene of turmoil before other provinces, and that order was always restored in that area later than the rest of the country' (quoted in Goodman, 1986, p. 27). Also, partly due to the sheer size of China, regional authorities have always been given a certain degree of autonomy, even recently in the Communist period (Ferdinand, 1992, pp. 283-4).

Regional disparities

It would be surprising indeed were regional disparities not to exist within such a vast and environmentally diverse country as China. Contrasts include the sub-tropical areas of the Southeast compared to the arid lands of the Northwest, the fertile highly populated river deltas of the East compared to what is called 'the land of no man and no dog' in the North of Tibet in the West, and the highly urbanized coastal zone contrasting with the more remote ruralized provinces of the interior. Despite the egalitarian impulse of Communism, coupled with geostrategic decisions to decentralize industrial development into the then secret 'third front' region centred on Sichuan, for example (Cannon, 1990; Linge and Forbes, 1990), regional disparities have become more pronounced, especially in the Dengist era. While many coastal provinces have developed rapidly over the past ten years or so, many regions in the hinterland are still very poor (e.g. Gansu, Guanxi, Guizhou, Inner Mongolia, Ningxia, Qinghai, Tibet, Xingjiang, Yunnan), lagging markedly in Gross National Product (GNP) per capita and also in the key area of exports per capita (Uri Dadush and Dong He, 1995). This situation arises despite the setting up in 1980 of a 500 million Yuan fund for 'underdeveloped regions' (Ma, 1990, p. 232) and a later decision to increase Central Government subsidies to many of these provinces by ten per cent per annum from 1985 (Yabuki, 1995, p. 119).

Further evidence for the perpetuation and indeed expansion of regional disparities comes from a number of sources. For example, a major aspect of regional wealth is the proportion of the population engaged in agriculture. The abolition of the communes and the reforms to the Rural Responsibility System introduced in the 1980s, towards *baochan daohu* and *baogan daohu* (contracting of output quotas to individual households with or without, respectively, the production team conducting unified accounting) (Sen, 1990, pp. 96-122), brought rural productivity gains but also increased rural inequalities. Indeed, as Bramall and Jones (1993) point out, this was one of the objectives of the reforms, designed to encourage good management practice and hard work. They analyze a wide range of rural income data to conclude that spatial inequalities have returned to those of the pre-World War Two years. Likewise, albeit in a more cautious vein, Selden (1993, p. 179) has concluded in his analysis that 'substantial intravillage and regional income differences exist in the countryside', and that 'there is evidence that certain income differentials have increased'. Recent work by Yao and Liu (1995) on township and village enterprises (TVEs), utilizing data at the macro-regional scale, also confirms this pattern, with TVE gross output values and pre-tax profits per worker displaying even wider differentials between the prosperous Eastern and poorer Western and Central macro-regions in 1992, compared to 1986. Similarly, Zweig's (1995) focus on TVE export-led growth drew him to the conclusion that 'TVE exports and the growth of rural joint ventures have made the coastal/inland gap within rural China more salient'.

The previous paragraph refers primarily to the rural dimension; when the urban dimension of development is added there is an even greater divergence between the highly urbanized coastal zone and the poorly urbanized interior as urban economic growth continues apace. The aggregation of a multiplicity of poor rural villages and/or TVEs, contrasting with provinces with rich cities, rich rural villages and TVEs expresses itself as a marked regional contrast between poor and rich regions. In consequence there exist tensions between the rich and poor provinces because of the increasing income gap between them. Provinces have also taken measures to compete with each other without prior approval from the centre, with incidents such as the 'rice war' between Guangdong and Hunan provinces in the early 1990s being indicative of inter-provincial resentments over wealth and resources (Goodman and Feng 1994, p. 187). Although the centre has tried to encourage inter-provincial cooperation, the problems of regional economic disparities and protectionism remain serious. As a result, the central government has found it increasingly difficult to coordinate the national economy (Chang, 1992, pp. 216-20; Segal, 1994, pp. 16-19).

It is unnecessary to go so far as to utilize the concept of 'internal colonialism' to realize that recent economic progress is unevenly distributed over the Chinese space and society; the richer regions are predominantly coastal and predominantly Han (ethnic Chinese), whereas the poorer regions are more likely to be in the interior and contain substantial minority populations. Moreover, it is the Han who seem to benefit most from development within the interior/minority areas as they flood in to build and run the new factories, mines and infrastructure of these areas. The marginalization and exclusion of other ethnic groups and provinces from the wealth of the richer areas could prove a potent brew for regional revolt. One question is whether certain well-developed provinces (e.g. Southern China — Guangdong, Fujian and to a lesser extent Hainan) can and will break away from the centre, and form separate economic and political entities (e.g. a new South China state with Hong Kong and possibly Taiwan?). This of course cannot be achieved without powerful military support (the role of the army will be explored in later sections).

Conversely, rapid economic growth may help to defuse decentralist tendencies. It must be pointed out that, despite regional disparities, , China as a whole is growing very fast, and the Chinese authorities have taken steps to spatially diffuse economic growth. For example, in 1992, five port cities along the Changjiang (Yangzi River), and thirteen inland border cities were declared as 'Open Cities', as were all inland provincial capitals (Wang and Cook, 1993; Yabuki, 1995, pp. 192-3). Also, within the coastal region, there is now a broad tripartite focus on the Beijing-Tianjin conurbation within the broader 'Bohai-Sea Rim Region' (Ye, 1993), the 'dragon head' of Shanghai in the Changjiang region, as well as the South China region. While the success of these measures remains to be seen, it is clear that the centre is well aware of the spatial dimension of economic transformation. In addition, although South China continues to attract a significant proportion of foreign direct investment (FDI) — a key element in economic change — FDI also flows into other regions. Indeed, approximately sixty percent of FDI is directed to provinces other than the two main recipients of Guangdong and Fujian (Wang and Cook, 1993).

Leadership succession and the role of the military

Whether China will remain united or not depends to a significant extent on the leadership changes after the death of Deng Xiaoping. Will a new 'dynasty' be established or will the 'Mandate of Heaven' be safely passed on within the leadership? Leadership succession has always been linked to significant political change in the history of the PRC. In fact, the struggle over the succession to Deng has already begun, and is likely to become more fierce as Deng's health deteriorates. Naturally, what most people are concerned about is the outcome of the succession struggle. Will there be a new supreme leader of China like Mao or Deng? If so, who? Which faction of the CCP will win the battle? These are of course important questions, but a more relevant question is whether the new leadership will wish, and be in a position, to continue the economic reform and Open Door Policy initiated by Deng, while maintaining its political control of China. Could the post-Deng leadership successfully tackle the serious social, economic, and political problems in Chinese society such as regional disparities, social inequality, widespread corruption, inflation and unemployment, rural discontent, economic crime, and so on? If the top leaders in China manage to reach a consensus and present a united front to the country, and show that they are willing and able to deal with the existing problems facing China, the centre might hold. Again, if one considers Chinese political history, whenever the centre was, or appeared to be, weak, regions tended to be more assertive, even challenging the authority of the central government, and countries bordered with China attempted to attack or invade the country. If the succession struggle among different individuals and/or factions within the leadership cannot be resolved after a certain period of time, then there is no guarantee that particular regional leaders will not take advantage of the situation, and try to break away from the centre. However, the CCP has successfully coopted various regional leaders, who now owe their allegiance to the centre rather than their previous regional bases. In any case, regional secession is impossible without sufficient support from regional military leaders., but, would the army leaders be prepared to get involved in the division of China?

The role of the army is a major factor determining the unity or division of China (Yang et al., eds, 1994). The involvement of regional military leaders, or warlords (*junfa*), in national politics in the 1920s following the collapse of the Qing Dynasty is well known (Waldron, 1990). Since 1949, the People's Liberation Army (PLA) has been closely involved in elite politics and factional struggle in China (Swaine, 1992, pp. 156-68). For example, the PLA was drawn into factionalism in Chinese politics during the Cultural Revolution in the 1960s, which 'deeply divided the military leadership at all levels of the chain of command' (Joffe, 1987, p. 19). Even after the Cultural Revolution, the army continued to play a significant role in politics. Indeed, the support of the PLA was crucial in Hua Guofeng's defeat of the Gang of Four after the death of Mao in 1976. Despite Deng's great effort to modernize the army and to remove it from politics in the 1980s, it was again brought back to the centre of political struggle in 1989 when the PLA was involved in the suppression of the student demonstrations in Tiananmen Square (Cheng, 1990, pp. 133-9). Since then the influence of the military in political affairs has undoubtedly increased. It has been argued that the role played by top PLA leaders is vital in deciding the outcome of the political succession to Deng and in maintaining the stability and unity of the PRC (Segal, 1994a, pp. 27-8). Some even suggest, as mentioned earlier, that certain military leaders may seek to control their regions and work with provincial officials to gain independence. This type of speculation is based partly on the PLA's extensive involvement over the past ten years or so in business activity and foreign trade in different regions (Cheung, 1994). Indeed, there is some evidence to suggest that the rise of economic regionalism has affected the behaviour of certain Area Military Commanders. For example, Beijing, Shenyang, Jinan, Nanjing, and Guangzhou Military Area Commands are said to have supported economic regionalism (Yu, 1992).

However, as some observers have pointed out, the emergence of 'new warlordism' in China can easily be exaggerated (Dreyer, 1994; Goodman, 1994). Indeed, it is difficult to know precisely what role the PLA will play in the succession to Deng and in the politics of post-Deng China (Li and White, 1993). For the moment, the centre still has tight control over the armed forces, especially the air force, navy and nuclear weapons, as well as the seven Military Area Commands, with regional military leaders being regularly shifted to prevent too much regional autonomy (Swaine, 1992, pp. 143-4). Indeed, the vertical networks of patronage within the army cut across different military regions and party and state organizations. It is unlikely that regional military leaders will challenge the authority of Beijing and support provincial leaders to break away from the centre, as long as the central government is regarded as legitimate by the PLA and the PLA remains united (Joffe, 1994; Segal, 1994a, pp. 24-5).

Culture, nationalism and ethnicity

For regional secession to occur, units of the PLA would have to be involved. So too, however, would the people themselves, for the Chinese armed forces are still perceived by many as a *people's* army, albeit a more sophisticated, professional and hence distant force than in the Maoist era. The role of the peasantry would perhaps not be crucial, but it would nonetheless be important. It is possible, for example, that there could be a neoMaoist revolt — particularly directed against urban corruption and 'cultural pollution', the countryside might rise up against the cities. Already in recent years have come reports of peasant revulsion against corruption, nepotism, and other negative acts of CCP cadres; were this allied to a local base, then regional conflict could occur. It seems to us, however, that such a scenario is unlikely. Instead, it is more probable that the peasantry will support the centre in a recognition of their historic role to defend the nation.

The future of China must also be considered within the broader context of culture and tradition. In China, there is a strong patriarchal tradition of deference, which runs through the family to the centre. The Confucian emphasis on filial piety and loyalty is deeply rooted in Chinese society. These social and cultural traditions, however, have been seriously questioned since the nineteenth century, and especially during the 'May Fourth' era, when some Chinese intellectuals advocated a totalistic antitraditionalist response to the challenge of Western culture and power. For many years, Chinese intellectuals and elites have been searching for their national identity (Dittmer and Kim, eds, 1993). Despite their criticism of China's past and enthusiasm for Western ideas, however, most of them have not been able to escape from the influence of Chinese traditions. For example, Chairman Mao claimed to be a Marxist, but he read more traditional Chinese books than any other, and quoted them extensively in his writing. The continuing legacy of Confucianism, therefore, makes it all the less likely that widespread revolt would occur and we note that in 1994, a high ranking CCP member stated that it was the duty of every Chinese to enhance the study of Confucianism (Levine, 1995, p. 392).

Chinese nationalism emerged as a response to the challenge and threat of European powers in the nineteenth century. Prior to that era, the concept of the 'Middle Kingdom' was largely a cultural one. Dr Sun Yat Sen and his followers began the search in the early twentieth century for a modern national identity. Since then, nationalism in its various forms has been used by Chinese leaders of all political persuasions. The Chinese revolution, for instance, was primarily a nationalist struggle to achieve national independence. As Mao put it in 1949: 'The Chinese people have stood up; they will never be humiliated again'. However, it has been suggested that family and community loyalties in China have always been more important than loyalties to the country (Segal, 1994, pp. 6-7). As China is such a vast country, *local* identity may be stronger than *national* identity. It is true that traditionally family and birthplace mean a lot to Chinese people, but most Chinese have multiple identities and can be loyal to their family (*jia*) as well as to their country (*guo*). For example, Dr Sun Yat Sen was of Hakka origin, but it did not make him put his local interests before the interests of the country as a whole. As White and Li (1993, p. 193) noted when they commented on the identities of Coastal Chinese: 'The multiple-level, mutually reinforcing, intense identities of south coast people have *for centuries* (our emphasis) contributed crucially to the larger nation of which they now form the most dynamic part. These communities are at once regional, national, and cosmopolitan. They have helped to protect China's pride and strength, while absorbing new notions and resources from elsewhere'. Nationalist sentiments have been, and will be used by Chinese leaders, Communist or otherwise, to mobilize support from the Chinese people against perceived or real foreign intervention. Indeed, the fear of the consequences of chaos (*luan*) and national disintegration is rather strong among both the leaders and ordinary citizens in China.

Western observers often emphasize the role of minorities in the potential break-up of China. Within the PRC fifty-six ethnic minorities are officially recognized. In 1990, they numbered more than ninety-one million people, accounting for eight per cent of the total population (Li, 1992). They cover large tracts of the interior (see Table 9.1; Zhang and Zeng, 1993), but, despite their spatial dominance and potential geostrategic

207

importance, they are nonetheless dominated economically and politically by the Han Chinese. Although ethnicity is certainly a factor to be recognized, it does not necessarily follow that minority dissent will lead to the regional disintegration of China. Since the Han comprise ninety-three per cent of the population of China, even if minority regions such as Tibet and Xinjiang *were* to secede in a Balkanization scenario, most of the rest of China would be unlikely to do likewise. In any case, Han hegemony is very powerful within all minority regions. We agree with other scholars

Table 9.1
China's minorities,* by region

Northeast	Northwest	Southwest	Central South and Southeast
Manchu, 9.8	Hui, 8.6	Miao, 7.4	Zhuang, 15+
Mongol, 4.8	Uygur, 7.2	Yi, 6.6	Tujia, 5.7
Korean, 1.9	Kazak, 1.1	Tibetan, 4.6	Yao, 2.1
		Bouyei, 2.5	Li, 1.1
		Dong, 2.5	
		Bai, 1.6	
		Hani, 1.3	
		Dai, 1.0	

Regional totals:

16.7	18.0	30.4	25 (approx.)

*   Those with more than one million people.

Source: Zhang, W.W. and Zeng, Q.N. (1993), *In Search of China's Minorities*, New World Press, Beijing.

when they suggest that ethnic minorities in China are unlikely to pose a great challenge to the centre, unlike the former Soviet Union (Breslin,1995a, p. 72; Cole, 1994, p. 52; Ferdinand, 1992, pp. 282-3). The PRC situation is dissimilar to that of the Soviet Union, for China has an historical depth of continuities, greater economic progress and a relative lack of politically and economically viable nationalisms to foment disintegration.

Modernization, external links and interdependence

The economic reforms initiated by Deng Xiaoping in 1978 have led to an increase in the people's living standards in general, and the emergence of the 'new rich' in particular. It has been suggested that China's growing middle classes will sooner or later demand more involvement in the political process and may even demand political change. This would represent a serious challenge to the power of the central government, and can only strengthen the existing decentralist tendencies. Analysts tend to cite the experience of certain East Asian states, such as South Korea and Taiwan, where economic transformation has been followed by political liberalization. However, what has happened in China over the past ten years or so is what David Goodman called 'economic restructuring' rather than economic modernization. Unlike its East Asian neighbours, China already had a modernized economy in 1978, however inefficient it might have been. When Deng Xiaoping launched the 'Four Modernizations' programme, the Chinese economy had already been transformed from agricultural to industrial production, with the existence of substantial numbers of white-collar workers and professional middle classes (Goodman, 1992). The experience of Singapore shows that the majority of the middle classes may not necessarily challenge the authority of their government, as long as they enjoy a high living standard., but of course Singapore is such a small country and can be much more easily governed.

The previous discussion focuses very much on China's internal situation; external links and foreign involvement would be key factors in a 'fragmenting China' scenario. It is impossible to imagine the development of a 'South China' state, for example, without the tacit agreement or even explicit support of foreign countries. External involvement would also be key factors in the potential secession of Tibet and Xinjiang. For example, Britain had an historic involvement in both regions in fomenting revolt against the Qing government, as had Tsarist Russia, while in recent times the US government supported the Khampas in an attempted uprising in Tibet in the 1950s. Such involvement today — by India in Tibet, by the countries of Central Asia in the development of a pan-Islamic federation including Xinjiang, by Russia and Mongolia in neighbouring parts of Heilongjiang, Jilin, or Inner Mongolia and by other surrounding or more distant countries — is possible to envisage. We note, however, that direct involvement is likely to be counter-productive to those who wish to encourage regional disintegration, in that the Chinese government would do all in its power to resist external intervention in its affairs. Indeed, one of the greatest fears of the Chinese government is foreign encouragement, and even military support of, separatism in China, these being regarded as major threats to China's national security and survival in the 'new world order' (Li, 1993).

This fear has been exacerbated, somewhat paradoxically, via China's Open Door Policy to the outside world, for the country has now become more vulnerable to the influence and pressure of transnational forces (Cook and Li, 1994). Already, many regions have been penetrated by foreign companies, including multinational corporations, and provinces are dealing with foreign businesses directly. Likewise, if more stock exchanges are established in China in future, the national economy is bound to be subject to the fluctuation of the global financial markets and the Chinese regions will gain even more financial autonomy. In addition, the technological and communications revolutions in the last few decades have made central control more difficult. Regional authorities can now easily communicate with foreign businesses and organizations through the most advanced communications technology. The recent openness also means easier access to the foreign media, which is frequently critical of the decisions and policies of the centre, thereby encouraging greater decentralization in China. This produces a fundamental tension between the Western view of 'freedom of the press' contrasting sharply with the Chinese government's view of the press as serving the 'national interest'. Such controversies are likely to multiply as the communications revolution continues apace. Nonetheless, this is not to say that Western media will necessarily move from critical reporting overseas to encouraging a climate of dissent and regional fragmentation within China itself. In any case, the Chinese authorities will not sit idly by while this occurs, and they have already placed restrictions on the ownership of satellite dishes, for example, as well as curbs on foreign correspondents.

Future scenarios and their regional and global implications

It is clear from the above discussion that there are both strong centralizing and decentralizing forces shaping the future of China. Whether China will remain united or follow the Soviet path of disintegration depends on a wide variety of internal and external factors. No doubt, China is in a period of great change and uncertainty. It is impossible to predict the exact course of development in the PRC; it is, however, possible to present three plausible scenarios for the future spatial structure of China. We will consider the preconditions under which each scenario might occur and its regional and global implications.

Scenario one: no substantial change

This scenario is based on the assumption that the leadership transition would be smooth, and that Deng would be succeeded either by a single individual who supports his line or by a collective leadership which is committed to economic reform and the Open Door policy. Of course, there would be disagreements among the top leaders, but they would be prepared to make compromises in order to maintain the 'leading and guiding role' of the CCP in Chinese society and the social and political stability of the country. Another precondition would be that the PLA remains united and loyal to the central leadership.

Under this scenario, the Chinese economy would continue to grow, and the living standards of the people as a whole would continue to rise, but the problem of regional disparities would remain unresolved. The centre would continue to take measures to reduce the imbalance between the rich and poor regions without jeopardizing the overall growth of the country. Some elements of decentralized economic growth would continue, such as encouraging tourism and cross-border trade, and providing subsidies to poorer provinces. However, inflation and unemployment rates might remain high as

210

a result of rapid growth of the Chinese economy. Social inequality and corruption within the CCP and government might remain serious. Those who could not benefit from the country's economic growth might take extreme actions such as committing economic crime and getting involved in illegal activities. Despite all of these problems, China would remain as a unitary state and the Communist regime would continue in control; the borders of the PRC would remain sacrosanct. Regional autonomy would be tolerated within the existing national framework as long as it would not turn into political or military autonomy. Problems of governance would be overcome via continued economic growth and sophisticated communication and control systems. This would be facilitated by the considerable spatial concentration of population within relatively easily controlled lowland deltas, river valleys and urban areas. This is not to say that the regime would not be challenged by the intellectuals and the middle classes in society. Indeed, a limited degree of democratization might be introduced in response to growing demands of the population, but dissent would be minimized via consumerism. On the whole, social stability would be achieved through tight political control and authoritarian measures.

In order to secure a stable and peaceful international environment for domestic economic development, China would continue to pursue its dual strategy of improving diplomatic relations with most countries in the world and building up its military strength (Li, 1995). It would not resort to the use of force unless the issue of territorial dispute with its neighbours came to a head. This scenario would probably be welcomed by transnational business corporations and the international community, as it would provide a relatively stable and predictable environment for businesses and foreign investors. The China market would remain important to the Asia-Pacific as well as to the United States and Europe, but there would be occasional tensions over issues of human rights, Most Favoured Nation trade status, and so on, with Western criticisms being muted by economic opportunities. On the whole, economic and political stability would be the norm, and there would be more continuity than change in China. This would by and large be accepted by Asia-Pacific countries and the West, as they would benefit from expanded trade and economic links with the PRC within a more predictable political environment. In addition, many Asian states would share the neoauthoritarian approaches of the Chinese government in maintaining order and stability, and economic prosperity of their own societies. Nevertheless, the outside world would be concerned about the growth of Chinese power and its long-term security implications, and would therefore try to tie China into the global network of interdependence, particularly in the areas of economic and technological cooperation in the hope that China would not become aggressive as it grows stronger, because of the huge economic costs involved (Cable and Ferdinand, 1994).

Scenario two: China shrinks

Another scenario perhaps reflects the general trend in the global system over the past twenty years or so, especially since the end of the Cold War. It has been argued that states find it increasingly difficult to protect their sovereignty in the face of global forces, such as rapid technological change, multinational corporations, transnational actors, international organizations and so on. The complexity of the global economy and global communications has undermined states, which are either transcended by supra-national organizations or fragmented by more responsive local/regional alternatives (Camilleri and Falk, 1992). The implementation of the Open Door policy since the late 1970s means that China has joined the 'global village' and has become part of the world economy. As China opens its door to the outside world, the aspirations and expectations of the Chinese people have also been raised. Perhaps China is too big to ensure homogeneity of direction and purpose in a fragmented global system; when this is coupled with the eccentric location of the 'northern' capital (Beijing), ethnic dissent and external involvement, the country may become ungovernable and regional fragmentation may occur. This scenario could occur if there was a prolonged crisis and division within the central leadership and no consensus could be reached by the top leaders in Beijing. But even then China would not disintegrate unless the PLA were deeply divided and involved in the CCP's factional struggle. If the centre were to fail both to present a united front to the country and to perform its leadership role for a lengthy period of time, regional leaders might try to take actions to protect their own economic interests and autonomy. Remote regions like Tibet and Xinjiang might try to take the opportunity to gain independence. Under such circumstances, military leaders would find it difficult to decide to whom they should be loyal, especially when their support were sought by different factions of the Party, or by some powerful regional leaders. This is probably the worst scenario of all, because no one knows exactly what the outcome would be. There could be serious social unrest and political upheaval, and even civil war, followed by the break-up of China into many political entities, some of which would possess nuclear weapons.

For this scenario to happen, the regime would have to depart radically from its existing position. There are two extreme sets of circumstances under which this might occur. First, if the CCP were to be dominated by a group of radical left-wing leaders following the passing of Deng, a neoMaoist agenda might be adopted with an emphasis on central planning and 'self-reliance', and the whole reform programme and the Open Door policy could be reversed. As this would affect the interests of a vast number of the population in China, including Party and government officials, the leadership would certainly face strong resistance at every level of Chinese society. If the regime were to respond by widespread purges and military crackdowns, it would lose its legitimacy completely, and the PLA would be reluctant to carry out the unpopular task of suppressing the people. After all, the army has been involved in business activities for many years and has benefited from trade links with the outside world. In order to protect their economic interests, richer regions might seek the support of their military leaders. The consequences of this could be a popular uprising in certain regions and a break-up of China.

The second set of circumstances is that the post-Deng leadership would adopt a sort of 'new-right' agenda based on economic individualism, privatization and capitalist competition. Politically, the state would not tolerate any criticism, dissent and opposition, and would place a great deal of emphasis on social stability, and law and order. Under such circumstances, most people would try to make as much money as they could by hook or by crook, and the poor and the weak would be abandoned for the sake of 'economic efficiency'. This type of agenda might be acceptable to Western governments, transnational corporations, and foreign investors, at least in the short term. However, unrestrained economic liberalism combined with unchecked political authoritarianism in China would ultimately lead to widespread corruption, extreme social inequality and injustice, serious economic imbalances, huge regional disparities, social disorder and political apathy. Rich regions like Guangdong and Fujian might attempt to break away from the centre to form a South China state with Hong Kong and Taiwan in order to maintain their economic prosperity, while poor regions would become poorer with the possibility of social unrest and even civil war.

Those who fear that the growth of Chinese power would destabilize regional security in Pacific Asia (Chanda, 1995; Roy, 1994) and would represent a long-term threat to Western economic and security interests might like to see the disintegration of China. However, the consequences of such a scenario are extremely serious, as potential military confrontations and great bloodshed within China could easily spill over into the rest of Asia, and ultimately disrupt the international system. This 'nightmare scenario' could result in mass migration into Japan and other Southeast Asian states, which would in turn affect the social stability and economic development of these countries. Could they cope with such a highly unstable and unpredictable situation? As the PRC is one of the major economies in Pacific Asia, its violent break-up would undoubtedly have a detrimental effect on the economic dynamism of the region. Should such a scenario become reality, businesses and investors would be likely to pull out from not only China but also other Asia-Pacific countries, so as to minimize potential losses. In a world of growing interdependence, what happens in Asia's economies would have serious implications for the global economy. In political and security terms, this scenario would also destabilize international relations and global security. For one thing, the world would have to establish and develop diplomatic relations with different Chinas, which would no doubt have many tensions and conflicts among themselves. It would be very difficult, if not impossible, to deal with such problems as environmental degradation and arms proliferation effectively with so many Chinas. Under that circumstances, China(s) would become a major destabilizing force in the world, and in Pacific Asia in particular.

Scenario three: China expands

This scenario assumes that the post-Deng leadership would be united and fully committed to the Four Modernizations programme, and that economic reform in China would be successful, so successful that China would 'expand'. The cohesion of Han culture, including the overseas Chinese, might facilitate the successful integration of Hong Kong and Taiwan into a new 'Greater China' based on the principle of 'one

213

country; two systems' (Crane, 1993; Harding, 1993; Shambaugh, 1993). In fact, even at the moment, the social, economic, and to a lesser extent, political interactions among the PRC, Hong Kong and Taiwan are quite strong (Ash and Kueh, 1993; Lin, 1993; Yahuda, 1993). In particular, a 'new regionalism' is said to have emerged in Southern China, which includes the South China provinces of Guangdong and Fujian, and Taiwan and Hong Kong (Asia Research Centre, 1992). By 1997, Hong Kong will have become part of China. Given time, the reunification of Taiwan and the PRC is not impossible. Indeed, in early 1995 Taiwanese leaders responded positively to the proposal made by the CCP General Secretary Jiang Zemin that both sides should try to end the existing hostile situation and to begin negotiations on the reunification of China. However, the spirit of cooperation between Beijing and Taipei was soon replaced by a situation of antagonism after the unofficial visit of Lee Teng-hui, the Taiwanese President, to the US in June 1995 and China's missile tests in the East China Sea in the following two months. It is possible that Taiwan's politicians would sooner or later be forced to the negotiation table given the enormous military threats from China and lack of support from the US and Western governments. Should Taiwan declare independence, China may resort to the use of force to take over the island (Guowuyuan, 1993). With the human resources, advanced technology and business experience of Hong Kong and Taiwan, China would become a formidable player in the Pacific economy (Cheng, 1993); and the military strength of the PRC and Taiwan combined would make China a true Pacific power in the twenty-first century.

The consequences of this scenario are more unpredictable. On the one hand, a Greater China could concentrate on economic development and enhanced regional trade and cooperation (Zhang, 1992; Ji, 1992), thus promoting regional integration in Pacific Asia and contributing to the development of the global economy. Many hope that economic interdependence between China and its neighbours would lead to security cooperation, and that China would be involved in multilateral security dialogues and confidence-building measures in the region. China's territorial dispute with its neighbours may also be resolved through negotiations and peaceful means. Even though China 'expanded', it would become a major force of economic progress and a responsible member of the international community. It would therefore be seen as a competitor rather than a potential enemy by Asia-Pacific and Western countries.

On the other hand, the emergence of Greater China could be perceived as a powerful force for instability. First, Southeast Asian states would feel uncomfortable with the concept of Greater China because of the large number of overseas Chinese living in their countries. They would naturally be concerned that these Chinese might be more loyal to the PRC than to their host countries. Second, as China's economic strength grows, so will its military capability. China would continue to develop conventional as well as nuclear weapons, and would become more confident and assertive on regional security issues. It would refuse to get involved in multilateral security cooperation and would reject the demand from other countries for military transparency. Driven by a strong nationalism and the need for more economic resources, China could attempt to regain its lost territories through diplomatic channels, and if necessary, through

214

military force. As a result, China could become much more assertive in dealing with the competing claims to the Nansha/Spratly and Diaoyutai/Senkaku islands, which might lead to military confrontations with Southeast Asian states and Japan. In any case, a rich and unified China with strong military capabilities, including nuclear weapons, combined with its size, population and natural resources, as well as the economic strength of Hong Kong and Taiwan, would be viewed by neigbouring countries with fear and suspicion. This could provoke new regional antagonisms and increased militarism in countries such as Japan and Russia, thus potentially destabilizing the entire international system.

Conclusion

To conclude, we would suggest that scenario one is likely to occur but cannot be sustained forever, while scenario two is unlikely but cannot be ruled out. Scenario three is potentially problematic but quite possible. China is such an important country that its unity or division will have profound regional and global implications. Although the future of China is largely in the hands of the Chinese, outside forces will have some influence on the development of the country in a world of growing interdependence. This is why the rise of regionalism in the PRC and its consequences have attracted a huge amount of attention in both the academic and policy communities outside China. Some scholars suggest that the decentralizing trend in China will continue, and that it is in the interest of the outside world to deal with more than one China. This, they argue, is the 'only way to ensure that China does not become more dangerous as it grows richer and stronger' (Segal, 1994b, p. 352). We must, however, remind analysts and policy-makers that the process of the disintegration of China may be extremely lengthy and violent with serious regional and global consequences. The high cost of a fragmenting China may have to be paid by the Chinese *people* as well as the *international community*. Scenario three may indeed frighten a lot of people, but the consequences of it would depend on how China handles its relations with neighbouring Asian states, and how the outside world responds to China's rise in the international system (Kristof, 1993; Segal, 1995). The West, therefore, must be cautious in case it actively encourages the break-up of China. Similarly, the Chinese government would be well advised to be sensitive to perceptions of other countries in its pursuit of great power status. The suspicions and fears of its Asian neighbours should not always be interpreted as Western-sponsored attempts to undermine the stability and unity of the PRC. We would argue that contemporary analysis of regionalism in China and future policy options should be based on deeper mutual understanding and cooperation in an increasingly interdependent world.

References

Ash, R. and Kueh, Y.Y. (1993), 'Economic Integration within Greater China: Trade and Investment Flows Between China, Hong Kong and Taiwan', *The China Quarterly*, No. 136, December, pp. 711-45.

Asia Research Centre (1992), *Southern China in Transition: The New Regionalism and Australia*, Department of Foreign Affairs and Trade, Canberra.

Bramall, C. and Jones, M.E. (1993), 'Rural Income Inequality in China Since 1978', *Journal of Peasant Studies*, October.

Breslin, S. (1995a), 'Centre and Province in China', in Benewick, R. and Wingrove, P., *China in the 1990s*, Macmillan, London, pp. 63-72.

Breslin, S. (1995b), *China in the 1980s: Centre-Province Relations in a Reforming Socialist State*, Macmillan, London.

Bucknall, K.B. (1989), *China and the Open Door Policy*, Allen & Unwin, Sydney.

Cable, V. and Ferdinand, P. (1994), 'China as an Economic Giant: Threat or Opportunity?', *International Affairs*, Vol. 70, No. 2. April, pp. 243-61.

Camilleri, J.A. and Falk, J. (1992), *The End of Sovereignty? The Politics of a Shrinking and Fragmenting World*, Edward Elgar, Aldershot, Hampshire.

Cannon, T. (1990), 'Regions: Spatial Inequality and Regional Policy', in Cannon, T. and Jenkins, A. (eds), *The Geography of Contemporary China: The Impact of Deng Xiaoping's Decade*, Routledge, London, pp. 28-60.

Cannon, T. (1993), 'Regions, Ethnicities and Conflicts: The Break-up of China?', paper presented at the *ESRC Pacific Rim Seminar Series*, Liverpool John Moores University, September.

Chanda, N. (1995), 'Fear of the Dragon', *Far Eastern Economic Review*, 13 April, pp. 24-6, 28.

Chang, M.H. (1992), 'China's Future: Regionalism, Federation, or Disintegration', *Studies in Comparative Communism*, Vol. XXV, No. 3, September, pp. 211-27.

Cheng, C.Y. (1990), *Behind the Tiananmen Massacre: Social, Political, and Economic Ferment in China*, Westview Press, Boulder, CO.

Cheng, C.Z. (1993), 'Zhongguo yu zhoubian guojia jingji xiezuoquan - zouxiang ershiyi shiji de kayou zhi lu ('A Conception of Economic Cooperation between China and Its Peripheral Countries — A Possible Road to the Twenty-first Century'), *Yatai yanjiu* (Asia-Pacific Studies), No. 5, pp. 21-8.

Cheung, T.M. (1994), 'Profits Over Professionalism: The PLA's Economic Activities and the Impact on Military Unity', in Yang, R.H., Hu, J.C., Yu, P.K.H. and Yang, A.N.D. (eds), *Chinese Regionalism: The Security Dimension*, Westview Press, Boulder, CO, pp. 85-110.

Chossudovsky, M. (1986), *Towards Capitalist Restoration? Chinese Socialism After Mao*, Macmillan, London.

Cole, J.P. (1994), 'China and the Former USSR: A Comparison in Time and Space', in Dwyer, D. (ed.) , *China: The Next Decades*, Longman, Harlow, Essex, pp. 31-53.

Cook, I.G. and Li, R. (1994), 'The Transformation of China's Cities: The International Dimension', paper presented at the *RUSI Asia Forum*, Royal United Institute for Defence Studies, Whitehall, London, January.

Crane, G.T. (1993), 'China and Taiwan: Not Yet "Greater China"', *International Affairs*, Vol. 69, No. 4, October, pp. 705-23.

Dittmer, L. and Kim, S.S. (eds) (1993), *China's Quest for National Identity*, Cornell University Press, Ithaca, NY.

Dreyer, J.T. (1994), 'The PLA and Regionalism in Xinjiang', *The Pacific Review*, Vol. 7, No.1, pp. 41-55.

Ferdinand, P. (1992), 'Russian and Soviet Shadows over China's Future', *International Affairs*, Vol. 68, No. 2, April, pp. 279-92.

Goodman, D.S.G. (1986), *Centre and Province in the People's Republic of China*, Cambridge University Press, Cambridge.

Goodman, D.S.G. (ed.) (1989), *China's Regional Development*, Routledge, London.

Goodman, D.S.G. (1992), 'China: The State and Capitalist Revolution', *The Pacific Review*, Vol. 5. No. 4, pp. 350-9.

Goodman, D.S.G. (1994), 'The PLA and Regionalism in Guangdong', *The Pacific Review*, Vol. 7, No. 1, pp. 29-39.

Goodman, D.S.G. and Feng C. (1994), 'Guangdong: Greater Hong Kong and the New Regionalist Future', in Goodman, D.S.G. and Segal, G. (eds), *China Deconstructs: Politics, Trade and Regionalism*, Routledge, London, pp. 177-201.

Guowuyuan (1993) *Taiwan wenti yu Zhongguo de tongyi* (The Taiwan Issue and the Reunification of China), Guowuyuan Xinwen bangongshi, Beijing.

Harding, H. (1993), 'The Concept of 'Greater China': Themes, Variations and Reservations,' *The China Quarterly*, No. 136, December, pp. 660-86.

Howe, C. (1978), *China's Economy: A Basic Guide*, Paul Elek, London.

Howell, J. (1993), *China Opens Its Doors: The Politics of Economic Change*, Harvester Wheatsheaf, Hemel Hempstead.

Ji, C.W. (1992), 'Jiaqiang Zhongguo yu yatai diqu de jingji hezuo' ('Enhance the Economic Cooperation between China and the Asia-Pacific Economies'), *Yatai yanjiu* (Asia-Pacific Studies), No. 1, pp. 10-14, 68.

Joffe, E. (1987), *The Chinese Army After Mao*, Weidenfeld & Nicolson, London.

Joffe, E. (1994), 'Regionalism in China: The Role of the PLA', *The Pacific Review*, Vol. 7, No. 1, pp. 17-27.

Kristof, N.D. (1993), 'The Rise of China', *Foreign Affairs*, Vol. 72, No. 5, pp. 59-74.

Levine, S.I. (1995), 'World Affairs: China', *Britannica Book of the Year: Events of 1994*, Encyclopaedia Britannica, London, pp. 391-3.

Li, C. (1992), *A Study of China's Population*, Foreign Languages Press, Beijing.

Li, C. and White, L. (1993), 'The Army in the Succession to Deng Xiaoping', *Asian Survey*, Vol. XXXIII, No. 8, August, pp. 757-86.

Li, R. (1993), 'Chinese Perspectives on the New World Order', paper presented at the *London China Seminar*, School of Oriental and African Studies, University of London, March.

Li, R. (1995), 'China and Asia-Pacific Security in the Post-Cold War Era', *Security Dialogue*, Vol. 26, No. 3, September, pp. 331-44.

Lin, C.P. (1993), 'Beijing and Taipei: Interactions in the Post-Tiananmen Period', *The China Quarterly*, No. 136, December, pp. 770-804.

Linge, G.J.R. and Forbes, D.K. (1990), 'The Space Economy of China', in Linge, G.J.R. and Forbes, D.K. (eds), *China's Spatial Economy*, Oxford University Press, Oxford, pp. 10-34.

Liu, G.G., Liang, W.S. et al. (1987), *China's Economy in 2000*, New World Press, Beijing.

Ma, H. (ed.) (1990), *Modern China's Economy and Management*, Foreign Languages Press, Beijing.

Roy, D. (1994), 'Hegemon on the Horizon? China's Threat to East Asian Security', *International Security*, Vol. 19, No. 1, Summer, pp. 149-68.

Segal, G. (1994a), *China Changes Shape: Regionalism and Foreign Policy*, Adelphi Paper 287, International Institute for Strategic Studies, London.

Segal, G. (1994b), 'Deconstructing Foreign Relations', in Goodman, D.S.G. and Segal, G. (eds), *China Deconstructs: Politics, Trade and Regionalism*, Routledge, London, pp. 322-55.

Segal, G. (1995), 'Tying China into the International System', *Survival*, Vol. 37, No. 2, Summer, pp. 60-73.

Selden, M. (1993), *The Political Economy of Chinese Development*, M.E. Sharpe, New York.

Sen, N.C. (1990), *Rural Economy and Development in China*, Foreign Languages Press, Beijing.

Shambaugh, D. (1993), 'Introduction: The Emergence of 'Greater China'', *The China Quarterly*, No. 136, December, pp. 653-9.

Swaine, M.D. (1992), *The Military and Political Succession in China: Leadership, Institutions, Beliefs*, RAND, Santa Monica, CA.

Uri Dadush and Dong He (1995), 'China: A New Power in World Trade', *Finance and Development*, June 1995, pp. 36-8.

Waldron, A. (1990), 'Warlordism Versus Federalism: The Revival of a Debate?', *The China Quarterly*, No. 121, March, pp. 116-28.

Wang, Y.J. and Cook, I.G. (1993), 'Foreign Investment in China and the Current Situation', paper presented at the *ESRC Pacific Rim Seminar Series*, Liverpool John Moores University, September.

Wen, Y.K. (1984), *Zhongguo de daqushi: Wen yuankai tan gaige* (China's Megatrends: Wen Yuankai on Reform), Shanghai renmin chubanshe, Shanghai.

White, L. and Li, C. (1993), 'China Coast Identities: Regional, National , and Global', in Dittmer, L. and Kim, S.S. (eds), *China's Quest for National Identity*, Cornell University Press, Ithaca, NY, pp. 154-93.

Yabuki, S. (1995), *China's New Political Economy: The Giant Awakes*, Westview Press, Boulder, CO.

Yahuda, M. (1993), 'The Foreign Relations of Greater China', *The China Quarterly*, No. 136, December, pp. 687-710.

Yang, R.H., Hu, J.C., Yu, P.K.H. and Yang, A.N.D. (eds) (1994), *Chinese Regionalism: The Security Dimension*, Westview Press, Boulder, CO.

Yao, S.J. and Liu, J.R. (1995), 'Uneven Development of TVEs in Rural China: Some Macro-economic Evidence', *The CEA (UK) Newsletter*, Vol. 7, No. 2, Chinese Economic Association in the UK, London, pp. 18-24.

Ye, S.Z. (1993), 'The Development Prospects of North China's Coastal Region and Beijing-Tianjin Conurbation' (unpublished paper, presented to a Hong Kong Conference).

Yu, P.K.H. (1992), 'Regionalism and the Chinese Military Area Commands: A Preliminary Macro-Analysis', *The Korean Journal of Defense Analysis*, Vol. IV, No. 2, Winter, pp. 175-205.

Zhang, P. (1992), 'Yatai diqu de jingji hezuo yu woguo de duiwai kaifang' ('Economic Cooperation in the Asia-Pacific Region and China's Open Door Policy'), *Yatai yanjiu* (Asia-Pacific Studies), No. 1, pp. 6-9, 29.

Zhang, W.W. and Zeng, Q.N. (1993), *In Search of China's Minorities*, New World Press, Beijing.

Zhong, P. R. (1990), *Shinian jingji gaige* (Ten Years' Economic Reform), Henan renmin chubanshe, Henan.

Zweig, D. (1995), '''Developmental Communities' on China's Coast: The Impact of Trade, Investment, and Transnational Alliances', *Comparative Politics*, Vol. 27, April, pp. 253-74.

Aung San Suu Kyi, 9, 42, 182, 183, 184, 189, 191, 194, 195, 196, 198, 199
Australia, 44, 46, 99, 143, 195, 215

—B—

Baht Economic Zone, 24, 141
Bali, 5, 107, 114, 116, 117, 118, 119, 120, 129, 130, 131, 133
Balkanization scenario, 208
Bangkok, 35, 118, 133, 193, 194
Bangkok Declaration, 35
Barricades mentality, 168
Bassein, 191
Bastian, A., 123
Batam, 153, 154
Beijing, 43, 46, 56, 57, 59, 60, 65, 69, 73, 74, 82, 84, 85, 96, 97, 98, 99, 147, 156, 158, 176, 177, 191, 204, 206, 208, 212, 214, 217, 218, 219
Bigemony, 12, 55
Bilateralism, 3, 12, 21, 24, 51, 54, 58
Bintan, 153
Bipolarity, 53
Black Sea, 102
Bohai Sea Economic Circle, 140
Brazil, 219
Britain (see also United Kingdom), 1, 54, 58, 65, 66, 70, 201, 209
British, 54, 59, 60, 66, 67, 70, 102, 153, 182
Brunei, 29, 31, 33, 34, 43, 57, 133, 174, 184, 192
Buddhism, 192
Burma (see also Myanmar), 8, 9, 18, 41, 42, 181-9
Bush, G., 58
Buzan, B., 34, 35, 43, 49, 50, 51

—C—

Cambodia, 18, 25, 29, 34, 36, 37, 38, 40, 41, 42, 43, 45, 47, 49, 50, 51, 57, 192, 194, 198
Cambodian issue, 29, 36
Canada, 8, 25, 44, 143
Canon, 159
Capital, 6, 8, 23, 57, 64, 65, 71, 83, 85, 87, 89, 92, 93, 96, 114, 119, 137, 140, 151, 152, 154, 155, 157, 159, 173, 174, 175, 195, 202, 212
Capitalism, 20, 21, 24, 170
Central Java, 102, 128
Central Kalimantan, 113, 118, 128
Central Malaysia, 118
Central Sumatra, 110
Centralization, 5, 110, 120, 200, 201
Chaovalit Yongchaiyut, 192, 194
Chen Xitong, 97
Chi Haotian, 190
Chiang Jiang (see also Yangzi), 10
Chiang Rai, 195
China, 3, 4, 6, 8, 9, 10, 12, 15, 19, 20, 22, 23, 24, 36, 37, 38, 39, 41, 43, 44, 45, 46, 47, 48, 50, 53-74, 75-101, 138, 139, 140, 141, 147, 148, 149, 150, 151, 152, 155, 156, 157, 158, 159, 169, 171, 172, 173, 174, 175, 176, 178, 181, 185, 186, 188, 189, 190, 191, 194, 195, 198, 199, 200-19
China Steel Co., 156
Chinese Communist Party (CCP), 10, 201, 205, 206, 207, 210, 212, 214
Chinese Economic Area, 140, 146, 147
Chinese strategic culture, 56
Christianity, 104
Chulalongkorn University, 193
Clark Field, 55

221

Greater East Asia, 2, 12, 15, 25
Greater East Asia Coprosperity
  Sphere, 2, 12, 15, 25
Greece, 173, 179, 219
Green Sea, 22
Gross Domestic Product (GDP), 6,
  31, 49, 111, 113, 114, 115, 116,
  117, 118, 122, 127, 128, 129,
  130, 131, 133, 134, 176
Gross National Product (GNP), 159,
  203
Growth Triangle, 6, 32, 54, 71, 140,
  141, 146, 147, 153, 154
Guangdong, 10, 58, 59, 61, 62, 64,
  74, 79, 80, 84, 93, 96, 140, 152,
  178, 204, 213, 217
Guangxi, 84
Guangzhou, 84, 206
Guizhou, 96, 203
Gulf, 25, 31, 56, 188
Gulf of Thailand, 188
Gulf War, 25, 56

—H—

Hai Rui, 171
Hainan, 84, 96, 156, 204
Hainan Scandal, 84, 96
Hakka, 207
Han, 10, 88, 96, 99, 142, 149, 204,
  208, 213
Hanoi, 36, 37, 38, 41, 42, 43
Harahap, 106
Hata, 14
Hatta, 103
Hayward, G., 146
Hegemony, 8, 12, 55, 57, 58, 68, 70,
  208
High-performing Asian economies
  (HPAEs), 12, 14, 20, 21, 25
Hill 492, 193
Hinduism, 103
Hitachi, 19
Hokkaido, 23, 24

Honda, 19
Hong Kong, 3, 6, 10, 12, 15, 20, 21,
  53, 54, 56, 58-67, 69, 70, 71, 72,
  73, 74, 97, 99, 100, 137, 140,
  141, 146, 147, 148, 152, 156,
  157, 158, 159, 169, 171, 175,
  176, 179, 188, 198, 204, 213,
  214, 215, 217, 219
Hu Angang, 90, 100
Hubei, 79
Human rights, 44, 157, 189, 191,
  195, 211
Hunan, 79, 204
Hyundai Group, 159

—I—

Identity, 3, 7, 8, 13, 14, 15, 16, 21,
  22, 24, 54, 64, 65, 66, 67, 68, 69,
  70, 74, 172, 174, 207, 216, 218
Identity struggle, 4, 54, 65, 66, 68,
  69
Ideology, 36, 103, 109
Idris Hydraulic, 194
Imperialism, 13, 17, 20, 22, 25, 56
Imports, 5, 6, 20, 106, 118, 157,
  158, 177, 219
Income, 12, 32, 61, 91, 94, 106,
  113, 114, 117, 120, 121, 122,
  123, 134, 203, 204
Independence movement, 57, 59, 60,
  103
India, 9, 39, 55, 57, 67, 88, 169,
  174, 175, 185, 186, 188, 190, 209
Indochina, 15, 30, 35, 36, 38, 43
Indonesia, 3, 5, 6, 8, 12, 18, 20, 29,
  31, 33, 34, 35, 36, 37, 41, 43, 44,
  50, 51, 52, 57, 71, 102-136, 140,
  141, 147, 148, 150, 153, 154,
  156, 169, 183, 191, 194
Indonesian National Party (PNI),
  105, 106
Industrialization, 5, 18, 20, 117,
  179, 180, 200

Myanmar (see also Burma), 8, 9, 29, 41, 42, 43, 45, 47, 52, 169, 184, 185, 188, 193, 195, 197, 198, 199
Myanmar National Democratic Alliance Army (MNDAA), 185

—N—

Naga, 185
Najib, 40, 49
Nanjing, 206
Nasroen, M., 106
National Democratic Front (NDF), 185
National economy, 88, 89, 116, 204, 209
National identity, 207
National resilience, 3, 30, 31, 32, 33, 34
National unity, 31, 181, 182, 187, 196, 200
Nationalism, 2, 4, 56, 64, 65, 66, 67, 68, 69, 70, 71, 103, 105, 110, 206, 207, 214
Ne Win, 9, 181, 182, 183, 184, 187, 196
NeoMaoist, 206, 212
Netherlands, 105, 136
New Order regional development policies, 108
New World Order, 1, 73, 74, 217
New Zealand, 44, 143
Newly Industrializing Countries (NICs) (see also Asian Newly Industrializing Countries and Newly Industrializing Economies), 62, 94, 139, 150, 169, 170, 173, 174, 178, 219
Newly Industrializing Economies (NIEs), 12, 20
Nigeria, 109, 111
Niigata, 22, 23
Ningxia, 203
Nixon, 19

North America, 1, 2, 8, 10, 13, 19, 25, 138, 141, 143, 144, 146, 157, 176
North American Free Trade Area (NAFTA), 13, 144, 146
North Korea, 8, 22, 23, 45, 57, 72, 141, 147, 158, 159, 177
Northeast Asia Economic Zone, 22
Northeast China, 22, 157
Northern Triangle, 141
Nusatenggara, 107, 116, 117, 122, 128, 129, 131

—O—

Official Development Assistance (ODA), 18
Ohira, M., 142
Ohmae, K., 175, 179
Ohn Gyaw, 184, 192
Oman, C., 219
Open door policy, 59, 60, 62, 138, 210, 212
Open regionalism, 13, 26, 71, 144
Orderly Marketing Agreements (OMAs), 18
Organization for Economic Cooperation and Development (OECD), 16, 27, 147, 148, 152, 157, 219
Osaka, 23
Outer Islands (Indonesia), 102, 103, 107, 120
Overseas Chinese networks, 174
Ozawa, I., 168

—P—

Pacific Asia, 1, 2, 3, 7, 10, 27, 76, 137, 139, 140, 142, 144, 167, 168, 170, 174, 175, 176, 177, 178, 200, 213, 214
Pacific Basin Economic Council (PBEC), 140

148, 149, 153, 156, 157, 158,
159, 160, 169, 174, 175, 176,
181, 186, 187, 188, 189, 190,
191, 201, 202, 206, 210, 211,
212, 214, 219
Trading bloc, 31
Transnational banks (TNBs), 53
Transnational corporations (TNCs),
53, 149, 153, 213
Transport, 25, 56, 60, 109, 111,
175, 187, 195
Treaty of Amity and Cooperation in
Southeast Asia, 30, 37
Tsarist Russia, 209
Tumen Delta, 141
Tumen River Delta Project, 23
Tun Daim Zainuddin, 154

—U—

U Nu, 182
United Kingdom (see also Britain),
19, 173, 188
United States (US), 2, 3, 6, 9, 11,
12, 13, 14, 16, 17, 18, 19, 21, 24,
25, 26, 36, 38, 39, 44, 45, 46, 47,
48, 49, 54, 55, 56, 57, 58, 61, 62,
65, 68, 69, 70, 71, 72, 118, 133,
134, 138, 139, 140, 143, 144,
145, 148, 150, 151, 152, 155,
157, 158, 159, 169, 176, 184,
186, 188, 189, 190, 194, 195,
209, 214, 219
United Wa State Party (UWSP), 185
Urbanization, 31, 32, 77, 110, 115,
117, 122, 131, 203, 206, 211
Uruguay Round, 138, 143, 145

—V—

Vancouver, 176
Venezuela, 111
Vietnam, 3, 15, 17, 18, 27, 29, 36,
37, 38, 39, 41, 42, 43, 45, 47, 49,

51, 55, 57, 118, 156, 169, 174,
177, 192, 195
Vietnam War, 17, 27
Vitit Muntarborn, 193
Voluntary Export Restraints
(VERs), 18

—W—

Wang Baosen, 96
Wang Huning, 84, 89, 100
Wang Shaoguang, 90, 97, 100
War of words, 58, 66
Washington, DC, 50, 100, 189
West Irian, 102, 107
West Kalimantan, 117, 118, 122,
128
West Nusatenggara, 116, 128
West Pacific, 137, 143
Western Indonesia, 114, 117, 127,
132
World Bank, 9, 12, 28, 96, 100, 111,
169, 180, 195

—X—

Xiamen Special Economic Zone, 61,
156
Xinjiang, 79, 208, 209, 212

—Y—

Yamagata Prefecture, 23
Yangon (see also Rangoon), 42
Yangzi River (see also Chang
Jiang), 204
Yellow Sea, 140, 141, 159
Yellow Sea Economic Circle, 140
Yellow Sea Zone, 141
Yetagun oil field, 188
Yogyakarta, 102
Young, A., 147, 170, 173, 179, 180
Yuen Foong Yu Paper
Manufacturing Co., 156